SECOND EDITION

Strategies for Inclusion

A Handbook for Physical Educators

Lauren J. Lieberman, PhD

Cathy Houston-Wilson, PhD

State University of New York at Brockport

Human Kinetics

Library of Congress Cataloging-in-Publication Data

Lieberman, Lauren J., 1965-
  Strategies for inclusion : a handbook for physical educators / Lauren J. Lieberman, Cathy Houston-Wilson. -- 2nd ed.
      p. cm.
  Includes bibliographical references and index.
  ISBN-13: 978-0-7360-6247-3 (soft cover)
  ISBN-10: 0-7360-6247-5 (soft cover)
  1. Physical education for children with disabilities--United States. 2. Physical education for children--United States.
3. Inclusive education--United States. I. Houston-Wilson, Cathy, 1962- II. Title.
  GV445.L54 2009
  371.9'04486--dc22
                                    2008044986

ISBN-10: 0-7360-6247-5
ISBN-13: 978-0-7360-6247-3

The Web addresses cited in this text were current as of February, 2009, unless otherwise noted.

Acquisitions Editor: Scott Wikgren
Managing Editor: Bethany J. Bentley
Assistant Editor: Anne Rumery
Copyeditor: Tom Tiller
Proofreader: Kathy Bennett
Indexer: Andrea Hepner
Permission Manager: Dalene Reeder
Graphic Designer: Robert Reuther
Graphic Artist: Patrick Sandberg
Cover Designer: Robert Reuther
Photographer (cover): Carla Rodriguez
Photographer (interior): Les Woodrum (pp. 5, 17, 22, 27, 29, 39, 41, 71, 72, 102, 105) and Amanda Tepfer (pp. 7, 10, 15, 20, 43, 44, 51, 55, 57, 69, 80, 81, 84, 89, 96, 103), unless otherwise noted
Photo Production Manager: Jason Allen
Art Manager: Kelly Hendren
Illustrator and Associate Art Manager: Alan L. Wilborn
Printer: McNaughton & Gunn

Printed in the United States of America   10 9 8 7 6 5 4 3 2 1

The paper in this book is certified under a sustainable forestry program.

Human Kinetics
Web site: www.HumanKinetics.com

United States: Human Kinetics
P.O. Box 5076
Champaign, IL 61825-5076
800-747-4457
e-mail: humank@hkusa.com

Canada: Human Kinetics
475 Devonshire Road Unit 100
Windsor, ON N8Y 2L5
800-465-7301 (in Canada only)
e-mail: info@hkcanada.com

Europe: Human Kinetics
107 Bradford Road
Stanningley
Leeds LS28 6AT, United Kingdom
+44 (0) 113 255 5665
e-mail: hk@hkeurope.com

Australia: Human Kinetics
57A Price Avenue
Lower Mitcham, South Australia 5062
08 8372 0999
e-mail: info@hkaustralia.com

New Zealand: Human Kinetics
Division of Sports Distributors NZ Ltd.
P.O. Box 300 226 Albany
North Shore City
Auckland
0064 9 448 1207
e-mail: info@humankinetics.co.nz

Lauren would like to dedicate this book to her mother Janet Mirjam Joseph, PhD. She valued education and instilled that love for learning in us all. Her drive, determination, and passion were inspirational throughout her life. Her energy and enthusiasm for life and everything life had to offer was infectious. She was a leader and a true role model for many people.

Cathy would like to dedicate this book to her mother Marie (Houston) Maxwell, who passed away right after the book was completed. Mom was always supportive of our efforts and proud of our accomplishments. She was a loving wife, mother, and grandmother and is truly missed.

Contents

Preface

Since 1975, the process of including children with disabilities in general physical education classes has become a reality for school districts across the country. Unfortunately for many students with disabilities, however, the transition from traditionally segregated classrooms to supportive, inclusive environments has been a continual struggle for all parties involved.

Consequently, when it comes to integrating these students, teachers of physical education have been forced to navigate the maze of legislation and its accompanying mountains of paperwork, all the while relying on the best intentions rather than the best information. The purpose of this book is to educate and empower physical education teachers by giving them the information and tools necessary for successful inclusion of children with disabilities in their programs.

In this second edition, we have again worked diligently to create a solid resource filled with practical applications and easily implemented planning and assessment strategies. These strategies can be used by physical education teachers; coaches; paraeducators; adapted physical educators; special education teachers; recreation directors; therapeutic recreation specialists; parents; and graduate and undergraduate students in physical education, recreation, and special education.

The book is divided into two parts. The first part provides background information, as well as a road map for planning successful inclusion of children with disabilities in traditional physical education settings. The second part of the book offers numerous teachable units, complete with assessment tools for use in curriculum planning.

The book is organized so as to provide the reader with the most useful and up-to-date strategies for including children with disabilities. To reinforce the information and strategies, we have created a unique recurring chapter element that goes beyond the chapter objectives and chapter summary typically included in textbooks. These brief chapter-opening scenarios or case studies are designed to help readers explore their thoughts and feelings regarding various aspects of inclusion and adapted physical education.

Part I focuses on understanding inclusion, and the first chapter, "The Move to Include," provides an overview of legislative mandates that directly affect physical education. Armed with knowledge of the legal requirements, teachers can advocate for and receive support to successfully educate children with disabilities. We present a sample of a continuum of supports and placements so that physical educators can see various options available for educating children with disabilities. It is not necessary for children with disabilities to stay in one environment at all times. Depending on a child's unique needs and on the unit of instruction, he or she might move from one placement option to another. This chapter also reviews current research about inclusion in physical education; we review the effectiveness of inclusive physical education and discuss the roles and responsibilities of the general physical educator.

The second chapter, "Assessment: The Cornerstone of Effective Instruction," addresses such topics as authentic assessment and traditional forms of assessment. In making placement decisions, teachers can take advantage of the sample Ability Description Form, which is introduced in this chapter and provided on the accompanying CD-ROM. This chapter highlights the purposes of assessment and the use of assessment data to drive instruction; it also provides sample rubrics and examples of portfolio uses for children with disabilities. In addition, the chapter introduces an alternative assessment created specifically for children with severe disabilities.

Chapter 3, "Exploring Individualized Education Plans," addresses a necessary component in the education of a child with disabilities. An IEP helps ensure that a child is making progress toward chosen goals, and this chapter provides physical educators with all the steps necessary to develop and implement a physical education IEP. We review the roles of each member of the IEP multidisciplinary team and offer a step-by-step guide for getting involved in the IEP process for the many teachers who are left out of this important piece of the program. The chapter also provides information on IEP goal banks and how to use them effectively. Finally, the chapter reviews several ways to ensure that a child's IEP objectives are implemented in his or her general physical education class.

Chapter 4, "Managing Student Behavior," helps teachers set up their environments to maximize success with minimal disruption. This chapter discusses how to use positive behavior support (PBS) and how to train others to use this system.

In chapter 5, "Adapting Activities: A Universal Design for Learning," we outline four main theories which support the concept of adapting activities to include children with disabilities. We then discuss the Universal Design for Learning philosophy that drives modifications for all in general physical education; this discussion includes specific guidelines for adaptation. Four major variables—rules, equipment, environment, and instruction—can easily be adjusted for inclusion of children with special needs. To ensure that readers understand the options, this chapter provides a variety of examples.

Chapter 6, "Support Service: Making Inclusion a Reality," is a much-needed new chapter on the value and roles of a variety of support personnel. It includes comprehensive guidelines for training, utilizing, and motivating a variety of staff members to support instruction in general physical education. This invaluable network of individuals includes peer tutors, paraeducators, volunteers, senior citizens, and practicum students.

Chapter 7, "Creating an Atmosphere for Achievement," offers strategies and techniques for successfully including children with disabilities in general physical education. Use of these strategies creates a welcoming environment for all children, as members of the class are intricately involved in the inclusion process. The six techniques discussed are as follows: overcoming blanket medical excuses, integrating disability and ability awareness activities, using homework in physical education, using community facilities, using role models with disabilities, and providing leadership opportunities.

Part II of the book introduces specific strategies for inclusion. Here, readers learn how to use the curriculum provided in part I. Part II includes a step-by-step guide for implementing an inclusive curriculum and provides readers with five elementary units, four sport units, five recreation units, and three fitness units—all with potential adaptations. The adaptations are divided into the following categories: equipment, rules, environment, and instruction. In addition, each unit contains an assessment rubric, with skills broken down both quantitatively and qualitatively.

The book's appendixes provide extensive information that teachers can use to successfully include children with disabilities in general physical education. The authors hope that this book will empower teachers to advocate for themselves and for their students with disabilities, and, as a result, receive the necessary support to lead all children to healthy, active lifestyles. It is also our hope that physical educators will use this book to empower all students with the knowledge that anything is possible, and that hopes and goals can be achieved through understanding, cooperation, and creativity.

Acknowledgments

We would like to acknowledge our valued colleagues Joseph Winnick, Doug Collier, Francis Kozub, and Susan Petersen for their continued support. We would also like to acknowledge Haley Schedlin, Lauren Evans, Dean Bowen, Sara Scott, Kira Labagh, Kaila Smith, Jason Clarcq, Rocco Aiello, Ellen Kowalski, Sara Daggett, and Roy Speedling. Finally, we would like to thank the participants at Camp Abilities as well as their peer models, Gia Colgan, Joanna Colgan, Christopher Joyce, Peter Raimondo, Mina Stavey, Emily Volpe, Meaghan Wilson, and Shannon Wilson.

How to Use This Book and CD-ROM

This book provides a valuable resource for preservice and practicing teachers, recreation specialists, and special educators responsible for teaching physical education and physical activity to students with disabilities. The book includes chapters on the inclusion movement, assessment, IEP development, behavior management, creating a universal design for learning, using support personnel to foster success, and creating an atmosphere for achievement.

The book also provides an array of basic skills, sport skills, health and fitness activities, and recreation and life skills that include rubrics and assessments to determine present level of performance, to track progress, and to evaluate students. The skill sheets are included in part II of the book and on the accompanying CD-ROM for easy printing. You can use them as a template to create more rubrics.

In addition to the skill sheets included on the CD, you will find the sample forms that are discussed throughout the book. These are marked with a CD-ROM icon. The sample forms provided are:

- an ability description chart that can follow a student from grade to grade
- a peer tutoring handout that can be used for training peers to assist in physical education
- a peer tutor application form
- a peer tutor permission form
- a peer tutor quiz to determine if peers have learned the basic skills presented in the training
- a process checklist for dribbling a basketball that can be replicated for other sport skills
- a peer tutor evaluation checklist to determine how effectively the peer works with the tutee
- a sample form letter to a physician requesting permission for modified physical education for students who have a temporary disability
- an aquatic skills checklist

We hope that by providing these resources, you will be able to be successfully include students with disabilities in physical education, physical activity, and recreation programs.

PART I

Understanding Inclusion

It has been documented that more than 93 percent of children with disabilities are included in public schools. This change from typically segregated placements to more inclusive environments has resulted from Public Law 94-142, the *Education for All Handicapped Children Act of 1975*, reauthorized as Public Law 108-446, the *Individuals With Disabilities Education Improvement Act of 2004*. The law requires that children with disabilities receive physical education and that, if necessary, it be adapted to meet their unique needs. The law also requires that children with disabilities be educated in the least restrictive environment (LRE) possible, which means an educational environment in which the child will be most successful. In physical education, the most successful environment could range from a totally inclusive class to a segregated class. The most important thing to remember, however, is that a child with a disability can receive adapted physical education in any environment, because adapted physical education is a *service*, not a placement.

Inclusion—the process of educating children with and without disabilities together at all times—has become a reality for most school districts across the country. And even if a district has not embraced the concept of "total inclusion," most children with disabilities are included in its general physical education classes. Thus teachers of physical education are faced with the challenge of providing an appropriate education for students with a variety of abilities; but many teachers lack the professional preparation to know how to successfully include children with disabilities (Block 2007; Lieberman, Houston-Wilson, & Kozub, 2002). They may have good intentions yet possess limited knowledge about how to adapt the curriculum. Most undergraduate professional preparation programs offer only one class in adapted physical education, which seldom qualifies an individual to adequately adapt the whole curriculum for children with a variety of disabilities. In addition, most schools do not offer in-service training to assist teachers and paraeducators in including all children successfully (Davis, Kotecki, Harvey, & Oliver, 2007). As a result, many teachers have very little knowledge of the variables that determine success in the gymnasium.

The challenge faced by physical educators is compounded by the fact that children with disabilities are often behind in their levels of fitness (Lieberman & McHugh 2001; Shephard 1990) and motor skills (Silliman-French, Candler, French, & Hamilton, 2007). The solution to these problems—and the purpose of the first part of this book—is to educate and empower teachers of physical education by introducing them to all the variables that can be adapted to ensure appropriate inclusion in physical education. It is only when teachers are willing to plan ahead and analyze their curriculum, instruction, rules, equipment, and environment that children with disabilities will have a chance at full participation in general physical education. The following table shows how children feel when they are included versus when they are excluded. Inclusion is worth the time and energy because all students should experience the feelings resulting from being included when they leave the gymnasium.

Feelings Associated With Exclusion Versus Inclusion

Excluded		Included	
Angry	Worthless	Proud	Appreciated
Resentful	Invisible	Secure	Reinforced
Hurt	Substandard	Special	Loved
Frustrated	Unwanted	Comfortable	Grateful
Lonely	Untrusted	Recognized	Normal
Different	Unaccepted	Confident	Open
Confused	Closed	Happy	Positive
Isolated	Ashamed	Excited	Nurtured
Inferior		Trusted	Important
		Cared about	Responsible
		Liked	Grown-up
		Accepted	

Falvey, Givner, & Kimm, 1995.

CHAPTER 1

The Move to Include

Ian is a 5-year-old boy with diplegic cerebral palsy; diplegia is a condition in which the arms are slightly affected and the legs are greatly affected. After attending an inclusive preschool program at a United Cerebral Palsy center for a year, Ian was ready to begin kindergarten in his local school district. He had made great gains in preschool, especially in the motor area, and he could now walk slowly without a walker, and even faster with a walker. At the start of the school year, Ian was assigned a teacher's aide named Ms. Adams, who had worked with a child with cerebral palsy before and was looking forward to working with Ian.

Preparing for kindergarten was a little scary for Ian, but once he met Ms. Adams he was more comfortable. Ms. Adams and Ian's mother made sure that the teachers in the school knew about Ian's disability—as well as his abilities—during a meeting about his individualized education program (IEP). It was decided that Ian would be included in his general physical education class because his skills were adequate for the intended curriculum.

The general physical education teacher, Mrs. Bishop, who attended the meeting, was honest and said that she did not have much experience in teaching children with physical disabilities but was willing to do her best to accommodate Ian. Mrs. Bishop had taught elementary physical education for 13 years and had received support and recognition from parents and administrators for her creativity and encouraging spirit. Mrs. Bishop was assured that she would receive support from an adapted physical education (APE) consultant.

As the school year progressed, the consultant showed Mrs. Bishop how to modify and adapt activities so that Ian could be included successfully in physical education. After a while, Mrs. Bishop began to think of her own strategies and also solicited advice from the students in the class, as well as from Ian, who often had the best suggestions. The children were very supportive and enthusiastic about helping Ian to succeed in physical education. Mrs. Bishop modified some equipment, the pace of some games, and the instructional grouping, and Ian did well. Mrs. Bishop reflected on the experience and concluded that all good teaching is adapted.

> **The purpose of this chapter is to help readers**
>
> ■ understand the historical and legislative mandates that have affected the education of students with disabilities,
> ■ understand physical education placement options available to students with disabilities,
> ■ become familiar with research on the effectiveness of including students with disabilities in physical education, and
> ■ understand the roles and responsibilities of the general physical education teacher and the adapted physical education teacher in the education of students with disabilities.

As dramatized in the opening scenario, schools are responsible for planning the intake of students with disabilities. The scenario also illustrates the need for and value of including physical education teachers in preliminary discussions. For example, when Mrs. Bishop described her limited ability and experience in working with students with physical disabilities, she was provided with the assistance of an adapted physical education consultant. Unfortunately, scenarios like this may not be the norm for everyone. Sometimes physical educators are unaware until the first day of school that they will have students with special needs in their classes; these teachers are often left out of the loop in planning for placement of students with disabilities. They often do not even see the student's individualized education plan, and such lack of information and communication is frustrating for even the most competent and motivated teachers. However, as frustrating as the bureaucracy surrounding school policy and procedures may be, it is important that teachers continue to work to involve themselves in the process. Only through persistence will teachers become fully valued members of the team. Similarly, teachers who involve themselves in the planning and implementation process will be more able to secure the necessary resources and supports to make inclusion a successful experience, both for themselves and for their students with disabilities.

A Historical Perspective

Educating students with disabilities was not always required. In fact, before much attention was paid to the subject, several parent activist groups filed suit on behalf of their children with disabilities who were being denied an education. Two specific landmark lawsuits filed in 1972 in the United States (*Pennsylvania Association for Retarded Children v. Commonwealth of Pennsylvania* and *Mills v. Board of Education of the District of Columbia*) set the stage for the passage of several laws that ensured the right to schooling opportunities for all students with disabilities. In both cases, children with disabilities were being denied the right to an education due specifically to their disability. It was determined that excluding children with disabilities from public education violated both the 5th (due process) and the 14th (equal protection under the law) constitutional amendments.

▶ Exclusion, such as leaving a student out of a basketball game, can have long-lasting negative effects.

Legislative Mandates

As a result of these watershed lawsuits, two legislative mandates were passed: the *Rehabilitation Act of 1973* (Public Law 93-112) and the *Education for All Handicapped Children Act of 1975* (Public Law 94-142). The latter has undergone a series of reauthorizations and is currently known as the *Individuals with Disabilities Education Improvement Act of 2004* (PL 108-446). All components of PL 94-142 have been retained, and other mandates have been added over the years. These laws have affected the provision of physical education services to students with disabilities. Part of PL 93-112 (the *Rehabilitation Act*) is Section 504, which stipulates that no person with a disability shall be discriminated against or denied opportunity equal to that afforded to nondisabled individuals in any programs or activities that receive federal funding. This stipulation has been especially significant, because all public schools receive some form of federal support; as a result, students with disabilities are guaranteed equal protection under the law. This law also stipulates that students with disabilities should be provided with physical education and opportunities in sport-related programs comparable to those available to their nondisabled peers.

Similarly, the *Education for All Handicapped Children Act of 1975* guaranteed that special education would be provided to qualified students to meet their unique needs. Special education is defined as specially designed instruction used to meet the unique needs of the learner. Instruction can take place in an array of environments, including schools, homes, and hospitals. Most significant, however, this law established that instruction in physical education *must* occur and that if necessary it may be adapted. The law went on to define physical education as the development of (a) physical and motor fitness, (b) fundamental motor skills and patterns, and (c) skills in aquatics, dance, sports, and individual and group games. Physical education was the only curricular area specifically identified in the law, a distinction which holds to this day. As a result, physical education is considered a *direct service*—a service that must be provided to all students with disabilities. *Related services*, on the other hand, are provided to students only to allow them to benefit from their educational experience; examples include occupational therapy, speech therapy, and physical therapy (Silliman-French, Candler, French, & Hamilton, 2007). While both physical therapy and occupational therapy can supplement a physical education program, these services can never supplant or replace a physical education program (Silliman-French et al.).

In addition to requiring physical education for all students with disabilities as a direct service, the law also stipulates that educational services must be provided by qualified personnel. Although federal legislation does not define the term *qualified personnel*, most states define it in their regulations governing physical education. New York, for example, defines it as anyone certified to teach physical education. Other states may allow classroom teachers to provide adapted physical education, and still others may require adapted physical education certification. Regardless of state definitions, however, anyone providing physical education to students with disabilities should be aware of appropriate adaptations and modifications to ensure successful physical education experiences (Winnick, 2005). The law also requires that students with disabilities be provided with an individualized education program that identifies specific educational needs and determines appropriate resources for addressing those needs.

Typically, upon notification that a student with a disability will be entering a district, an IEP team is assembled to determine an appropriate plan for the child. IEP team members usually include the following parties: parents; general education teachers, including the general physical education teacher if the student will be participating in regular physical education; special education teachers; special education providers, including adapted physical educators; school psychologist; school district representative; others, at the request of the parents or the school district (Sherrill, 2005); and, when appropriate, the child. During IEP deliberations, participants make placement decisions, determine modifications, and formulate adaptation strategies; they also finalize goals and objectives based both on the regular goals and objectives specific to each curricular area and on the results of an assessment of the student. Chapter 3 provides more information about the IEP process.

Initially, the law identified and defined 11 disability populations—specifically, those with deafness, deafblindness, emotional disturbance, hearing impairment, learning disability, mental retardation, speech or language impairment, multiple disabilities, orthopedic impairment, visual impairment including blindness, or other health impairment. In 1990, two other disability populations were added: those with autism and those with traumatic brain injury. Currently, any student between the ages of 3 and 21 who meets the criteria for one or more of the specified disabilities shall be provided with a free, appropriate public education in the least restrictive environment. Students with disabilities should be educated with their typically developing peers unless it would not be beneficial to do so. According to Yell (1998), students with disabilities should be removed from the general education class only when the student needs additional one-to-one services; when the placement has a negative effect on the other students in the class; when the inability to perform physically is deemed significant enough to warrant alternative placements; or when the student is not receiving educational benefit from the regular class placement (Block, 2007; Friend, 2005). Similarly, French, Henderson, Kinnison, and Sherrill (1998) noted that a student should be segregated from his or her typically developing peers for physical education only if there is a probability of harm to the student with the disability—if, for example, the student's disability might be exacerbated by involvement in regular physical education.

■ Adapted physical education constitutes not a placement but a service.

This model of providing services to students with disabilities in the typical environment, rather than removing them from the regular class to receive the service, is known as *inclusion*. When students with disabilities are provided with specialized instruction in physical education to meet their unique needs, they are receiving *adapted physical education*. Thus, adapted physical education constitutes not a placement but a service. While every effort should be made to educate students with disabilities in regular physical education by providing the necessary supports to ensure success, there will be instances where the regular class placement is not in the best interest of the learner, and perhaps not in the best interest of his or her peers (i.e., when a student is extremely disruptive or distracting). The law provides for a continuum of placement options to be made available to students with disabilities, ranging from a totally inclusive environment to a totally segregated environment. Students can move from option to option based on their unique needs within a given curricular area. Here is an example of a continuum of placement options that could be made available to students with disabilities in physical education.

Lieberman and Houston-Wilson Model of Continuum of Supports and Placement Options

A. Inclusion Options
  1. Full inclusion with no adaptations or support (no IEP needed)
  2. Full inclusion with curriculum adaptations and modifications
  3. Full inclusion with trained peer tutors
  4. Full inclusion with paraeducators
  5. Full inclusion with specialists

B. Part-Time Segregated and Part-Time Integrated Placement Options
  1. Split placement without additional support
  2. Split placement with additional support

C. Community-Based Options
  1. Part-time community-based, part-time school-based
  2. Full-time community-based

D. Full-Time Segregated Placement Options Within a Regular School District
  1. Reverse integration: typically developing peers attend class with peer with a disability
  2. Specialist-directed

E. Segregated Placement Options
  1. Day school for specific disabilities
  2. Residential school for specific disabilities
  3. Home schooling
  4. Institution
  5. Hospital

These options provide a basis for making educated decisions about the most appropriate learning environments for students with disabilities in physical education. Regardless of the placement option chosen, teachers must understand their unique roles and responsibilities when teaching students with disabilities in their physical education classes.

▶ The most appropriate placement for this student is with a peer tutor, who demonstrates the shot put throw.

Please note that the interest or the skill level of the teacher should not be considered; the placement of the child should be the first priority of the committee. If the teacher of the class does not have enough experience or does not feel confident, he or she may attend in-services, workshops, or conferences; hire an APE consultant; or take additional college courses. Such steps enable the teacher to accommodate the child by means of the most appropriate placement.

Roles and Responsibilities of the General Physical Education Teacher

General physical education teachers assume multiple roles. They prepare and implement units of instruction and lesson plans in line with state and national standards; ensure the safety of all participants by minimizing foreseeable risks, checking on the integrity of equipment, and maintaining a safe and secure physical environment; assess student performance and modify or enhance the curriculum based on students' needs; manage an array of student behaviors to ensure a successful and positive learning environment (Lavay, French, & Henderson, 2006); engage in public relations to promote their physical education programs; and participate in professional development training—just to name a few! Some physical educators also coach and are involved in other school-related functions. Add to this the challenge of teaching (with limited training) students with disabilities, and it is easy to see how even the most seasoned teacher might struggle to create the best experience possible for a student with disabilities, the rest of the class, and the instructor him- or herself.

However difficult the challenge, general physical education (GPE) teachers do indeed play a role in the education of students with disabilities, and to fulfill it they may need to master new skills, such as adapting activities, working with paraeducators and special education teachers, and understanding how to read and write individualized education programs and 504 plans. When necessary, GPE teachers must also collaborate with professionals who are experts in the motor domains, such as occupational and physical therapists (Silliman-French, Candler, French, & Hamilton, 2007). Information and support is available to those who seek it. For example, school districts are responsible for providing ongoing educational support and training for their employees, and physical educators can request in-service training in adapted physical education. Physical educators can also take advantage of an array of books and resources geared to teaching students with disabilities in physical education. In addition, specially trained physical education teachers, known as *adapted physical educators*, are available to consult with school districts and, if necessary, provide hands-on assistance. In order to gain the services of an adapted physical education consultant, the teacher should add it to the IEP under "support services" once the team agrees the service should be implemented.

Roles and Responsibilities of the Adapted Physical Education Specialist

Adapted physical education specialists typically hold an undergraduate concentration, and perhaps a master's degree, in adapted physical education. They have logged additional hours in working with students with disabilities in physical education, and many are certified specialists who have passed the Adapted Physical Education National Standards (APENS) test (Kelly, 2006). See appendix J for more information on APENS.

While all adapted physical education specialists have received training in general physical education, they have also learned a great deal about specific disability populations and communication methodologies. Through this knowledge, they are able to make adaptations appropriate for a given condition. Specialists are also well trained in serving as members of multidisciplinary teams, which meet to discuss assessment data, placement, and IEP programming for students with disabilities. They are empathetic to parents and work with them to determine family needs and priorities related to movement and to incorporate them into programming (Salend & Garrick-Duhaney, 2002). Specialists are well prepared to provide sport opportunities for students with disabilities and can help develop movement programs that embed unique sport experiences that can create lifelong movers (Foley, Tindall, Lieberman, & Kim, 2007). Often, specialists travel from school to school, either to consult with general physical educators or to provide direct services; in this approach, known as the "itinerant teacher model," school districts can hire their own specialist or contract out these services as needed. Together, general and adapted physical educators can work to create the most effective programming for students with disabilities.

Effectiveness of Inclusion

With all this talk about inclusion, one may wonder how effective it is to include students with disabilities in general physical education, rather than providing adapted physical education in a special setting. Researchers hold that inclusion often results in a dichotomy of emotions and findings (Morley, Bailey, Tan, & Cook, 2005; Verderber, Rizzo, & Sherrill, 2003). For example, Goodwin and Watkinson (2000) determined that included students rated their experiences as "good days" or "bad days" depending on the situation. On good days, they felt a sense of belonging, shared in the benefits of the activity, and were able to master tasks. On bad days, their participation was restricted, they felt isolated, or their competence was questioned. These findings mirror those produced by other research (e.g., Falvey, Givner, & Kimm, 1995).

Some researchers have indicated that students' social skills can be improved when they are educated in an inclusive environment (Suomi, Collier, & Brown, 2003). Others have found that students with and without disabilities demonstrated favorable attitudes toward peers, coaches, and teachers as a result of inclusion (Obrusnikova, Valkova, & Block, 2003). Furthermore, when games are appropriately modified to create successful experiences for all learners, students with and without disabilities are more receptive to accommodating students with disabilities (Kalyvas & Reid, 2003; Obrusnikova et al., 2003). Utilizing peer tutors has also been determined to have a positive effect on students with disabilities who are included in general physical education. Planned peer tutoring programs that include training have increased physical activity levels (Lieberman, Dunn, van der Mars, & McCubbin, 2000), opportunities to respond (Houston-Wilson, Dunn, van der Mars, & McCubbin, 1997; Ward & Ayvazo, 2006), academic learning time in physical education (Wiskochil, Lieberman, Houston-Wilson, & Petersen, 2007), and fitness levels (Halle, Gabler-Halle, & Bembren, 1989). More information about peer tutoring programs can be found in chapter 6.

Inclusion also promotes personal development in students with and without disabilities (Martin & Smith, 2002; Tapasak & Walther-Thomas, 1999) by providing opportunities for leadership (Lieberman, Arndt, & Daggett, 2007). For example, when using a sport education model where each student takes on multiple roles, cohesiveness within the group was strengthened, so that regardless of ability the team worked together to accomplish the goal. Finally, research on inclusion suggests that students without disabilities are more able to handle the onset of disability in their own lives when they have ongoing contact with others with disabilities (Block, 1999).

▶ Having peers stretching together prior to the start of an activity can improve attitudes and understanding.

While these results are positive in nature, a poorly administered inclusion program will not yield these same outcomes. For example, in a poorly administered inclusion class, students with disabilities may be ridiculed, left out, and made to feel bad if they are on a team that loses a game (Place & Hodge, 2001). This in turn can affect the activity level of students with disabilities, who may hesitate to play ball for fear of letting the team down (Block, 1999; Goodwin & Watkinson, 2000; Place & Hodge). Additionally, poorly administered peer tutoring programs can be harmful to students with disabilities. If students with disabilities are always being assisted, they may lose confidence in themselves and question their own self-worth (Goodwin, 2001), and this effect is often observed when a student without disabilities always serves in the role of peer helper. Such students often dominate the decision-making process, thus preventing the student with a disability from making his or her own decisions. It is imperative, then, that general physical education teachers work to ensure successful experiences for all students in their classes and that students with disabilities are warmly embraced and valued. As research has shown, an instructor's competence in including all students grows as he or she gains more experience in working with students with disabilities (Hardin, 2005). Furthermore, students tend to follow their teacher's lead, and modeling the behaviors you want your students to demonstrate is one way to encourage a positive experience for all students. This approach, coupled with professional support by an adapted physical education specialist and trained paraeducators, helps ensure successful inclusion.

Summary

With its brief historical overview of relevant legislation, this chapter was written to help physical educators understand the legislative mandates currently affecting the education of students with disabilities, as well as the many placement options available for students with special needs under current legislation. The chapter also reviewed the roles and responsibilities of general and adapted physical educators. Finally, a review of the literature regarding inclusion revealed that properly implemented inclusion practices—those that involve multiple parties and support systems—can yield positive effects, whereas poorly implemented inclusion practices can yield adverse effects.

Assessment: The Cornerstone of Effective Instruction

Olivia is a seventh grader who has arthrogryposis, a condition that primarily affects range of motion. Individuals with arthrogryposis typically demonstrate extreme rotation at the shoulder joint, making their arms turn inward, and abnormal positioning of their knees and feet. Olivia, who just started middle school, has many friends. She uses an electric wheelchair to ambulate but also has good use of her left leg, which she uses as much as possible. Olivia loves swimming, and during summer she swims independently in her family's outdoor pool. She also swam independently during her swimming unit in elementary school. Unfortunately, her elementary school teacher, Mr. Long, never documented student skill ability; as a result, there were no records of students' abilities in swimming or any other unit of instruction.

Unaware of this issue, Olivia was excited about middle school physical education because she knew that swimming was offered once a week during the first quarter. She could not wait to show off her skills to Mrs. Bowman, her new physical education teacher. On the first day of swim class, however, Mrs. Bowman was very reluctant to allow Olivia to go into the pool. Judging Olivia's physical appearance, Mrs. Bowman had a hard time believing that Olivia could swim independently, despite explanations by Olivia and her peers. Mrs. Bowman was just not going to take any risks and was fearful of possible liability. She allowed Olivia to swim only in the shallow water with a flotation device and a paraeducator to offer assistance if needed. Olivia was crushed and embarrassed. This was the one activity she could do independently, and do well, and the opportunity was gone. Olivia's mother contacted Mrs. Bowman at once. Mrs. Bowman agreed to a private evaluation to assess Olivia's swimming abilities. The whole situation was frustrating, embarrassing, and demeaning to Olivia, and it could have been avoided through the use of appropriate assessment practices.

The purpose of this chapter is to help readers

■ understand what assessment is;
■ understand the role that assessment plays in educating students with disabilities;
■ know the types of assessment, both traditional and authentic, that can be used to assess students with disabilities; and
■ understand how to use assessment data for program planning and implementation.

As noted in the scenario involving Olivia, assessment is needed to ensure that students receive an appropriate educational experience. Lack of information about students' abilities can compromise physical education programs, especially for students with special needs. Assessments need to accurately reflect what students can and cannot do in relation to the curriculum content. Poor, incomplete, or biased assessments yield weak and inaccurate information, which does little to shape the curriculum in a useful way. On the other hand, effective assessments—those prepared and administered with a clear purpose that is related to curriculum content—are useful in developing appropriate goals and objectives for all students; they can be used to help shape and grow student abilities (Henderson, French, & Kinnison, 2001). Once information is obtained about what students (regardless of special needs) can and cannot do, educators can carry out effective program planning and implement specific, appropriate activities. In contrast, failure to embed assessment in the physical education curriculum produces programs that do not address learners' individual needs and thus offer little benefit to the participants. Such programs can easily be targeted for elimination, since unless professionals can document learning, little value is placed on the subject matter.

What sets apart an effective assessment from an ineffective one is how accurately the assessment reflects the capabilities of the students being assessed. An effective assessment is objective and free from guesswork by the instructor as to the student's level of performance. To facilitate objective assessment, educators can use checklists that identify component parts of skills and that may also include a point system. Skills should be clearly identified, and the instructor should note which component parts of the skill the student has mastered. If points are attached, a score can be obtained; alternatively, the checklist can simply identify which component parts of the skill are yet to be mastered. Specific activities can then be developed to help the participant achieve a high level of mastery for any given skill observed.

Ability Description Chart

Student: _____
School: _____
Birth date: _____
Grade: _____
Previous physical education teacher: _____

Phone number: _____
Previous adapted physical education teacher (if applicable): _____

Phone number: _____
Form completed by: _____
Title of person completing the form: _____

During this semester, this student will receive his or her adapted physical education program in the regular physical education class. Please answer the following questions and give the requested descriptions as thoroughly as possible.

Disability: _____
Level of current function: _____
Ambulation method(s):
____ Wheelchair (pushes independently)   ____ Crutches   ____ Other
____ Wheelchair (needs assistance)   ____ Walker
Medical concerns:
____ Seizures   ____ Shunt   ____ Eye condition   ____ Ear condition
____ Diabetes   ____ Other: _____
Please elaborate: _____

Communication methods: _____

From Lauren J. Lieberman and Cathy Houston-Wilson, 2009, *Strategies for Inclusion, Second Edition* CD-ROM (Champaign, IL: Human Kinetics).

Before a child with a disability can be assessed, it is extremely important to acquire information about the child, and instructors can record such information on an Ability Description Chart. The instructor can ask parents, previous teachers, therapists, or administrators for any information that is not yet known to the teacher. Once this information is in hand, assessments will be much easier to implement. A printable version of the Ability Description Chart is included on the CD-ROM.

Features of Effective Assessment

Effective assessments produce data that are valid, reliable, and functional. *Valid* assessments are those that measure what one seeks to measure. For example, to assess students on throwing maturity, the assessment task must yield a throw. However, if the instructor adds the variable of accuracy to the throw (such as hitting a small target on the wall), the throwing assessment becomes invalid, because a person can demonstrate a mature throw without having to hit a specific target. Thus the addition of accuracy makes the test invalid if maturity is the variable being assessed. Assessments must also be *reliable*; that is, the test must give consistent results repeatedly. Finally, assessments should be *functional*. Tasks that require students to place pegs in a pegboard are not in themselves part of everyday functionality; seldom, if ever, is a person asked to place pegs in a pegboard. Although fine motor coordination is a necessary skill, assessments that measure fine motor skills should relate to everyday life. One example of a functional fine motor skill in physical education is tying knots during a ropes unit; another is zipping up one's personal flotation device in a swimming unit. Ensuring that tests are valid, reliable, and functional is the cornerstone of appropriate assessment.

An effective assessment is also easy to administer and easy to understand. The instructor must not only understand how to implement the test and interpret the results but also be able to present the information in a way that parents and administrators can understand. Various assessments can produce either limited or extensive statistical data. The key—regardless of the extent of the data generated—is being able to fully understand the assessment and clearly articulate its findings.

Utilizing appropriate assessments in physical education is imperative in determining the need for adapted physical education for students with disabilities. Appropriate assessments can (a) determine the unique physical or motor needs of students with disabilities, as well as appropriate placements based on those needs, (b) assist in the development of physical education goals and objectives, and (c) serve as a useful tool in monitoring student progress. These major outcomes are highlighted separately in the following sections.

▶ A teacher should assess students at the start of a unit to ensure that they have an appropriate baseline understanding of the skills to be covered.

Determining Unique Needs and Placement

Screening is the first step in determining whether a child has a unique need and is entitled to special education services such as adapted physical education. Screening involves the professional observation of student actions to determine whether these actions differ considerably from typical behavior. Physical educators are often asked to screen youngsters to determine whether motor delays are evident and whether further testing is warranted. To conduct screening tests, physical educators may develop checklists of skill performance and observe students as they perform various skills. Those who do not demonstrate developmentally appropriate or age-appropriate skill behaviors are identified for further testing.

This identification process is known as a *referral*, and referrals can be made to the Committee on Special Education (CSE) by any person who has a vested interest in the child, including parents, teachers, therapists, and physicians. Every district must have a CSE (or equivalent), which is made up of the child's teacher; a school psychologist; and a district representative qualified to provide, administer, or supervise special education. The CSE convenes to determine whether further testing is warranted; if so, physical educators or adapted physical education specialists may choose from a variety of formal tests and conduct formal assessments to determine unique needs and eligibility for services. Once students are deemed eligible, placement decisions are made about the appropriate environment in which the student will receive services (see chapter 1).

The *Individuals With Disabilities Education Improvement Act of 2004* requires that all students with special needs receive instruction in the least restrictive environment. For example, let's revisit Olivia, the student introduced in this chapter's opening scenario. She was to receive general physical education with her peers two times a week and separate physical education once a week to further her progress toward her goals and objectives. Because Olivia has limited range of motion, her goals centered on increasing flexibility, muscular strength and control, and body coordination. In her general physical education classes, she participated in the same unit as her peers, and her individual goals were incorporated where possible. In her separate physical education class, she worked predominantly on her individual goals. This combined program was least restrictive for Olivia, and she improved and excelled throughout the year. The lack of assessment data about Olivia at the start of the year created an embarrassing and negative situation. In contrast, assessing students to determine their ability and placement needs gives them an advantage, because they can be set up for success from the beginning (Auxter, Pyfer, & Huettig, 2005; Friend, 2005; Seaman, Depauw, Morton, & Omoto, 2003).

■ Collecting assessment data is the cornerstone of appropriate program planning, implementation, and evaluation.

Determining Program Goals and Objectives

Assessment in adapted physical education also aids in the development of program goals and objectives. Through assessment, physical educators can note individual strengths and weaknesses. Areas of weakness become *goals*, and improving on specific activities employed to reach goals are *objectives* (Burton & Miller, 1998). For example, Olivia's goal of developing muscular strength and control was incorporated into a gymnastics unit with her peers. A rubric was developed for the class, which included such tasks as performing front supports on a mat, doing a crab walk, performing movements with ribbons to accompanying music, and doing various rolls on the mat. These activities provided a way for Olivia to increase her muscular endurance and control in a typical physical education environment. Knowing students' goals and objectives and enhancing them are crucial to student learning. Thus Olivia can work on her goals and objectives with her peers *and* improve her ability to do activities of daily living.

Monitoring Progress

Finally, assessment provides physical educators with a way to monitor students' progress. Through ongoing assessment, students and teachers can note individual progress, and as one goal is achieved others can be developed.

The monitoring of a student's progress can take many forms. One easy and motivating approach is to create an Individual Skill Chart for students to keep in their portfolios. Olivia's upper-body strength was first evaluated using a lat pulldown machine. With straps tied around her wrists because of her difficulty with grasp, she could lift 10 pounds (4.5 kilograms) 3 to 5 times for 3 sets. During the gymnastics unit, she practiced making circles with streamers tied to her wrists and could do 10 circles with both arms. After 4 weeks of work on this goal in the gymnastics unit and in her separate class, she could do 10 to 12 repetitions on the lat pulldown machine and 15 circles with the streamers. Documenting this progress on an Individual Skill Chart showed Olivia how much she had improved through training and thus motivated her to continue working to develop her strength.

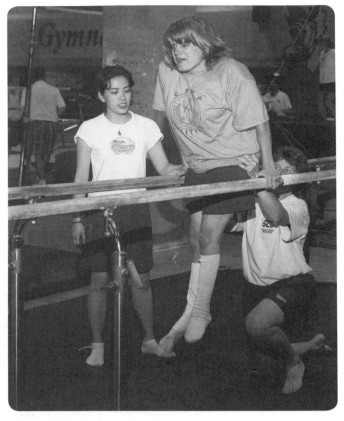

▶ To meet objectives, students must challenge themselves to improve their abilities.

Traditional Assessment Techniques

Since the 1950s, assessment in general physical education has traditionally focused on the physical fitness domain, and there has been a notable lack of testing instruments in the other areas of physical education. In fact, testing in physical education has often been viewed as confusing, time consuming, and unnecessary. The publication of the National Association for Sport & Physical Education's content standards (2004), however, has prompted a resurgence in the perceived need for and value of assessment for all students in physical education. NASPE's content standards posit the following capabilities and attitudes in a physically educated person:

1. Demonstrates competency in motor skills and movement patterns needed to perform a variety of physical activities.

2. Demonstrates understanding of movement concepts, principles, strategies, and tactics as they apply to the learning and performance of physical activities.

3. Participates regularly in physical activity.

4. Achieves and maintains a health-enhancing level of physical fitness.

5. Exhibits responsible personal and social behavior that respects self and others in physical activity settings.

6. Values physical activity for health, enjoyment, challenge, self-expression, and social interaction.

To maximize the effect of these new standards, teachers must utilize appropriate methods of assessment to ensure that students are meeting the standards. Physical educators realize that for programs to be held accountable, data need to be available to document student learning, and these data can be generated only through assessment.

In the field of adapted physical education, assessment continues to be the cornerstone for effective programming and instruction. A variety of assessment instruments are available to assist professionals in determining whether unique needs exist, identifying areas of strength and weakness, and documenting students' progress and learning. When choosing an assessment tool for students with disabilities, professionals look for qualities such as purpose, technical adequacy (validity and reliability), ecological validity (testing in a natural environment), nondiscriminatory features, ease of administration, cost, and availability. It is also important to consider whether the test is norm- or criterion-referenced, is curriculum-based, or has an instructional link (Zittel, 1994). Some tests are designed primarily for screening, whereas others are used for placement and program decisions. Some tests are considered formal because they must be set up and administered by using a specific protocol; these tests may require additional time to administer and in some instances may require training before test administration. Other tests are considered informal because the teacher can gain the necessary information through observation or the use of checklists with no strict protocol. Informal assessments can be conducted during class and can be administered by the instructor, a peer tutor, a paraeducator, or support personnel. All tests yield data that can be used in the development of individualized education plans (IEPs) in physical education.

To choose the most appropriate, efficient test for a particular situation, instructors may want to ask themselves some important questions. The following questions can help instructors make the right decisions:

Assessing the Assessment

1. What is the purpose of the assessment (screening, placement, programming, documenting improvement)? Does its purpose meet my purpose?
2. Is this test valid and reliable for the population I am testing?
3. Can I implement this test in my current setting?
4. Is the test qualitative or quantitative?
5. Does the test give criterion-referenced results or normative results?
6. Can my district afford this test?
7. Are the results understandable to parents and administrators?
8. Does the test come with any curriculum suggestions or ideas?

After answering these questions, the teacher can select the most appropriate test. The following list presents appropriate assessments that can be used to measure abilities from birth to 21 years of age.

Commonly Used Tests in Adapted Physical Education

APEAS II (Seaman, 2007)

Ages: Children ranging from 4 years and 6 months to 17 years of age

Tests: Perceptual motor function, object control, locomotor skills, physical fitness

Features: Norm-referenced

Contact: www.aapar-apeas.org

Brockport Aquatic Skills Checklist

Ages: Any

Tests: Pool preparation, pool entry, adjustment to water, floating skills, basic propulsion, swimming strokes, diving skills, water safety, and deepwater skills

Features: Checklist for each skill with corresponding levels of assistance needed to complete task

Availability: Included in appendix C and on the CD-ROM

Bruininks-Oseretsky Test of Motor Proficiency, 2nd Edition (Bruininks & Bruininks, 2005)

Ages: 4 to 21 years

Tests: Fine motor precision and integration, manual dexterity, bilateral coordination, balance, running speed and agility, upper-limb coordination, and strength

Features: Gamelike tasks, normative data, and profile analysis to evaluate an individual's strengths and weaknesses

Contact: www.pearsonassessments.com

Denver Developmental Screening Test, 2nd Edition (Frankenburg & Dodds, 1990)

Ages: Birth to 6 years

Tests: Fine motor, gross motor, social, and language skills

Features: Screening test to determine whether a child's development is within the normal range

Contact: www.denverii.com

I CAN Primary Skills K–3 (Wessel & Zittel, 1998)

Ages: 5 to 8 years

Tests: Locomotor, object control, orientation, play participation, and equipment

Features: Instructional link to an early elementary school motor curriculum

Contact: www.proedinc.com

Peabody Developmental Motor Scales, 2nd Edition (Folio & Fewel, 2000)

Ages: Birth to 5 years

Tests: Fine and gross motor skills

Features: Instructional link to motor activities

Contact: www.theraproducts.com

Smart Start: Preschool Movement Curriculum Designed for Children of All Abilities (Wessel & Zittel, 1995)

Ages: 3 to 6 years

Tests: Locomotor, object control, orientation, and play skills

Features: Instructional link to a preschool motor curriculum

Contact: www.proedinc.com

The Test of Gross Motor Development (TGMD), 2nd Edition (Ulrich, 2000)

Ages: 3 to 10 years

Tests: Locomotor and object control skills

Features: Criterion-referenced and normative standards.

Contact: www.proedinc.com

The Brockport Physical Fitness Test: A Health-Related Test for Youth with Physical and Mental Disabilities (Winnick & Short, 1999)

Ages: 10 to 17 years

Tests: Health-related physical fitness (aerobic capacity, muscular strength and endurance, flexibility, body composition)

Features: Criterion-referenced fitness standards for youth with special needs; computer applications to generate fitness reports

Contact: www.HumanKinetics.com

▶ A teacher must monitor students' progress to determine if they are meeting standards.

Although these commonly used tests can be quite useful in screening and evaluating students, making placement decisions, and developing program goals and objectives, they do have their limitations. For example, some students with severe disabilities may be unable to be tested in traditional ways, and when a test is not conducted in the way in which it was intended, the results are invalid. In addition, some traditional tests are more developmental in nature and, as such, are targeted toward elementary students. Unfortunately, tests for middle and high school students are not readily available, and tests linking assessment to the middle or high school curriculum have been almost nonexistent. Because of these factors, a new and creative way to assess students, known as *authentic assessment*, was developed.

New Assessment Options

Researchers have indicated that standardized testing protocols may present challenges in adapted physical education. For example, Block (2007) noted that outcomes from standardized tests have been misused in determining IEP goals and objectives; in addition, some standardized tests do not provide an instructional link to the physical education curriculum (Kowalski, Lieberman, Pucci, & Mulawka, 2005), and some items are not functional in relation to physical education or daily living skills (Block, Lieberman, & Connor-Kuntz, 1998). For example, although the Bruininks-Oseretsky Test of Motor Proficiency II (Bruininks & Bruininks, 2005) is considered a blue-ribbon standardized test for determining the need for special education services (such as adapted physical education), components of this test bear little relation to typical physical education curriculum content; tasks such as stringing beads (fine motor) or stopping a falling ruler (reaction time) do not correspond with physical education curricular content. These tasks are used, however, to develop an overall picture of the child's motor proficiency, and their value should not be minimized. Thus, although there is a purpose for standardized tests, other forms of assessment need to be examined that can provide more content-specific data, and authentic assessment fills this gap.

Authentic assessment is an ongoing feedback system that monitors and records student learning and outcomes under what are termed *authentic conditions*. Authentic assessment is conducted in real-life situations and gives students a chance to demonstrate skills, knowledge, and competencies in age-appropriate, functional activities. It is a performance-based approach to testing, which means that students are evaluated on skills directly related to outcomes of the program. The results provide unparalleled information about students' learning and achievement. Many in the teaching field today agree that this assessment technique should be infused into the teaching process (Jackson & Larkin, 2002; Wiggins, 1997).

Authentic assessment offers many benefits. They include the following:

■ Authentic assessment can be used in the current curriculum.

■ It is created specifically for the goals and objectives of each unit.

■ It can be created in such a way as to include every level of ability in the class.

■ Students are held accountable for their own learning.

■ Students know what is expected ahead of time.

■ Authentic assessment is motivating and challenging, and it keeps students interested in learning.

Authentic assessment is a clear, concise, measurable, and motivating way of assessing student learning, improvement, and achievement. Authentic assessment utilizes tasks that are based on roles and responsibilities required in real-world settings; as a result, students must rely on higher-level thinking and concept application in order to complete tasks. In addition, because the assessed skills are directly tied to the curriculum, students are informed in advance and get time to practice the skills. This advance knowledge gives students ownership of the process. They can prepare mentally and physically for testing, thus performing at their highest competency level (Block et al., 1998; Melograno, 1994; Smith, 1997).

The following sections describe several kinds of authentic assessment: rubrics, ecological task analysis, portfolios, and alternative assessment.

Rubrics

A rubric is a detailed guideline for making scoring decisions. It indicates specific scoring criteria to be used in evaluating student performance and progress (Smith, 1997). Scoring is qualitative rather than quantitative. Our culture already uses rubrics in formal ways, such as assigning levels of achievement in karate, gymnastics, or swimming. These rubrics have been successful because they are directly tied to instruction and because students know in advance what is expected and thus can be made accountable for their own learning. Rubrics can be created uniquely for each lesson and class; therefore, they can easily be individualized.

Rubrics used in previous years were better known by the terms *checklist, task analysis,* and *rating scale.* The current rubric evaluation system combines all of these approaches to give students a comprehensive idea of how to perform, what to perform, and the number of trials to be performed. The instructor develops and shares rubrics before the unit is taught so that students know what is expected of them.

Rubrics offer many advantages. Because they must be clear, observable, and measurable, students can learn to critically evaluate their peers' performance and achievement (Jackson & Larkin, 2002). Students can also self-assess, note their current level of achievement, and work to improve, and this process has proven to be quite motivational. A rubric can cover a wide range of abilities and accommodate heterogeneous classes by including multiple levels of achievement. Rubrics are also useful in developing a progressive curriculum so that students must attain prerequisite levels of skill before they can move on to more advanced forms of the skill. This process can help ensure the safety of the learners. Finally, rubrics can be developed to assess the *process*, or quality, of a movement skill; the *product*, or quantity, of a movement skill (how far, how fast, how many); and the *parameters*, or the conditions under which the movement skill was performed. As a result, both qualitative and quantitative data can be obtained. The rubric for juggling presented in figure 2.1 illustrates how a rubric can include both a qualitative and a quantitative approach to scoring.

Rubrics created for typically developing students may need to be modified in order to allow students with disabilities to be included in the assessment. The following list, based on the work of Block et al. (1998), presents adaptations that can be made in typical rubrics to ensure success.

1. **Rubric extension.** There may be times when the rubric starts too high for a student with a disability or too low for a highly skilled student. The concept of rubric extensions allows for more levels of observation within a given activity. Figure 2.2 presents an example; items marked with an asterisk constitute the extensions. This rubric also allows the instructor to determine the level of assistance that a student may need in order to achieve each objective.

▶ Students with disabilities should be included in a general physical education class and assessed from their individual skill level.

FIGURE 2.1

Rubric for Juggling

Jester
☐ Student can throw and catch scarf with one hand.
☐ Student can throw and catch scarf with either hand.
☐ Student can throw and catch one scarf from one hand to the other.

Street Performer
☐ Student can throw two scarves in the air and catch one at a time.
☐ Student can throw two scarves in the air and catch both at the same time.
☐ Student can simultaneously throw one scarf from left hand to right and another from right hand to left.

Juggle Bug
☐ Student can cascade-juggle three scarves 1 time.
☐ Student can cascade-juggle three scarves 5 times.
☐ Student can cascade-juggle three scarves more than 10 times.

Cool Clown
☐ Student can throw and catch a beanbag in both hands.
☐ Student can throw and catch two beanbags (one at a time) from one hand to the other.
☐ Student can simultaneously throw one beanbag from left hand to right and another from right hand to left.

Circus Clown
☐ Student can cascade-juggle three beanbags 1 time.
☐ Student can cascade-juggle three beanbags 5 times.
☐ Student can cascade-juggle three beanbags more than 10 times.

Ringling Brothers' #1 Juggling Clown
☐ Student can cascade-juggle more than three beanbags.
☐ Student can cascade-juggle two or three clubs.
☐ Student can juggle while riding a unicycle.
☐ Student can perform various juggling tricks, such as behind the back, under the leg, twirls, or partner juggle.

FIGURE 2.2

Scooter Traveler

Instructions: Next to each statement, write the code (check mark or letters) that best describes the student's performance. Items marked with an asterisk are rubric extensions.

√ = No assistance needed

PA = Partial assistance needed

TA = Total assistance needed

Slick Rider

*_____ Student lies on scooter while teacher, paraeducator, or peer pulls or pushes across gym 1 time.

Hammer Hold

*_____ Student sits or lies on scooter and holds a hula hoop or jump rope while teacher, aide, or peer grasps the other end and pulls the student across the gym 1 time.

Speedster

_____ Student sits on scooter and pushes self across gym with legs, demonstrating control, 1 time.

_____ Student lies on scooter and pulls self across gym with arms, demonstrating control, 1 time.

Roadrunner

_____ Student sits on scooter and pushes self across gym with legs, demonstrating control, 2 to 5 times.

_____ Student lies on scooter and pulls self across gym with arms, demonstrating control, 2 to 5 times.

*_____ Student lies on scooter while teacher, paraeducator, or peer pulls across gym, 2 to 5 times.

*_____ Student sits or lies on scooter and holds a hula hoop or jump rope while teacher, paraeducator, or peer grasps the other end and pulls the student across the gym 2 to 5 times.

Quicksilver

_____ Student sits on scooter and pushes self across gym with legs, demonstrating control, 6 to 10 times.

_____ Student lies on scooter and pulls self across gym with arms, demonstrating control, 6 to 10 times.

*_____ Student lies on scooter while teacher, paraeducator, or peer pulls across gym 6 to 10 times.

*_____ Student sits or lies on scooter and holds a hula hoop or jump rope while teacher, paraeducator, or peer grasps the other end and pulls the student across the gym 6 to 10 times.

Blast-off

_____ Student sits on scooter and pushes self across gym with arms and legs, demonstrating control, 6 to 10 times.

2. Rubric within a rubric. Some students with disabilities may need to implement their IEP goals within the regular class setting, and the idea of a rubric within a rubric is that a student can work on the overall class objective through the class rubric and on his or her IEP goals through an individual rubric. Here's an example: Sam, a seventh grader with Down syndrome, has low physical endurance. In order to enhance it, a rubric was created that leads him toward keeping his heart rate in the working heart rate zone for 3 periods of 6 minutes per class. This rubric was incorporated into the existing class rubric during a soccer unit, enabling Sam to go into the game and be encouraged to actively participate in play for intervals of 6 minutes. In this way, he is meeting his individual endurance goal through participation in the class unit.

3. Rubric analysis. In some cases, students with disabilities may need a skill to be further task-analyzed or broken down into smaller parts in order to achieve levels of success (Block et al., 1998). See, for example, the rubric analysis of foul shooting presented in figure 2.3; as each component is mastered, the student moves to the next level.

4. Individual rubric. Students with special needs may require rubrics developed specifically for their individual needs. Although the child may be able to participate in a specific unit of instruction (for example, dance), he or she may work specifically on balance while the rest of the class works on mastering a variety of dance steps. A child with limited balance who is engaged in a dance unit is able to do such things as toe walking for distance, standing on one foot for a certain period, and challenging equilibrium without losing balance. An individual rubric would reflect these specific skills and the child's ability to perform them. Rubrics can be a motivating, challenging, and rewarding approach to teaching almost anything. See part II of the book for more examples.

Ecological Task Analysis

Another form of authentic assessment that has been used with students with disabilities is ecological task analysis (ETA) (Davis & Broadhead, 2007; Davis & Burton, 1991). ETA provides students with choices within the environment for executing various skills. Thus the teacher sets the parameters or objectives, and students then choose the type of equipment, the rules, and the pace of activity with which to execute the designated skill. Teachers observe and maintain data about these behaviors and use the data to continually challenge students within their comfort level. Here is an example of utilizing ETA for the skill of striking a ball:

Striking a Ball

1. Present the task goal: "striking" or "propelling" a ball.
2. Provide options, such as size, color, and weight of ball; size and weight of bat; and choice of batting tee, thrown pitch, or hanging ball to hit.
3. Document student choices (e.g., "red ball off of a tee with tennis racket").
4. Manipulate task variables to further challenge the student (e.g., decreasing the size of the ball or hitting implement).

This system offers several advantages: the instructor learns what movement form and equipment are most comfortable to the student, the student starts out with success, and the teacher knows that the student is being realistically challenged because the teacher has set the task goal. There are no right or wrong choices for equipment or execution of performance; however, the type of equipment made available by the teacher limits the student's choices (Carson, Bulger, & Townsend, 2007). ETA is used

FIGURE 2.3

Rubric Analysis of Foul Shooting

Minnesota Lynx

*Knees bent.

Charlotte Sting

1. Knees bent.
2. Eyes on basket.

Cleveland Rocker

1. Knees bent.
2. Eyes on basket.
3. Body extended upward (for example, knees straightened, hips straightened, standing on toes).

New York Liberty

1. Knees bent.
2. Eyes on basket.
3. Body extended upward.
4. Correct hand position on ball.
   - a. Nonshooting hand supporting ball held in shooting hand.
   - b. Shooting hand positioned with palm up, fingers pointing back toward shooter.
   - c. Wrist flexed forward.

Houston Comet

1. Knees bent.
2. Eyes on basket.
3. Body extended upward.
4. Correct hand position on ball.
   - a. Nonshooting hand supporting ball held in shooting hand.
   - b. Palm up, fingers facing shooter.
   - c. Wrist flexed forward.
5. Shooting motion marked by extension of shooting arm up and forward.
6. Follow-through marked by full extension and reaching of shooting arm toward basket.

▶ It is important to work within a student's comfort level when teaching new skills.

to determine preferences and skill level and as a starting point in deciding how to further challenge the student (Mitchell & Oslin, 2007).

To illustrate this point, consider the following example: Felicia is a middle school student with mild intellectual disability, and her class is participating in a volleyball unit. Felicia is being taught the underhand serve and is given a choice between a beach ball, a volleyball trainer, and a regulation volleyball. She is also given a choice about how far from the net she will be when she serves; tape marks are placed on the floor in 1-foot (0.3-meter) increments from the net to the serving line. She chooses a beach ball and serves from a line located 2 feet (0.6 meter) from the net. Based on these choices, the teacher now knows that Felicia is a beginner. The teacher can further refine Felicia's skills and slowly work toward using smaller and harder balls until she feels comfortable making an underhand serve from the service line with a regulation volleyball.

Portfolios

A portfolio is a compilation of a student's best work; as such, it can reflect how close a student comes to achieving the necessary outcomes for being regarded as a "physically educated person" (Franck et al., 1992). Portfolios are also the most promising method of exhibiting and recording student performances. Because they reflect the outcomes of performance in each domain (psychomotor, cognitive, and affective), they provide a broad overview that gives teachers, parents, and learners a genuine picture of achievement. The visual presentation of student performance can be used as a motivational tool, a method of communication with the family, a means for grading, and a vehicle for program promotion. Portfolios can be used to chart progress in all domains over the course of a unit, a semester, a year, or a period of multiple years (Melograno, 2006).

> ## Contents of a Portfolio
>
> | | |
> |---|---|
> | Journals | Videos |
> | Self-reflections or self-assessments | Skill analysis |
> | Rubrics, checklists, or rating scales | Game statistics |
> | Peer evaluations | Special individual and group projects |
> | Fitness, cognitive, or affective tests | Teacher comments |
> | Articles, article critiques, or collages | Interest surveys |

Portfolio entries can be made daily, or specific achievements can be included when they occur. Students can be evaluated on portfolio contents in various ways, depending on the age of the student and on the content and purpose of the portfolio. If it is used as an evaluation or grading tool, the instructor can give an objective point or percentage value to contents in each domain in order to produce a composite score. For example, the portfolio can be divided into sections such as psychomotor, cognitive, affective, and physical fitness. Within each section, various components can be included, and a certain point value can be attached to each item. Portfolio scores can then be generated based on the portfolio content.

Alternative Assessment

Although authentic assessment helps fill the gaps left by traditional and standardized forms of assessment, students with severe disabilities may need alternative assessment. This section presents two forms of alternative assessment that can be used with students with severe disabilities. These assessments are intended to provide data that can be used in determining present levels of performance, creating goals and objectives for instruction and for IEP development, and evaluating progress made by students who cannot complete traditional tasks even with modifications and by those who need physical assistance to perform tasks. In addition, these assessments allow teachers to assess all students in their physical education classes, provide programmatic assessment data, and encourage inclusion by clearly demonstrating that students with disabilities are a part of the assessment process. They are useful in any state that utilizes performance-based assessment to help demonstrate competency and proficiency.

The two forms of assessment in question are the basic skills assessment (Kowalski, Daggett, Speedling, &, Houston-Wilson, 2002), used with students who have less severe disabilities, and the task analysis assessment (Houston-Wilson, 1995), used with those who have more severe disabilities. Once students are able to master the components of the task analysis assessment, they should use the basic skills assessment; in turn, once students are able to master the components of the basic skills assessment, they should be assessed using other forms of authentic and traditional assessment described in this chapter. These two approaches are not intended to create a separate-but-equal assessment, but to provide ideas for achieving equity in assessment within the physical education curriculum based on the unique needs of the learner.

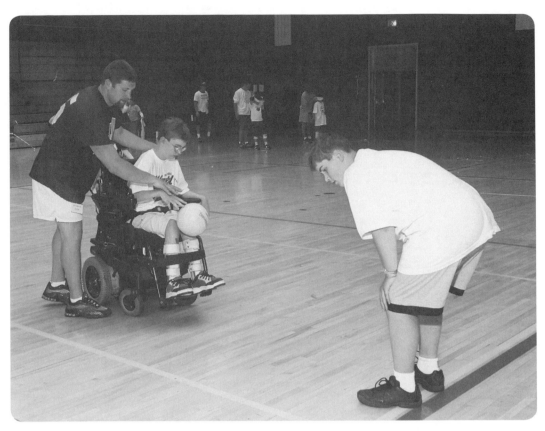

▶ During assessment, provide physical assistance as needed to students with disabilities.

Basic Skills Assessment

The basic skills assessment, modified from the 1989 Special Olympics Sports Skills Program (Special Olympics International), assesses performance of individual physical skills evaluates cognitive understanding of the game, and demonstrates personal and social skills that lead up to playing a game. Rather than assessing abilities in playing the game, students are assessed on the acquisition of individual skills at three levels: emerging, basic, and acquired. Here is a sample basic skills assessment for softball:

BASIC SKILLS ASSESSMENT FOR SOFTBALL

Instructions

This test consists of seven items, and each test item includes several tasks. To administer the test, observe the student as he or she performs each of the tasks within each test item and check off each task that the student completes successfully. If you have a question as to whether or not a student is able to complete a task, require the student to perform the task successfully in three out of five attempts. After the student has completed the seven test items, total up the number of checked boxes and apply the score to the chart provided in figure 2.4 to determine the student's present level of ability (emerging, basic, or acquired).

FIGURE 2.4

Basic Skills Assessment Chart

NAME: _____ **AGE:** _____ **DATE:** ____/____/____

CHECK BOX WHEN A STUDENT CAN SUCCESSFULLY COMPLETE THE FOLLOWING SKILLS:

TEST ITEM 1—THROWING

_____ Grips ball. _____ Throws softball in any direction.	**EMERGING SKILLS**
_____ Throws softball in desired direction. _____ Throws softball to designated teammate.	**BASIC SKILLS**
_____ Throws softball underhand. _____ Throws softball overhand.	**ACQUIRED SKILLS**

TEST ITEM 2—PITCHING

_____ Attempts to pitch a softball.	**EMERGING SKILLS**
_____ Pitches a softball underhand for a distance of 20 feet (6.1 meters) into a target area. _____ Pitches a softball underhand for a distance of 40 feet (12.2 meters) into a target area.	**BASIC SKILLS**
_____ Pitches a softball underhand with good form and height. _____ Pitches a softball into a regulation strike zone from 40 feet (12.2 meters).	**ACQUIRED SKILLS**

TEST ITEM 3—CATCHING/FIELDING

____ Attempts to catch a softball.
____ Attempts to field a softball.

EMERGING SKILLS

____ Fields a rolled softball correctly.
____ Makes an above-the-waist catch.
____ Makes a below-the-waist catch.
____ Catches an underhand throw.
____ Catches an overhand throw.

BASIC SKILLS

____ Catches a hit softball.
____ Fields a hit softball.
____ Catches or fields a softball and throws to an appropriate teammate.
____ Moves to position, with body in front of a hit ball in a softball game.
____ Catches or fields a hit softball cleanly in a softball game.

ACQUIRED SKILLS

TEST ITEM 4—BATTING

____ Assumes proper batting stance.
____ Attempts to hit a softball off of a batting tee.
____ Hits a softball off of a tee in any direction.

EMERGING SKILLS

____ Hits a softball off of a tee in desired direction.
____ Hits a softball off of a tee into fair territory in a game.
____ Attempts to hit a pitched softball.

BASIC SKILLS

____ Hits a pitched softball.
____ Hits a pitched softball into fair territory during a game.
____ Hits a pitched softball for a base hit in a game.

ACQUIRED SKILLS

(continued)

Figure 2.4 *(continued)*

TEST ITEM 5—BASERUNNING

____ Identifies order of running bases.	
____ Walks to first base.	
____ Attempts to run to first base.	**EMERGING SKILLS**
____ Runs to first base.	
____ Runs to first base within the base path.	

____ Tags first base and runs beyond it.	
____ Attempts to run to first base after hitting a pitched softball.	**BASIC SKILLS**
____ Runs safely to first base after hitting a pitched softball.	

____ Rounds first base when there is a chance for additional base(s).	
____ When appropriate, tags up and runs on a caught fly ball.	**ACQUIRED SKILLS**
____ Follows base coach's advice while on the bases.	

TEST ITEM 6—KNOWLEDGE OF SOFTBALL

____ Shows basic understanding of softball (hitting, catching, throwing, running bases).	**EMERGING SKILLS**

____ Can describe an out.	
____ Can describe a foul ball, hit, strike, out, fly ball, run, and walk.	**BASIC SKILLS**
____ Can locate pitcher's mound, batter's box, infield, outfield, foul lines.	

____ Understands rules and regulations of softball.	
____ Adapts to changes in game situations appropriately.	**ACQUIRED SKILLS**
____ Can assist in keeping score for a softball game.	

TEST ITEM 7—PARTICIPATION, SAFETY, AND SOCIAL RESPONSIBILITY

_____ Attempts to participate in softball game.

_____ Participates a little; recognizes teammates and opponents.   **EMERGING SKILLS**

_____ Practices softball skills.

_____ Understands the importance of safety and good sporting behavior while playing softball.

_____ Adapts ability to throw, catch, field, run, and bat.   **BASIC SKILLS**

_____ Participates enthusiastically.

_____ Participates in a slow-pitch softball game.

_____ Exhibits safety and fair play while playing softball.

_____ Participates regularly on a softball team.   **ACQUIRED SKILLS**

_____ Exhibits enthusiasm while playing softball.

_____ Helps teammates with rules and play during a softball game.

SCORING

_____ number of emerging skills

_____ number of basic skills

_____ number of acquired skills

_____ total number of checks

Level 1 (Beginner) 1–15 total checks primarily in the emerging and basic skills

Level 2 (Fundamental) 16–24 checks with a minimum of 3 test items for basic skills level

Level 3 (Developmental) 25–45 total checks with a minimum of 5 test items in basic skills and 2 test items in acquired skills

Level 4 (Skill Competency) 46–61 total checks with a minimum of 5 test items in acquired skills and 2 in basic skills

Task Analysis Assessment

The task analysis assessment, designed for students who need physical assistance to accomplish tasks, provides both a qualitative and a quantitative way to measure abilities. Qualitatively, each skill is task-analyzed into its component parts. Each level—total physical assistance, partial physical assistance, and independence—is given a numerical value of 1, 2, or 3, respectively. The assessor determines what degree of assistance is needed by the learner to accomplish each component of the skill. Figure 2.5 presents a sample task analysis assessment for the bench press.

In this example, the learner completed 2 of the 7 components independently, 3 of the components with partial physical assistance, and 2 of the components with total physical assistance. The sum of these scores is 14 points, whereas the highest possible total score (if each component is completed independently) is 21 points. By dividing the score achieved by the total possible score, we find that this student was able to perform the bench press with 66 percent independence. The form also includes a space for product scores, and in this example the student completed 5 bench presses.

Summary

The variety of assessment options addressed in this chapter makes it feasible for teachers to assess a wide range of ability levels, including those of students with severe disabilities. This chapter also provided an overview of both traditional and authentic assessment techniques that can be used to assess students with and without disabilities. Assessment is a necessary component of ensuring that students with disabilities are provided with an appropriate physical education experience and of justifying the need for adapted physical education. Assessment data are also used to develop Individualized Education Program goals and objectives. The next chapter continues to highlight the importance of assessment in the overall education of students with disabilities, specifically in IEPs.

FIGURE 2.5

Task Analysis Assessment

KEY TO LEVELS OF ASSISTANCE

IND = Independent—the individual is able to perform the task without assistance (3 points).

PPA = Partial physical assistance—the individual needs some assistance to perform the task (2 points).

TPA = Total physical assistance—the individual needs assistance to perform the entire task (1 point).

Bench press	IND	PPA	TPA
1. Lie on back on bench.	③	2	1
2. Place each foot on proper side of bench with knees bent.	③	2	1
3. Extend arms to reach for bar.	3	②	1
4. Grasp bar with both hands directly above the shoulders.	3	②	1
5. Raise bar to a straight-arm position.	3	2	①
6. Lower bar until it touches chest.	3	②	1
7. Raise bar to a straight-arm position.	3	2	①
Scoring sum (per column)	6	6	2
Total score achieved	14		
Total possible points	21		
% independent score	66%		
Product score	5		

CHAPTER 3

Exploring Individualized Education Plans

Ms. Kelly has been teaching at Susan B. Anthony Elementary School for the past 14 years but has had little contact with children with disabilities because they were previously taught by an adapted physical education specialist. Recently, Ms. Kelly's principal informed her that the adapted physical education specialist had become the district's consultant, and Ms. Kelly would be directly responsible for teaching the students with disabilities in her building. Now Ms. Kelly could not rely on the adapted physical education specialist to come in and teach her children with disabilities one on one or to write all of the individualized education plans. Because the adapted physical education specialist had acquired such a large case load, Ms. Kelly would also be responsible for developing IEPs and serving as a member of the multidisciplinary team. In short, she would now be responsible for developing IEP goals and objectives in physical education for eight students with special needs.

The purpose of this chapter is to help readers

- understand what an IEP is and why it is necessary for students with disabilities,
- know the components of an IEP,
- be able to serve as a member of the multidisciplinary team,
- understand the role of physical educators and adapted physical educators in the IEP process,
- understand the use of goal banks when writing IEPs, and
- incorporate IEP goals and objectives into the general physical education curriculum.

The Individualized Education Plan (IEP)

The scenario involving Ms. Kelly may seem familiar to many general physical education teachers—and if not, it may be something they encounter in the near future. Because more and more students with disabilities are being included in general education, and specifically in physical education, many teachers are being asked to teach *all* children, whether or not they have extensive training in doing so. According to Block (2007) and LaMaster, Gall, Kinchin, and Siedentop (1998), many adapted physical education specialists are taking on roles as consultants rather than serving as direct care providers. As a result, general physical educators are now being required not only to give input about physical education for students with disabilities but also to write IEPs and serve as members of the IEP multidisciplinary team (Dunn & Leitschuh, 2006; Kowalski, Lieberman, Pucci, & Mulawka, 2005).

In order to participate effectively in the IEP process, teachers need to understand the purposes of the IEP and the legalities associated with it. All students identified as having disabilities must receive an IEP, which is a legal written document developed to ensure high-quality educational programming for the child. The IEP addresses the following issues: present level of performance (PLP), annual goals and short-term objectives, support services and supplementary aids, statement of participation in regular settings, assessment modifications, schedule of services, transition services, procedures for evaluation, and parental reports.

Because physical education is a direct service, federal law mandates that it be identified in every IEP. The extent to which physical education is addressed, however, varies depending on the needs of the student. Some students with disabilities can participate in unrestricted general physical education with no modifications. The IEP for a student in this category will indicate *general* physical education, and physical education goals and objectives will not be developed specifically for the IEP. In contrast, for a student who does have unique needs that require modifications or specially designed physical education, the IEP will indicate *adapted* physical education, and goals and objectives related to physical education will be developed as part of the IEP. It is important to note here that an *adapted* designation on the IEP does not necessarily mean the student receives separate physical education. Remember, adapted physical education is a *service*, not a placement, and the environment in which adapted physical education is provided varies depending on the needs of the student.

The IEP Process

Because no two students, including those with disabilities, are exactly alike, the first step in the IEP process is to assess the student. Then, based on the assessment data, unique needs are identified, and individualized goals and objectives are generated for various academic and social areas of development, including physical education, to ensure that the student receives an appropriate education. Once a service or support is identified in the IEP, the school district is held accountable for providing it. Periodic reviews and due process (the right to appeal decisions when disagreements occur) help to ensure that an appropriate educational program is being provided to the student. The following sections explain the IEP process in greater detail.

Assess Students' Abilities

In order for a student with disabilities to be eligible for adapted physical education, a thorough assessment must be conducted, and questions may arise as to who should conduct it. Some districts employ adapted physical education specialists whose primary role is to coordinate adapted physical education. A district may also contract out the work to adapted physical education specialists who assess students, determine unique needs, and serve as members of the multidisciplinary team. These specialists may or may not be responsible for program implementation; if not, they should meet with the general physical education teacher, present their results, and collaborate on goals and objectives. Most schools, however, have the general physical education specialist conduct the assessment and fulfill the roles identified earlier in this paragraph. These teachers are also responsible for implementing the adapted physical education program where indicated.

Various formal assessments are available to help professionals determine a student's unique motor and fitness needs; they include the APEAS II (Seaman, 2007), the Test of Gross Motor Development II (TGMD II; Ulrich, 2000), the Bruininks-Oseretsky Test of Motor Proficiency II (Bruininks & Bruininks, 2005), and the Brockport Physical Fitness Test (Winnick & Short, 1999). In lieu of formal assessment, authentic assessments may also be used to determine whether unique needs exist (Short, 2005). (See chapter 2 for more on assessment.) Regardless of the type of assessment chosen, assessment data provide a means for developing relevant IEP goals and objectives in physical education.

▶ Always assess a student's abilities to determine present level of performance.

Use Assessment Data to Write IEPs

Writing IEP statements on present level of performance, annual goals, and short-term objectives for physical education can be done easily by following a simple procedure known as the three Ps (Houston-Wilson & Lieberman, 1999). This procedure has the teacher analyze the *process* of the movement; the *product*, or outcome, of the performance; and the *parameters*, or conditions, in which the performance is completed.

Process   Process information relates to the form or quality of a movement. Skills can be broken down into component parts through task analysis or the use of ready-made checklists. Fronske (2005) provides task analyses for a variety of sport skills that teachers can use to determine which parts of a particular skill a student is lacking. Skill deficiencies can then be used as the basis for formulating annual goals; the component parts of the skill that are lacking serve as the objectives.

Product   The product of a skill relates to the quantitative value produced by the student's performance. Skills are quantified differently depending on the desired outcome, the student's age, and the class goals. Product information answers questions such as these: How many? How far? How fast? How long?

Parameters   The term *parameters* refers to the conditions in which the skill was performed, such as type of equipment used, distance at which the skill is executed, environmental arrangement (e.g., indoors, outdoors, group, one-to-one setting), and levels of assistance (e.g., independent, verbal cue, demonstration, physical assistance). It should be noted that a student's parameters for a skill may change with developmental or motoric gains or increases in independence. This aspect should be continually monitored, as should the process and product of the skill.

The three Ps system is an effective way to develop IEPs based on assessment data. Typically, a physical education IEP includes at least three PLPs with corresponding goals and objectives. Students in elementary school receive goals and objectives that are related, but not limited, to the following:

- Locomotor skills
- Object control skills
- Perceptual motor skills
- Lead-up games and sport-related skills
- Physical fitness
- Aquatics
- Rhythm and dance

Secondary students may receive IEP goals and objectives related to the following:

- Sport skills
- Physical fitness
- Aquatics
- Lifetime activities
- Rhythm and dance
- Community-based activities

Targeted areas are those in which the student shows the greatest deficit, but in no way does this mean that these are the only areas worked on throughout the year. Students with disabilities should receive a comprehensive program, just as any other student in the district does.

Determine Present Level of Performance, Annual Goals, and Short-Term Objectives

A present level of performance (PLP) statement must be written in objective, observable, and measurable terms and should reflect what the individual is able to accomplish. If a formal assessment is conducted for the student, then the PLP statement should relate to the data produced by the assessment. For example, if a student is assessed with the Test of Gross Motor Development II (Ulrich, 2000), then a PLP statement may be written as follows: "Leslie scored in the 10th percentile on locomotor skills and in the 8th percentile on object control skills on the TGMD II." If the Brockport Physical Fitness Test (Winnick & Short, 1999) is used to assess fitness levels, then a PLP statement might read like this: "Zoe completed 12 laps on the 16-meter [17.5-yard] PACER test on the Brockport Physical Fitness Test with verbal assistance."

In some instances, authentic assessment data or individual test items are used to create PLP statements. For example, let's assume that the task of serving a volleyball underhand involves five components: (1) step toward net with foot opposite the serving arm, (2) put palm up and make fist with serving hand, (3) shift weight forward, (4) contact ball in front of body, (5) follow through. Let's now use a fictitious student named Joey to illustrate the use of the three Ps:

> Joey is a 12-year-old boy who has cerebral palsy. He is able to step toward the net with the foot opposite his serving arm and contact the ball with his fist. Joey is given five attempts to serve a volleyball trainer underhand from midcourt. He is able to push the ball off of his hand in three of five attempts.

With this authentic information in hand, a present level of performance statement for Joey could look like this:

> Joey can underhand-serve a volleyball trainer independently from midcourt (parameter) by stepping toward the net with the foot opposite his serving arm and with his palm up to make a fist with the serving hand (process), then push the ball off of his hand in three of five attempts (product).

▶ Adapt the game to coincide with a student's present level of performance by using a modified ball or moving the student up to half-court.

Once the PLP statement is documented, the educator can develop annual goals and short-term objectives that correspond with the present level of functioning. Annual goals are broad generic statements, and short-term objectives are narrower and more specific; both must be written in objective, observable, and measurable terms. Short-term objective statements are based on annual goals and serve as a direct link between the present level of performance statement and desired outcomes. Short-term objectives indicate realistic yet challenging increments of improvement that students strive to achieve. Increments for improvement should be attainable within 6 months to a year from the date of the IEP's development. A short-term objective can involve improvement in one or all three of the Ps, depending on the skill and the student's abilities.

It is important to note here that not all districts require short-term objectives. According to recent legislation, IEPs are required to include short-term objectives only for students with disabilities who need alternate assessment protocols and for preschool students with disabilities. Some districts, however, may choose to require short-term objectives for all students who have an IEP (*Individuals With Disabilities Education Improvement Act*, 2004; Sherrill, 2005).

Returning to the example of Joey, an appropriate annual goal could be written as follows:

> Joey will be able to independently serve a volleyball trainer over the net from the serving line using a mature pattern in four out of five attempts.

A corresponding short-term objective might look like this:

> Joey will be able to independently underhand-serve a volleyball trainer with proper form at a distance of 7 feet (2.1 meters) from the net in two of five attempts.

At this point, the process has been expanded so that Joey is expected to perform all components of the underhand volleyball serve. The parameter was also expanded to serving independently from 7 feet, and the product for executing the skill successfully has been made more rigorous.

If formal assessment data are used, an annual goal can be made broader and more generic. For example, "Leslie will improve her object control skills by reaching the mature stage of development in the overhand throw in three of five attempts." Her short-term objective (STO) would then indicate the increments used to meet this goal in terms of process, product, and parameters.

Important Components of the IEP

Present level of performance
Short-term objectives
Long-term goals
Support services
Personnel support
Equipment support
Participation in general physical education class
Assessment modification
Determining schedules
Transition services
Evaluation of progress

Enlist Support Services and Supplementary Aids

Students with disabilities may need support services in order to meet IEP goals and objectives, and this section outlines various forms of support that may be requested. Support services and supplementary aids form an extremely important component of an IEP, and the type of support varies depending on the unique needs of the student. Two typical types are personnel support and equipment support. Personnel support ensures that there are enough hands in the gymnasium to provide a safe and successful program. For example, Joey might have a paraeducator to support him in his classroom, and his IEP might state that the paraeducator must accompany him into all of his physical education classes in order for him to be most successful.

Equipment support ensures that specialized or adaptive equipment is available to allow the student to experience a high degree of participation and success. In the example involving Joey, he used a volleyball trainer in order to be able to serve the ball over the net. It is important to review your curriculum to determine specialized equipment that may be needed in order for the child to be appropriately included and experience success in your physical education program. Once these areas of support are agreed on, the district is responsible for supplying the requested resources.

Examples of Personnel Support Personnel support may include adapted physical education consultants, teacher's aides and paraeducators, interpreters for deaf students, and trained peer tutors. See chapter 6 for more on this subject.

Examples of Equipment Support Specialized equipment includes beep balls, adjustable basketball goals, modified bicycles, bowling ramps, and switches that when touched can move or propel objects. Such equipment can be utilized by students with severe disabilities who lack the ability to use large muscle groups. Most of this equipment can be purchased through physical activity catalogs. See chapter 5 for more on this topic.

▶ The student's IEP may specify assistance from a peer tutor.

Prepare Statement of Participation in General Physical Education

This component of the IEP designates where the student's physical education class will take place. The placement of a student with disabilities in physical education classes can be one of the most difficult decisions a district makes. The goal is to provide the most appropriate and beneficial placement for each child with a disability (Block, 2003a). IEP team members should look at specific variables that can point them toward placing the student in the least restrictive environment that enables success. Variables to consider include the learner's sensory needs (i.e., the effect that acoustics, spatial relationships, and class size may have on the student's performance), the learner's individual skill set (e.g., motor and physical fitness), and behavioral factors (e.g., ability to work independently or with peers).

It is not appropriate, however, to determine placements based on the wishes of the teacher because he or she may have inadequate training. Since support services are a component of the IEP, teachers who lack the necessary training to accommodate students with disabilities in their classes initially should be provided with appropriate

▶ A modified bike allows students with certain disabilities to experience the joy of cycling.

support to ensure everyone's success. The law states that a student with disabilities must receive at least as much time in physical education as do his or her same-age peers, and the student with disabilities can spend additional time in physical education if feasible and if the student would benefit. If a student has severe disabilities or medical or behavioral conditions that would impede success, the IEP can include documentation to justify totally segregated placements.

Modify Assessment

For students who cannot be assessed in a traditional manner or who cannot participate in state- or district-required assessments, the law allows for alternative assessments. However, the IEP must include a statement indicating why the default assessment is not appropriate for the student and identifying the alternative strategies. Chapter 2 provides more information on alternative assessment for students with severe disabilities.

Determine Schedule of Services

An IEP must identify the nature, frequency, and duration of services that the student will receive. The IEP's schedule of services also allows educators to identify groupings for instruction, which can range from individual to small group to traditional class size. In our earlier example, Joey receives adapted physical education once a week for 45 minutes in a small-group setting and adapted physical education twice a week for 45 minutes in a general physical education class. It is appropriate for Joey to receive instruction in both settings because, again, adapted physical education is a service rather than a placement. The law requires that students with disabilities must be provided with physical education to the same extent as their typically developing peers. This requirement can be a double-edged sword, since if there is a particular semester or year in which the student's typically developing peers do not have a physical education requirement, then neither will the student with disabilities be provided with physical education. This issue can be resolved if the teacher is able to justify the need for physical education on an ongoing basis in order to maintain progress; this need must be documented in the IEP.

Begin Transition Services

Transition services are components of a student's educational program that prepare him or her for life after school. They may include vocational training, activities for daily living, and recreational programming. The physical educator should consider the student's physical activity and recreational opportunities available in the community after formal schooling is over and embed those activities in the curriculum. Current legislation requires that transition services begin at 16 years of age (*Individuals With Disabilities Education Improvement Act*, 2004); thus, if the child is 16 or older, transition services must be described in this section of the IEP. Transition services in physical education emphasize lifelong activities and community-based physical activities, including skills that enable the student to access such opportunities after leaving school.

Evaluate Progress and Send Parental Reports

The last component of the IEP involves procedures for evaluating the student and making parental reports. Procedures for evaluation describe how the teacher will know whether the student is making progress toward, or has met, stated objectives. These procedures also allow the teacher to recognize when goals and objectives are no longer appropriate, in which case they must be rewritten. Most schools require teachers to examine and update IEP goals and objectives on a quarterly basis. Examples of evaluation methods include teacher-made tests, rubrics, authentic assessments, standardized tests, criterion-referenced tests, teacher observations of specific skills, and checklists.

This part of the IEP must also state how parents will be informed about their child's progress. By law, the school must send reports to parents at least as often as their same-age peers' reports are sent home. For example, if a school sends out quarterly report cards, then the parents of a child with disabilities must also receive progress reports at least quarterly. The school may issue a report card or a progress report or hold a quarterly meeting with the student's parents. In any case, the physical educator must share the progress of the student with the parents at least as often as the progress of their peers is shared.

Members of the Multidisciplinary Team and Their Roles

In order to ensure the best educational experience for a student with a disability, a team of individuals is assembled to discuss appropriate IEP goals and objectives. Mandated by law to convene, this group is known as "the multidisciplinary team"; it may also be called "the IEP team." By any name, the team consists of a group of individuals who are responsible for the educational experience of the student with a disability. These members meet at least three times a year to develop appropriate goals and objectives, discuss programs, and address any concerns that may arise. At a minimum, the team must include parents or guardians, a district representative, a school psychologist, a special education teacher, and (when appropriate) the student. Others who may participate include general education teachers, adapted or general physical education teachers, paraeducators, physical therapists, occupational therapists, speech therapists, and medical personnel (e.g., school nurse, audiologist, vision specialist, orientation and mobility specialist).

Required Members of the Multidisciplinary Team

Parents or guardians: According to the IDEIA Amendments (2004), the IEP must address the parents' concerns, as well as the information they provide about their child.

The student with a disability: The student knows most about his or her level of ability, wants, needs, and preferences. Levels and types of participation on the multidisciplinary team may vary from student to student depending on age, disability, and ability to communicate.

Special education teacher: This teacher is the primary advocate, planner, supporter, and organizer for students with disabilities. Other than the parents and the student him- or herself, the special education teacher will know the most about the student with disabilities. The special educator will know how to contact and communicate with other team members.

District representative: A designee for the district must be identified and be present at all IEP meetings. This person is responsible for ensuring that all components of the IEP are addressed and that appropriate services are provided as indicated in the IEP.

School psychologist: The psychologist is a vital member of the team and is responsible for testing in the psychological domain, interpreting tests, and helping develop appropriate programs. In some cases, the student will have ongoing meetings with the school psychologist, and in others the student will receive consultation from the psychologist. Either way, the psychologist is a good resource for test interpretation and psychological evaluation.

Transition service representative: Once a student is 16 years of age or older, plans for the transition to post-school options may include professionals from outside the school. In this case, a representative from the relevant agency might attend the IEP meeting to ensure clear communication among all team members about the services that can be provided (Friend, 2005).

Recommended Members of the Multidisciplinary Team

Adapted physical education (APE) specialist: The APE specialist is a critical member of the team who should be qualified to provide information regarding the motor performance of the student with a disability. It is suggested that a qualified APE specialist hold a master's degree in adapted physical education or have passed the Adapted Physical Education National Standards (APENS) exam (Kelly, 2006).

General physical education (GPE) specialist: GPE specialists can share critical information pertaining to physical education that no other team member can provide. They know and can describe the general physical education curriculum and can facilitate the inclusion of a child with disabilities in a physical education class. It is imperative that the GPE teacher be part of the IEP team if the child with a disability is to be served in the GPE class setting.

General education teacher: When students with disabilities are included or are going to be included in general education classes, the general education teacher must be present at the IEP meeting to present the curriculum and secure the supports needed for successful inclusion.

Paraeducator: Paraeducators are also known as educational aides, instructional assistants, and teacher assistants. Paraeducators work under the supervision of the general education teacher or special education teacher to implement classroom goals and IEP goals and objectives. They may also be responsible for monitoring behavior and carrying out behavior plans if needed. Paraeducators are expected to attend physical education with the student or students they are assigned to supervise. Chapter 6 provides more information about paraeducators in physical education.

Physical therapist (PT): The PT works in the area of gross motor development, daily living skills, and utilization of assistive devices such as wheelchairs, walkers, crutches, and braces. The PT can help inform others about issues such as contraindicated activities, positioning, and reflex integration. Not every student with a disability will receive physical therapy, but if physical therapy is part of a student's program, then the PT is a vital member of the team and can help with consultation in physical education. Physical therapy, however, cannot replace physical education.

■ Physical educators should serve as members of the multidisciplinary team.

Occupational therapist (OT): The OT focuses on activities of daily living, self-help skills, fine motor skills, sensory integration, and adapted equipment. The OT can serve as an important resource on the IEP team.

Speech-language therapist: The speech-language specialist primarily assesses communication and language skills, plans habilitation programs, provides services, prevents further disorders, and consults with other members of the team on issues involving communication. The speech-language specialist can be a key player in helping the physical educator incorporate communication and language goals into their classes.

School nurse: The involvement of the school nurse varies according to level and extent of disability. The nurse's responsibilities often include dispensing medication; monitoring health, as in cases of asthma, cystic fibrosis, or AIDS; and carrying out medical procedures such as catheterization, cleaning a tracheotomy, or inserting a feeding tube. The nurse is a vital member of the IEP team and should be consulted regarding any health concerns about the student. Sometimes a student is medically fragile enough that he or she is assigned a one-to-one nurse; in this case, the one-to-one nurse should be the one involved in the IEP process. The nurse is also the bridge to the student's physician and can share any medical concerns about the student.

Audiologist: An audiologist works with students who have a hearing loss or who are at risk for a hearing loss. The audiologist assesses level of function, recommends assistive devices such as hearing aids or cochlear implants, and helps physical educators with the proper use of amplification systems and hearing aids.

Vision specialist: A vision specialist helps students with visual impairments by assessing vision, helping students use their vision effectively, and working with assistive devices such as closed-captioning televisions, braillers, magnifiers, and computer technology. A vision teacher can help physical educators with guiding techniques for running and walking, use of auditory equipment, game adaptations, and rules for blind sports.

Orientation and mobility (O&M) specialist: O&M specialists help students with visual impairments travel in a variety of environments safely and efficiently. They can help students with visual impairments move independently to the gymnasium (as well as in and around it), the locker room, the pool, or the playground. An O&M specialist can also give the physical educator ideas about using guide wires, setting up activities, and adapting and modifying rules and activities.

This list was taken in part from M.E. Block, 2007, *A teacher's guide to including students with disabilities in general physical education*, 3rd ed. (Baltimore, MD: Paul H. Brookes).

The Role of the Physical Educator in the IEP Process

The thought of using an IEP for physical education may make even the most enthusiastic teacher cringe. The time required to participate in meetings and write the IEP is typically added onto an already busy day. However, the IEP can serve as a useful tool in securing the supports and services needed to provide high-quality programs for students with disabilities, and as such it can become a physical educator's best ally. Even so, general physical educators are often left out of the IEP process altogether and therefore do not gain its intended benefits (Block, 2007; LaMaster et al., 1998). For example, Block (2007) found that general physical educators were often

- unaware of the existence of an IEP for a particular student;
- aware that the student had an IEP but given no input in developing it for physical education;
- aware of an IEP but not encouraged to review goals and objectives from past IEPs; or
- familiar with the IEP but hindered by the fact that it did not address physical education.

Not only are teachers often left out of the loop regarding physical education for students with disabilities; the students themselves are often unaware of their own physical education goals and objectives. Lieberman, Robinson, and Rollheiser (2006) found that of surveyed students who were blind or visually impaired, only those who were totally blind were aware that they had an IEP with physical education goals and objectives. Students with low vision (i.e., who had travel vision or were legally blind) were less aware of their IEP physical education goals and objectives. Furthermore, fewer than 40 percent of the students surveyed knew they had IEP goals and objectives related to physical education, and fewer than 25 percent knew what those objectives were. It is clear then, that physical educators must be more involved in the IEP process if gains are to be made, and one way to achieve this involvement is to attend IEP meetings.

Attending IEP Meetings

IEP meetings for students with disabilities are always held at the beginning, middle, and end of the school year. The exact dates and times are available from the Office of Special Education in each school district. Teachers of students with disabilities should be informed of the meeting dates and times for students under their care. If this information is not readily transmitted, teachers are encouraged to contact the appropriate personnel and find out for themselves (Kowalski, Lieberman, & Daggett, 2006). According to Sherrill (1998, p. 89), "most adapted physical activity authorities believe that a physical educator should be present at the IEP meeting to provide input concerning performance and needs in the psychomotor domain." If general physical educators are unable to attend the IEP meeting, written recommendations should be provided to the classroom teacher or other individuals, such as a parent or guardian, who can speak on behalf of physical education. Other options include having a colleague with a free period take the class and combining classes so that a member of the physical education staff can attend the meeting. Districts can also provide substitute teachers if multiple meetings are scheduled on one day (Kowalski, Lieberman, & Daggett, 2006). Unless physical education is clearly represented at the meeting—whether in written form or by in-person attendance—chances are that teachers will not receive the necessary supports to successfully include the student.

Some school districts require that IEP team members limit themselves at meetings to addressing issues and recommendations relating to the student's present level of performance. After a meeting, in which the student's performance and goals are discussed, the team is given 10 days to complete the full IEP for the parents to read. During the meeting, the team, especially the parents, can give valuable information and insight about their child's performance, and all of this information is taken into consideration when writing the IEP. Only after the team has met and agreed on the student's performance do the members write the IEP. The teacher who wrote the IEP, as well as the administrators and parents, sign the written document to signify agreement. In other instances, teachers may be asked to bring a draft of the IEP to the meeting, then make necessary adjustments based on the meeting results. A similar procedure then follows, in which all parties sign the IEP to signify agreement.

What to bring to an IEP meeting:

- List of student's strengths and weaknesses
- Description of student's learning style
- Assessment results for the student's present level of performance (PLP)
- Suggestions for goals and short-term objectives
- Suggestions about extent of inclusion in general physical education
- Suggestions for supports needed in physical education
- Suggestions regarding transition services (if applicable)
- Report on assessment modifications
- Suggested evaluation schedule
- Paper and pen to make notes
- A positive, open mind

▪ Unless physical education is clearly represented at the meeting—whether in written form or by in-person attendance—chances are that teachers will not receive the necessary supports to successfully include the student.

Computer-Generated IEPs

Since time is a restraint for many people, school districts have begun using computer-generated IEPs. One popular program, IEP Direct, maintains a goal bank for all curricular subject areas. A goal bank is a system in which goals, objectives, and evaluation procedures are listed by number. Teachers choose the appropriate items and identify them by number on a standard grid sheet; computers are then used to print the goals, objectives, and evaluation criteria for each subject area. This procedure is considered somewhat controversial, since IEPs need to be individualized, and there are cases where needed goals and objectives are not included in the goal bank. Furthermore, teachers should refrain from using the same goal bank numbers for every student with a disability. They must put thought and effort into their use of a goal bank. If needed goals and objectives are not identified in the goal bank, then either IEPs should be written by hand or new goals and objectives should be added to the bank. See table 3.1 for a summary of advantages and disadvantages of using goal banks.

TABLE 3.1

Advantages and Disadvantages of Using Goal Banks

Advantages	Disadvantages
1. Accessibility: quick access to a student's file from home or school	1. Generality: possible lack of fit between goals and individual student's needs
2. Streamlining: not a compilation of paperwork that lacks continuity	2. Lack of flexibility: inability to edit or modify existing goals (although you can create new ones)
3. Efficiency: easy to track, and multiple professionals can work on the same IEP at the same time	3. Complex: program is difficult to navigate
4. Quantity: extensive library of goals to choose from	4. Lack of training: too little training, insufficient ongoing support
5. Consistency: common bank of goals ensures consistency of language and minimizes redundancy and errors	

Adapted, by permission, from E. Kowalski, R. McCall, R. Aiello, and L.J. Lieberman, 2009, "Utilizing IEP goal banks effectively," *Journal of Health, Physical Education, Recreation and Dance* 80, p.46.

Here are some suggestions for using goal banks effectively:

1. The navigation system should be easy for everyone to use, from the technologically advanced to the technologically challenged. In other words, everyone should be able to use the system.

2. Goal bank statements must be measurable.

3. The system should allow physical educators to easily modify a goal or customize their own goals to meet each learner's needs.

4. Customized goals should follow the same descriptors as pre-identified goals in the bank.

5. The system should have built-in supports from the software maker, either via e-mail or phone assistance (Kowalski, McCall, Aiello, & Lieberman, 2009).

Incorporating Goals and Objectives Into the General Physical Education Class

In addition to goals and objectives for children with disabilities, general physical education teachers also set specific goals and objectives for their inclusive classes. These objectives may involve various issues, including cooperation, balance, endurance, and teamwork. So what happens when a student with a disability has goals and objectives that differ from the class goals and objectives? This is a common dilemma for teachers who teach inclusive classes and do not want to separate students with disabilities from their peers.

But look beneath the surface. Whether instructing the class using a partner or group activity, station work, an obstacle course, or a lead-up game or drill, good physical educators are constantly modifying and changing activities to meet their goals and objectives. This same process can be used to incorporate a student's IEP objectives into class activities. Once the student's IEP goals are known, one can look for situations where tasks can be incorporated within the current lesson or unit. And if the original lesson, game, or activity does not directly work with a student's objectives, one can add equipment, add a challenge or task, or add a rule that can allow the student to work toward his or her objectives. Here are some examples and commonly faced challenges related to embedding IEP goals and objectives within the general physical education class.

Challenge: Incorporate IEP objectives into an existing unit.

Explanation: The student with the disability has his or her own IEP objectives. Incorporate these objectives into the current unit.

Example 1: The IEP goal is "To improve eye–hand coordination," and the objective is "To be able to catch an 8-inch [20-centimeter] playground ball with hands only when tossed overhead from 8 feet [2.4 meters] away." The current class unit is volleyball. The instructor can have the whole class work on this objective in the following ways:

A. Have students work in pairs.

Student 1 tosses a ball to student 2, who sets it back to student 1. Student 1 must catch the ball to start over. Each pair can be given various balls to use (e.g., beach balls, volleyball trainers, volleyballs, and 8-inch [20-centimeter] playground balls).

B. Play a game of Newcomb (throwing and catching a ball over a volleyball net).

Challenge the students by using balls of various sizes and types, including an 8-inch playground ball.

▶ Incorporating modified games, such as sitting volleyball, into a unit can help meet IEP goals and objectives.

Example 2: The IEP goal is "To improve eye–hand coordination," and the objective is "Overhand-throw a beanbag and hit a target that is 3 feet [0.9 meter] square from a distance of 8 feet [2.4 meters]." The current class unit is ball-handling skills. The instructor can have the whole class work on this objective in the following way:

Use stations.

Stations can include dribbling, catching, throwing for distance, and throwing for accuracy. The accuracy station can involve a variety of targets, distances, and throwing objects (e.g., tennis balls, Wiffle balls, Koosh balls, yarn balls, and beanbags).

Challenge: Correlate class and IEP objectives.

Explanation: The objective for the student with a disability can often be the same as the objective the rest of the class is working toward.

Example 1: The IEP goal for a student with a visual impairment is "To increase spatial awareness during a dance unit," and the objective is "To be able to move for a specific amount of time without bumping into others."

Allow students to move in their own space.

The students have to clap and move to the music while not touching or invading another student's space.

Example 2: The IEP goal is "To improve balance," and the objective is "To be able to walk 10 consecutive steps on a balance line without stepping off."

Use additional activities to meet the desired objective.

Set up an obstacle course that requires students to walk along a line to get to the next obstacle. In station work, create lines that students need to walk along to get to the next station.

Challenge: Incorporate IEP objectives into class rubrics.

Explanation: Include at least one of the IEP objectives in the class rubric and extend the rubric if necessary to meet the needs of students with disabilities.

Example: A student with cerebral palsy has an objective of increasing flexibility by 5 to 10 percent. Using a gymnastics rubric, extend the original rubric to include the following: "Extend sit-and-reach ability on both sides by 1 inch [2.5 centimeters]."

Challenge: Incorporate the student's objectives within individual segments of the class.

Explanation: If the focus of the unit is not conducive to infusing the student's objectives, the objectives can be incorporated during segments of the class such as the warm-up and cool-down periods, station work, squad drills, or individually assigned activities (Kowalski, Lieberman, Pucci, & Mulawka, 2005).

Example: The IEP goal for the student is "To increase upper-body strength," and the unit is volleyball. During the warm-up, all students can perform various push-up activities (e.g., isometric push-ups or knee push-ups). During the drill period, students can practice serving the ball over the net. Weighted balls may also be used to make progress toward this goal.

Challenge: Use paraeducators to work on objectives.

Explanation: The primary role of the paraeducator is to help individualize instruction so that students with disabilities can successfully meet their IEP goals and objectives.

Example: A student with a physical disability who uses a wheelchair is involved in a flag football unit. Her IEP objective is "To be able to maneuver her chair in a game situation for 10 consecutive pushes without assistance." The paraeducator or peer tutor may be used to walk alongside the chair and help to direct or push the chair only when the student is in the midst of catching the football. After the student gains control of the ball she then continues to push herself until she is flagged or scores.

Challenge: Individualizing instruction in noninclusive settings or situations.

Explanation: In certain situations, it is more appropriate to teach students with disabilities in a noninclusive or segregated setting. In these cases, the instructor can use typically developing students as peer tutors to help students with disabilities reach their goals.

Example: If a student's identified goals are to work on socialization skills and eye–hand coordination, a peer tutor can assist with both of these objectives. The peer tutor and the student with a disability can work on ball-handling skills in a noncompetitive manner to foster peer relationships through their interaction and to enhance eye–hand coordination through the ball work itself.

Summary

The IEP is a required part of educational programming for any student with a documented disability. This chapter has presented an overview of the components of the IEP, with particular emphasis placed on the development of goals and objectives. We have also examined the role of the physical educator in the IEP process. It is essential that if a student with a disability is in need of adapted physical education, physical educators or adapted physical educators be responsible for developing appropriate goals and objectives and implementing the program. Computer-generated IEPs are commonly used. Finally, the chapter addressed various strategies for program implementation to meet everyone's goals and objectives together while ensuring successful interactions with able-bodied peers.

Managing Student Behavior

Mary is 12 years old and is identified as having attention-deficit/hyperactivity disorder. When she enters the gym, she becomes very excited and wants to move from station to station every 30 seconds. When you try to talk to her about staying on task, she stares blankly at you.

Thomas is 8 years old and has autism; he does not use words to communicate. When he enters the gym, he begins to cry and hit himself on the side of the head.

Doug is 14 years old and is considered to have a behavioral disability. During a small-sided game of floor hockey, a puck got by him and went into goal. Doug became very angry, ran over to John the goalie, and started yelling and cursing at him.

These scenarios suggest the range of behavioral situations that teachers may face at any given time in a physical education class. Being able to positively manage student behavior is an essential component of teaching. Without order, no real teaching can occur.

The purpose of this chapter is to help readers

- ■ learn proactive strategies to avoid behavioral problems,
- ■ determine the cause of inappropriate behavior,
- ■ use positive behavioral supports to improve behavior, and
- ■ implement intervention strategies for managing student behavior.

Strategizing to Avoid Behavioral Problems

Teachers who are focused, interesting, and skilled at using appropriate pacing greatly reduce the incidence of behavior problems in their classrooms. Most students in these classes (80 percent or more) do not engage in any major behavioral episodes (Collier, 2005). However, even teachers who follow best practices will come across students who, whether due to disability or other factors, engage in inappropriate behaviors in class. Teachers can minimize the chances of such incidents by being proactive in behavior management, and the key to effective management is structured teaching. From the beginning, students need to know and understand what is expected of them. Examples include

- ■ entry and exit routines,
- ■ signals for stops and starts,
- ■ rules of acceptable behavior, and
- ■ consequences for unacceptable behavior.

Determining, reviewing, and posting class rules and consequences can help teachers be consistent in their handling of situations as they arise. Teachers should serve as role models by exemplifying the good behavior they would like to see in their students. They can also reduce the chances of inappropriate behaviors by providing developmentally appropriate activities that meet the needs both of typically developing learners and of learners with disabilities, thus promoting active engagement by all students. Students are much more likely to engage in off-task or inappropriate behavior if the classroom is marked by disorganization, long periods of waiting, or skill demands that are too hard or too easy.

Physical educators also need to establish a positive climate for learning, and one way to create such an environment is to provide positive reinforcement for both behavior and skill performance. Most researchers believe that 80 to 90 percent of reinforcement should be positive (Lavay, French, & Henderson, 2006). *Positive reinforcement* refers to the process of offering something intrinsically valued (extrinsic reinforcers are praise, stickers, rewards, awards) as a consequence of a desired behavior, resulting in an increase in the frequency of that behavior. For positive reinforcement to be effective, the consequence or reinforcer must be perceived as valuable to the individual. Reinforcers often change with time, and something that students consider desirable on one day may not be seen as desirable on another day.

■ Behavior always has a communicative function. It is our job to figure out what the child needs.

Thus teachers should have a variety of reinforcers available and switch them around from time to time. Reinforcers can be used as a classwide strategy or as an individual strategy to manage behavior. Here is a list of best practices for administering positive reinforcement:

Best Practices for Administering Positive Reinforcement

1. Positive reinforcement should be used when the appropriate behavior is demonstrated.
2. Reinforcers must be valued and age appropriate.
3. Physical activity should be used as a reinforcing reward, not as punishment. For example, upon successful completion of a task or activity, students can be rewarded with 5 minutes of free jump-rope time at the end of class.
4. Initially reinforce more to achieve the desired goal, then gradually reduce reinforcers so that the appropriate behavior is demonstrated without the reliance, or dependence, on reinforcers (Lavay et al., 2006; Lavay et al., 2007).

Teachers can also promote a positive learning environment by employing a behavior management strategy known as the Premack Principle, which essentially uses activities with a high probability of occurrence to elicit low-probability behaviors. For the Premack Principle to be effective, a teacher needs to be aware of high-probability activities that students enjoy doing—for example, roller skating or shooting baskets—and that, as a result, can be used as reinforcers for appropriate behavior. For example, Thomas, the 8-year-old boy with autism mentioned at the start of this chapter, enjoys rolling down a wedge mat, but he does not like to do fitness activities. The instructor tells Thomas that after he completes 10 curl-ups, he can roll down the mat. Thomas completes his curl-ups and is then permitted to roll down the mat. It is important that various reinforcers are used so that a highly preferred activity does

▶ Give positive reinforcement, such as "good job leveling your knees" or "super ready position," to motivate appropriate behavior and performance.

not become a neutral or less-preferred activity. Similarly, one should not rely strictly on the Premack Principle to elicit appropriate behaviors because not all nonpreferred actions are reinforced with preferred actions.

A final strategy for mitigating inappropriate behavior is negative reinforcement, which can be used to strengthen or maintain appropriate behavior by giving students cause to avoid an aversive stimulus, or one that they perceive as undesirable. For example, negative reinforcement is being used effectively if a student perceives detention as aversive, if it is clear to the student that inappropriate behavior will lead to detention, and if the student refrains from inappropriate behavior in order to avoid detention.

Despite using best practices in proactively managing student behavior, teachers will be faced with students who, whether due to disability or another factor, exhibit inappropriate behaviors. The following section is intended to help teachers reduce and eliminate inappropriate student behaviors over time.

Determining the Cause of Inappropriate Behavior

All negative behavior has a communicative function. It is up to the teacher to determine what message the behavior is conveying.

The ABC Model

Determining what may be the cause of an inappropriate behavior usually involves some detective work. One common method for determining the cause of a behavior is known as the ABC model. Based on the principle of applied behavior analysis (ABA), the ABC model works in the following manner: First, the instructor examines the antecedent (A), or what was happening right before the incident occurred; second, the instructor notes the actual behavior (B); and third, the instructor notes the consequence (C) of the behavior, or what happened right after the behavior occurred. Detecting the antecedent enables instructors to modify that variable in order to eliminate the inappropriate behavior or reduce the chance of its reoccurring.

If, for example, the teacher determines that every time Josh stands in the back of the room, he pokes at his peers, then moving him to the front of the room may alleviate the inappropriate poking. In addition, noting the consequence can help reduce or eliminate the inappropriate behavior if it is determined that the consequence positively reinforces the behavior. For example, peers' laughter about the behavior can positively reinforce the inappropriate behavior, making it more likely to continue rather than to subside. For behaviors to be modified or changed, consequences must be such that the student avoids the behavior in order to avoid the consequences. Teachers need to constantly scrutinize their surroundings and take proactive steps to eliminate or minimize the chance of behavioral problems.

Positive Behavior Supports

As an outgrowth of the need for further behavior management in schools, the notion of positive behavior supports (PBS) has emerged. PBS relies on the use of person-centered interventions to modify environments, teach alternatives to inappropriate behavior, and employ meaningful consequences when inappropriate behaviors occur (Wheeler & Richey, 2005). PBS is tied heavily to functional behavioral assessment (FBA), which relies on structured interviews with key individuals (e.g., parents, teachers, and students themselves) and on observations in a variety of settings. Questions asked might include the following: What triggered the behavior? What does the student get out of the behavior? How often does the behavior occur? Who are the individuals present when the behavior occurs? Are there settings where the behavior does not occur? PBS emphasizes collaborative problem solving and prevention through effective educational programs that teach students more appropriate alternative behaviors (Block, French, & Silliman-French, 2007). A functional assessment allows teachers to

1. identify the targeted behavior,
2. identify conditions that yield or prevent the targeted behavior,
3. identify consequences of the targeted behavior,
4. hypothesize about what motivates it, and
5. gather baseline data regarding the targeted behavior.

Once the targeted behavior is identified for termination, person-centered interventions are established.

Intervention Strategies to Increase the Likelihood of Appropriate Behavior

The goal of an intervention strategy is either to increase the occurrence of appropriate behaviors or to decrease or eliminate the occurrence of inappropriate behaviors. Four commonly used procedures for increasing the likelihood of appropriate behaviors are shaping, chaining, prompting, and fading. Shaping involves reinforcing sequential steps that lead to the terminal behavior, whereas chaining reinforces approximations of the terminal behavior. Prompting involves giving cues to a student prior to any output—for example, as students enter the gym, the teacher might prompt Josh to refrain from poking his peers by saying, "Josh, please pick up a jump rope and jump to the music." Fading involves gradually removing prompts and reinforcement so that appropriate behavior occurs naturally.

Behavioral Consequences

Using the PBS model, the consequence for inappropriate behavior should be tailored to the unique characteristics of the learner. What serves as a displeasing consequence to some students may be appealing to others. For example, if a student who does not like physical education supposedly forgets her sneakers and is given the consequence of going to study hall, the consequence is likely to *increase* the chance that she will manage to forget her sneakers again. With this in mind, teachers should consider an array of consequences and choose those that will be most effective in promoting positive behaviors by the learner.

▶ You may need to prompt the student to stay on task. This instructor prompts the student to do a roll for the game of goal ball.

Time-Out

One consequence that is typically overused in education, as in society as a whole, is the time-out, which is defined as the removal of the student from positive reinforcement. In order for a time-out to be effective, the student must consider the removal from the activity as an aversive consequence for inappropriate behavior. For students who do not enjoy physical education, removing them from class activity or from the gymnasium might be considered positively reinforcing and in that case will do nothing to alleviate the inappropriate behaviors. Experts agree that a time-out should not be viewed simply as a form of punishment (Lavay et al., 2006). Rather, it can be used and self-regulated by students who feel that they are about to lose control; prior to taking inappropriate action, the student has the opportunity to regroup and regain composure. In this case, a time-out is not used as a punishment at all.

In current practice, however, a time-out is often the only strategy that teachers use to manage behavior, even for minor infractions. Before using a time-out as a method to manage student behavior, teachers need to consider the following:

1. **What is the purpose of a time-out?** It can be used as a cooling-off space, a place to go in order to regain composure after a blow-up, or a place to go when inappropriate behaviors occur. It should be discussed with students in advance.

2. **Where will students go to take the time-out?** A designated area should be set up in the gymnasium so that it is clear to students where to go for a time-out.

3. **How long will the student need to stay in a time-out?** Some suggest a ratio of one minute for each year of the child's age, but we do not recommend this strategy. Consider that in a typical 30- to 40-minute physical education class, a child who is 10 years old could miss one-third of the class. Teachers need to determine how long a time-out should last for each infraction. Similarly, in situations where students are using the time-out to self-regulate their behavior, they should have the opportunity to determine for themselves (within reason) the sufficient amount of time to serve the purpose.

4. **What type of infraction will lead to a time-out?** Make sure that "the punishment fits the crime." For example, Ben pushed his peer while waiting in line for a game. He was given one warning but did it again. Because he likes the game and it was his first time exhibiting that behavior, he was given a 30-second time-out. After apologizing, he was allowed back in the game. Don't overuse time-outs by assigning them for minor infractions. Identify which behaviors will lead to a time-out.

5. **How will the student know when to return to the activity?** Once a time limit has been established, the teacher can have a stopwatch or timer available so that the student can recognize when it is time to return. In some instances, teachers have inadvertently left students in a time-out for an entire class period simply because they forgot about the student.

6. **What happens after a time-out has been served?** The final step in using a time-out effectively to manage student behavior is to plan to debrief with the child after the time-out has been completed. Not only should the instructor discuss what happened that led to the time-out; he or she should also help the student develop strategies for handling the same situation if it arises again. Teaching students alternatives to inappropriate behavior is the key to managing student behavior (Lavay et al., 2006).

Token Economy

A token economy deploys tokens as positive reinforcers for appropriate behavior. Tokens can consist of chips, stickers, check marks, or any other item that can be collected or tallied and redeemed for something of value to the student. In order for a token economy to be effective, the teacher must identify and make the student aware of the targeted acceptable behavior and the number of tokens needed to gain the privilege or item of interest.

Contracts

As with the token economy, the use of contracts relies heavily on consequences. Contracts are written documents that outline terms of acceptable behavior, as well as consequences for both acceptable and unacceptable behavior. Contracts are signed by the student, the teacher(s), and in some cases the parents. Teachers need to be sure that a contract is achievable—that, with appropriate support, the student can meet the terms of the contract. Approximations of the desired behavior should also be included in the contract in order to ensure that goals are realistic. If it becomes apparent that the contract goals are unattainable, then the contract can be renegotiated.

Decreasing the Likelihood of Inappropriate Behavior

This section discusses several other behavioral intervention strategies that can be tailored to the unique characteristics of the learner and contribute to the maintenance of a positive climate: differential reinforcement of other behaviors, differential reinforcement of incompatible behaviors, and differential reinforcement of low rates of responding. Typically, these techniques are paired with one of the forms of intervention already described in this chapter because a reinforcer must be used with these approaches.

Differential Reinforcement of Other Behaviors

This approach calls for the instructor to provide reinforcement to the student who exhibits any (appropriate) behavior other than the unacceptable behavior. For example, if the unacceptable behavior is banging equipment on the floor, the student might be reinforced for demonstrating an activity, answering a question, or helping a peer, as long as the student was not banging the equipment on the gym floor.

Differential Reinforcement of Incompatible Behaviors

This strategy can be used when the student engages in behaviors that are the opposite of the unacceptable behavior. For example, if talking out is an unacceptable behavior that has been targeted for change, the student can be reinforced every time he or she raises a hand in order to ask or respond to a question.

Differential Reinforcement of Low Rates of Responding

This approach is used when the student reduces his or her rate of unacceptable behavior or increases the frequency of acceptable behavior. For example, if the unacceptable behavior is refusal to participate in activities, then each time the student participates in any form of (appropriate) activity, the student can be reinforced.

Summary

The purpose of this chapter is to provide strategies to manage student behavior in physical education. Proactive strategies have been presented to help instructors create environments that reduce the chance of inappropriate behaviors. However, even the best class managers will encounter students who, due to disability or other risk factors, engage in inappropriate behaviors, and the chapter has presented intervention strategies using a positive behavior support model. Based on the unique characteristics of the learner, interventions are tailored to help that individual positively modify his or her own behavior.

Adapting Activities: A Universal Design for Learning

Eric is a sixth grader who has spina bifida. He uses a wheelchair to get around, but he can also walk with a walker. Eric has many friends and loves being active. His physical education teacher, Mr. Anderson, had always allowed Eric to be included in individual sports, such as swimming and track, but when a unit involved team sports he would have Eric keep score or watch from the sideline. Eric had also been involved in elementary school physical education classes, but most of the activities at that level were developmental and non-competitive in nature. Thus Eric was not used to sitting out, and he wanted to be involved in his middle school physical education class with the other kids. He complained to his parents, and they called a meeting with the principal and the teacher. Mr. Anderson said that Eric could not safely or successfully compete in team sports units in his class. Eric was entitled to adapted physical education, but Mr. Anderson was responsible for providing the program within the inclusive class. Through the use of an adapted physical education consultant, strategies were created to allow Eric to participate fully.

Although skeptical, Mr. Anderson was willing to try some of the suggestions. Using volleyball as an example, the adapted physical education consultant suggested that for the skill development part of the unit Eric could use a volleyball trainer (an air-light volleyball). In addition, Eric was allowed to catch the ball off of one bounce instead of bumping or setting the ball over the net immediately. In order to ensure that Eric was a part of the game, his team could not score a point unless Eric made or attempted to make contact with the ball. A few of the adaptations, such as the catch-and-bounce, were expanded to include the whole class, and points often lasted for 2 or 3 minutes. With these slight modifications, Eric was able to participate in all aspects of the inclusive physical education class.

The purpose of this chapter is to help readers

- understand the theoretical constructs driving the move to adapt activities;
- understand the philosophy behind adapting activities;
- understand Universal Design for Learning (UDL);
- understand basic principles of adapting games and activities; and
- understand and be able to implement adaptations related to equipment, rules, environment, and instruction.

The opening scenario demonstrates that, with a little creativity, games and activities can be adapted and still be fun and effective in helping all students meet their physical education goals. The adjustments made were ideal for Eric, and it was not difficult to come up with a few variables that would ensure appropriate inclusion of everyone. Many teachers may not know what to do for a student like Eric or other students with disabilities. The purpose of this chapter is to provide instructors with teaching strategies for including students with disabilities in general physical education. Many of these strategies can also be used to promote the success of typically developing peers.

Theoretical Constructs Driving the Move to Adapt

The following theories indicate the necessity of adapting activities to include all students. When environments are adapted, individuals with disabilities are empowered to be full and active members of society. By embracing the idea of empowerment through adaptation, we are able to more fully include individuals with disabilities—not only in physical education but also in society as a whole.

A quick glance at the theory summary in the sidebar gives you an overall understanding of the power inherent in each one. It is imperative to note that some individuals cannot be empowered unless some variables are adapted. Volleyball would not have been a realistic choice for Eric without some adaptations. Since adaptation drives the theories, it follows that if students are to reach the empowerment stage, then games, skills, sports, and activities must be adapted.

Theoretical Constructs

Adaptation theory: Many activities will be accessible to children with disabilities only if they are adapted.

Normalization theory: Children with disabilities should be afforded the same opportunities in life that their same-aged peers enjoy.

Self-determination theory: Individuals with disabilities should be provided with choices, enabling them to exercise autonomy in their own lives.

Empowerment theory: If individuals with disabilities take advantage of available choices whenever possible, empowerment will become intrinsic.

Adaptation Theory

Adaptation theory is the practice of managing variables, or adapting them, in order to achieve desired outcomes. "All good physical education is adapted physical education" (Sherrill, 2004, p. 10). Adaptation theory, or the process of adapting, was first introduced by Kiphard (1983), who described this theory as individual and environmental interactions that maintain involvement in the activity. Individuals adapt to and alter the environment each time they respond to it, which makes their relationship reciprocal, or bidirectional (Sherrill, 1998); Sherrill further describes the process of adaptation as continuous and dynamic (1998). She identifies seven variables that can be addressed to maximize success:

▶ Students are empowered by adventurous and challenging activities such as rock climbing.

© Jim McGuire/Index Stock/age fotostock

1. **Temporal environment.** These variables relate to the timing involved in an activity. Timing can be slowed down or quickened depending on task demands. For example, a large ball will move more slowly through the air than will a small ball thrown with the same force, and students who have difficulty with catching will be more likely to catch the slower-moving ball. Another example involves replacing a hockey puck with a Frisbee, which moves much more slowly and does not provoke the fear of injury. Also in hockey, the use of carpet squares under the feet of all players will slow down the game considerably and equalize the playing field for some children who move more slowly than their peers do.

2. **Physical environment.** The physical environment can also be adapted to facilitate success. For example, in volleyball, students who have attention-related difficulties may do better in environments where arrows are placed on the floor to show how players rotate from one spot to another.

3. **Object or equipment.** The equipment used in each lesson is essential to success. In the opening scenario, Eric was allowed to use a volleyball trainer, which is soft and floats through the air more slowly than does a traditional volleyball.

4. **Psychosocial environment.** Here, the variables that may need to be manipulated involve peer-to-peer interactions. Situations should be made available where peers have opportunities to work together to achieve a common goal. Project Adventure,

■ All good physical education is adapted physical education.

which offers adventure-based experiential programming, provides a variety of class activities emphasizing cooperation and support rather than competition. For more information, go to www.pa.org/programs/advclassroom.php.

5. Learner. Examining the learning style of each student is essential to effective instruction. For example, students with autism are often visual learners and thus need to see the activity rather than just be told what to do. In contrast, students with visual impairments obviously need to hear about the task, and perhaps experience it kinesthetically, in order to be successful. It is imperative to engage the preferred learning style of all students. This is often called differentiating instruction (Thousand, Villa, & Nevin, 2007).

6. Instruction or information. How you present information to the class will affect outcomes. It is considered best practice in instructing all students to give instructions that are short and concise and do not involve a lot of waiting time.

7. Task. It should be a goal for all good teachers to provide tasks that allow for differentiated learning (Gregory & Chapman, 2007; Thousand, Villa, & Nevin, 2007). If the task involves ball-handling skills, for example, then a variety of balls of different shapes and sizes should be made available to the learners.

These seven variables can be adapted individually or in combination, and adaptation in one area may facilitate adaptation in another. Adaptations can be made in a lesson, skill acquisition or skill practice, activity, game, scrimmage, practice, sport, or entire program. Adaptations are not an afterthought. They are part of the planning process and are written into the curriculum and into each lesson plan to accommodate individual differences among all students.

Normalization Theory

Normalization theory involves providing persons who have disabilities with educational conditions that are as close as possible to the ones normally provided for

Robertstock.com/Brand X Pictures

students without disabilities (Sherrill, 2004). In other words, what is "normal" for people without disabilities should be available to people with disabilities. The concept driving this important theory is that students with disabilities should be afforded the same opportunities provided to their same-age peers. Thus they are not isolated from the norm; rather, they are embraced. This theory was first introduced to the United States by Nirje (1969) and has been recognized as a major contribution to the integration of individuals with intellectual disability into the mainstream community. Normalization theory is important to adaptation because it supports including students with disabilities in culturally acceptable games and activities with their peers. We adapt so that students will have the same social and educational opportunities in physical education and in society. In many cases, adaptations are the only reason that "normal" activities are available to some students with disabilities.

According to Auxter, Pyfer, and Heuttig (2005, p. 23), the following attitudes must be present if normalization is to become a reality. Individuals with disabilities must be

■ perceived as humans,

■ perceived as having a legal and constitutional identity,

■ viewed as individuals who can acquire skills throughout their lifetimes,

► Working together with teammates to reach a goal is key to achieving normalization.

- provided with an opportunity by society to take full advantage of their culture,
- provided with services by competent, trained personnel in education and habilitation,
- cared for and provided with opportunities by public services that are valued and well understood by society, and
- provided with opportunities to play valued roles and lead valued lives in our culture.

Self-Determination Theory

The third theory, self-determination, involves the right to possess control, power, and decision-making ability in one's life (Wehmeyer, Agran, & Hughes, 1998). When individuals with disabilities are included side by side with their peers in normal activities, they are viewed as valued in society (Wolfensberger, 1972). The practice of valuing all persons can be promoted by adapting activities so that *all* can participate and achieve. Being valued in society also provides opportunities for choice in participation, affiliation, and adaptations. This experience is frequently referred to as *self-determination* and is particularly significant when considered from a global perspective (e.g., all areas of the child's life). In order to define this perspective in terms of a student with disabilities, teachers must ask themselves, "Does this student have the same choices and options that his or her same-age peers do?" In many cases, the answer is no (Wehmeyer et al.).

All people, whether or not they have disabilities, should get to make their own choices. Opportunity is, in fact, one of the essential characteristics that must be present for an individual to be self-determined (Wehmeyer et al., 1998). Therefore, it is essential for teachers to ensure that all students be given equal opportunities (Getchell, & Gagen, 2006; Gregory & Chapman, 2007; Thousand et al., 2007). If Eric's peers are taught 13 different units in their sixth-grade year, then Eric should be involved in the same 13 units. Again, we must emphasize that in many cases normal opportunities can be provided to students with disabilities only through adaptations.

Empowerment Theory

The fourth theory, empowerment theory, emphasizes the belief that individuals are their own change agents and that such agency emerges only when responsibility for planning and decision making is shared (Powers et al., 1996). That is to say, the adults running the programs should involve the desires and interests of the child with the disability.

Teachers of students with disabilities and other social minorities must study this theory to enable students to take charge of their lives. Individuals with disabilities must be empowered to change what needs to be changed so that they can live normal, active, healthy, and fulfilling lives. As with the adaptation, normalization, and self-determination theories, empowerment theory advances the vision that individuals with disabilities have the right to live in the mainstream of society; to be included in everyday activities; and to have choices, control, power, and dreams. Teachers can help students realize this potential every day by showing them how to make the most of opportunities to learn; they must teach students how to take advantage of community resources and consistently encourage empathy in every student they teach. Empowerment theory has especially strong implications for the student's life beyond school. A strong educational background, along with adapted experiences, should lead these children to be strong, independent self-advocates.

Taken together, these four theories serve as the basis for understanding the nature of disability and the need of those with disabilities to feel a sense of belonging (see figure 5.1). As educators, we must ensure safe, successful, and enjoyable educational

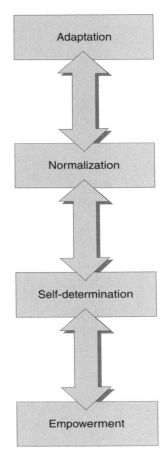

▶ **Figure 5.1** Adaptation drives empowerment through involvement in physical activity.

experiences for all students in our care. Realizing the importance of these theories helps educators frame their ideas about inclusion and may serve as a means of changing attitudes from fear to acceptance.

Philosophy of Adapting Activities

It is imperative that instructors consider the entire class before they engage in planning. In the chapter's opening scenario, for example, Eric should have been considered before the volleyball unit was taught. Individual units in the curriculum must be considered fluid in their make-up, instruction, and implementation, and planning for both units and lessons should involve the modification of equipment, rules, and instruction as integral components. In order to ensure that each student is fully included in the class, consider the following preplanning questions (Getchell & Gagen, 2006):

- What can the student see?
- What can the student hear?
- Does the student have additional disabilities?
- How does the student ambulate?
- Are any activities contraindicated (i.e., not recommended) based on the student's disability?
- What is the student's previous experience in physical activity?
- What can the student do?
- How does the student perform?
- What does the student like?

The next consideration is to determine the goal of the game or unit (Grenier, Dyson, & Yeaton, 2005)—for example, endurance, upper-body strength, cooperative learning, or skill development. Educators must also consider specific objectives and how they relate to the student's IEP (Kowalski, Lieberman, Pucci, & Mulawka, 2005). Returning to the chapter-opening scenario, Eric could ambulate by using his chair or walking on crutches. He also had good upper-body strength. These capabilities represented the "function" of Eric (e.g., how he moves and manipulates objects). Thus IEP goals for Eric could be related to abdominal strength, endurance, eye–hand coordination, and socialization. By participating in a modified volleyball game, using a volleyball trainer, and playing a sitting volleyball game (where all players sit on the ground and attempt to get the ball over the net), Eric was able to accomplish his goals of working on eye–hand coordination and on socialization with his peers. He was also able to talk to the class about his experiences with sitting volleyball and his upcoming competition, thus promoting disability awareness among his peers.

Figure 5.2 depicts the ongoing connection between the function of the student, the objectives of the activity, and the modifications that need to be made based on the student's function. Considering each of these variables *before* the unit is taught lies at the heart of the concept of Universal Design for Learning (Lieberman, Lytle, & Clarcq, 2008).

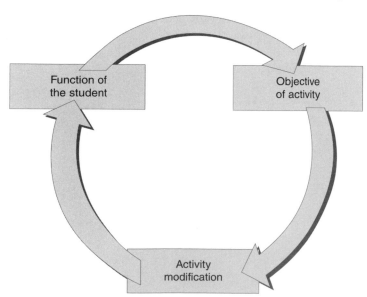

▶ **Figure 5.2** This model depicts the interaction between student, objective, and activity modification.

Universal Design for Learning

Universal Design for Learning emerged from the field of architectural design when federal legislation began requiring universal access to buildings and other structures for individuals with disabilities. Architects began to design accessibility into buildings during their initial design stage rather than retrofitting standard structures. Building on this architectural principle, UDL is a strategy for eliminating barriers to students' learning that includes Universally Designed Instruction (UDI), Universally Designed Curriculum (UDC), and Universally Designed Assessment (UDA; Meyer and Rose, 2000; Rose & Meyer, 2002). For example, a curb cut enables a person who uses a wheelchair to access a sidewalk while also making travel easier for individuals who use walkers, parents with strollers, bicyclists, and other people who might have trouble negotiating curbs. Another example is closed-captioned television programming, which helps persons who are hard of hearing or deaf follow what is happening, just as it also helps people with typical hearing who are watching in a noisy room or have the volume turned down. Lastly, universal symbols that communicate function, such as restroom signage, are helpful both to individuals who have trouble reading and to those who do not speak the local language (Spooner, Baker, Harris, Ahlgrim-Delzell, & Browder, 2007).

Universal design in education means that the physical, social, and learning environments are designed so that diverse learners are supported through powerful possibilities for teaching and learning. Universal design is a concept, a set of principles, a framework, a frame of mind that supports accessibility for the widest possible range of individuals. Universal design is achieved not through uniformity but through flexibility. It provides alternative methods of instruction (in the broad sense), delivery of instruction, materials (equipment), and methods of student response (how students show what they can do)—all within the general curriculum and for every student, regardless of his or her specific areas of diversity (Odem, Brantlinger, Gersten, Thompson, & Harris, 2005; Rose & Meyer, 2002).

UDL is an efficient way to provide students with access to the curriculum. It considers the range of students' abilities at the design stage of curriculum making and incorporates accommodations at that point. This built-in access for a wide range of users—with and without disabilities—is the underlying principle of UDL (Lieberman, Lytle, & Clarcq, 2008).

In terms of curriculum, universal design implies an approach to instructional materials and activities that allows learning goals to be attained by individuals with wide differences in their abilities to see, hear, speak, move, read, write, understand English, attend, organize, engage, and remember. Such a flexible yet challenging curriculum gives teachers the ability to provide each student with access to the subject area without having to adapt the curriculum repeatedly to meet needs. Tools and materials that meet the standards of UDL help students learn by getting them to feel interested in, and good about, the work they are doing. Such tools and materials support motivation to learn by offering multiple ways to engage with the task at hand, thus enabling learners with various preferences and styles to find avenues that suit them (Meyer & O'Neill, 2000).

Had the Universal Design for Learning philosophy been in place in Eric's classroom, he would have been automatically included in his class from the beginning of the school year rather than being treated as an afterthought during team sports units. His function and objectives would have been considered, and all units would have been designed to fully include him.

Figure 5.3 provides examples of instructional methods that employ the principles of UDL. Applying these strategies can make your class content accessible to students with a wide range of abilities and disabilities.

■ The UDL approach promotes a more inclusive environment for all students.

FIGURE 5.3

Instructional Methods That Employ the Principles of Universal Design

1. **Inclusiveness.** Create a classroom environment that respects and values diversity. Avoid stigmatizing or segregating any student.

2. **Physical access.** Ensure that classrooms, gymnasiums, fields, pools, and courts are accessible to individuals with a wide range of physical abilities and disabilities. In addition, make sure to provide a wide range of options for equipment use (e.g., a variety of racquets, balls, bats, flotation devices, and mats).

3. **Delivery modes.** Use multiple modes to deliver content. Alternate your methods of delivering instruction by using demonstrations, posters, discussions, explanations, videos, and hands-on activities. Make sure that each mode is accessible to students with a wide range of abilities, disabilities, interests, and previous experiences.

4. **Interaction.** Encourage various ways for students to interact with each other and with you. Possibilities include class questions and discussions, group work, individual demonstrations, routines, station work, and group dances and demonstrations.

5. **Feedback.** Provide effective prompting during an activity; also provide feedback after an assignment is complete.

6. **Assessment.** Provide multiple ways for students to demonstrate knowledge, understanding, and skills. Besides traditional tests, consider group work, demonstrations, routines, station work, portfolios, and presentations.

The benefits of employing the principles of Universal Design for Learning cannot be underestimated. They include

- full access to content for all,
- increased motivation in all learners,
- increased active participation by all learners,
- increased learning of curricular content,
- increased acceptance of students with disabilities by their peers,
- reduced time spent in trying to figure out how to accommodate various learners once the unit has been started, and
- reduced frustration for all parties.

Types of Adaptation

For many students with disabilities, making the most of their lives involves manipulating environmental variables so that they can be successful and attain control (Grenier, Rogers, & Iarrusso, 2008). This section of the chapter applies the concept of UDL to making the physical education environment accessible to all students. For example, if equipment, rules, environment, and instruction had not been modified, Eric would have fewer sports, games, and activities available to him. But because basic principles for adapting activities were applied, Eric now knows how to play the same games as his peers. Therefore, he has the same options available to him as his peers, which contributes toward his becoming a self-determined young man as he grows up, and his self-determination will empower him to make decisions, advocate for himself, and enjoy a better quality of life.

In many cases, parents are the strongest advocates for their child and should be consulted for functional ideas when incorporating modifications into lessons at the beginning of the school year. In turn, modifications that are successful should be shared with parents so that they can implement them during the child's leisure time (see figure 5.4). The next section of this chapter gives instructors ideas for adapting variables that will allow a student to participate with peers in a game, activity, or sport.

Adapting Activities

This section addresses four areas of the teaching and learning process: equipment, rules, instruction, and environment (Lieberman, Lytle, & Clarcq, 2008). Some variables could fit into more than one area, and we have tried to put each into the most appropriate area. In the following photo, it is evident that the task of jumping has been modified to include various adaptations in equipment, rules, and environment. Thus the objective has been universally adapted to be responsive to a wide variety of abilities.

Equipment Modifications

An equipment modification can involve any change that would make the participant more successful than he or she would be if using the unmodified equipment. Modifications of equipment are among the most common modifications that physical

▶ Students can participate in a jumping activity with various adaptations, such as jumping traditionally, jumping over a stationary rope, or jumping in and out of hoops.

FIGURE 5.4

Basic Principles for Adapting Activities

1. When possible, include the student with the disability in adaptation decisions. Some students will not mind having the activity modified to ensure success. In middle school and high school, however, many students with disabilities would prefer to "fit in" rather than be successful, and they may not welcome any adaptation that makes them look different or be perceived as different. Thus any well-meaning teacher must first consider the student's attitude toward the activity, toward peers, and toward him- or herself.

2. Give the student as many choices as possible. The more types of equipment offered, teaching styles used, rule modifications available, and environmental options provided, the greater the chance that the student can make a choice that will enable him or her to be successful in the activity. The teacher may want to discuss all options with the student prior to the unit and allow him or her to try out a few in order to make the best decisions. This way, the student can start the unit with success, and the teacher can adapt further if needed.

3. Physical assistance is acceptable and preferred over sitting out of an activity. The use of physical cues, hand-over-hand aid, and even total physical assistance is appropriate to ensure participation in the activity. The amount of assistance should be decreased to "normal" cues when possible.

4. If a modification is not working, be sure to change it as soon as possible in order to facilitate success.

5. Students with disabilities should be offered the same variety of sports, games, and recreational activities that their peers are offered. This approach maximizes the chance that students will learn lifetime activities and a variety of skills.

6. Community-based activities should be included in the curriculum whenever possible. For example, by practicing an activity in the environment where it will be executed will increase the likelihood that they will be successful when they get there (i.e., ice skating).

7. Adaptations should be ongoing and continually evaluated rather than being limited to a one-time occurrence. Consistency ensures that as a student increases his or her independence, becomes frustrated, or becomes embarrassed, the instructor can modify any adaptation to meet the child's need.

8. Include all modifications of the lesson plan at the beginning of the unit. Consider all students in the class when developing lessons; do not adapt as an afterthought.

Adapted from M.E. Block, 2007, *A teacher's guide to including students with disabilities in general physical education* 3rd ed. (Baltimore, MD: Paul H. Brooke); and L.J. Lieberman, 1999, Physical fitness and adapted physical education for children who are deaf-blind. In *Deaf-blind training manual* (Logan, UT: SKI-HI Institute Press).

educators make in order to encourage desired movement (Getchell & Gagen, 2006). Students with disabilities may need to have equipment adapted for any number of reasons, including limited mobility, limited grip strength, lack of vision or hearing, decreased cognitive function, and inability to attend for a long period. Examples of equipment modification include the use of beeper balls, guide wires, Velcro mitts, longer rackets, and softer balls. It is important to remember that equipment should be age-appropriate.

Equipment Modification Example

Tamiqua is a ninth-grade girl with a spinal cord injury that has resulted in impairment of all four of her limbs. She has some use of her arms—she is able to move them up, down, and to the front—but limited grip strength. She uses a wheelchair to ambulate and can move her chair independently. Before the tennis unit, the teacher, Ms. Meehan, brainstormed with Tamiqua, the paraeducator, and Tamiqua's mother to identify necessary modifications. They decided to try using a badminton racket, indoor Nerf tennis balls, and an Ace bandage (to attach the racket to her hand). At first, Tamiqua could not get the timing right and became frustrated, so they switched to a balloon. By the second week of the unit, they switched back to the Nerf tennis ball and used a two-bounce rule. Tamiqua could rally at least five times in a row! She has been practicing on weekends with her brothers and is now learning how to serve the ball.

As the sidebar scenario involving Tamiqua shows, a few minor equipment modifications and rule changes can greatly improve the opportunities available for students with disabilities. In this case, the modifications led Tamiqua down a path toward beginning tennis, and there is no ceiling on how much she can improve her tennis, as well as her upper-arm strength, mobility, and speed.

■ Adapt the game to the child, *not* the child to the game!

Rule Modifications

A rule modification can involve any deviation from the original or culturally accepted rules of the game. The instructor must create an atmosphere of flexibility among all participants. There are many ways to play a game, and with the wide variety of diversity in classes today, all players must be open-minded and willing to try new things.

▶ Tamiqua gains skills in tennis enabled by a rule modification allowing two bounces.

Students with disabilities may need to have the rules adapted so that they can be successfully included. Examples of rule modifications include slowing down the pace of a game, allowing more chances, taking away rules, allowing for no defender, limiting or adding responsibility, and making sure all players are involved before a team can score (Lieberman, 1999). In addition, the instructor may want to change a task completely for a specific person rather than just modifying the rules. For example, a student might throw a ball instead of striking it (Rink, 1998). Low-organized games with few rules lend themselves to accommodating many children (White, Casebolt, & Hull, 2004).

Rule Modification Example

Jane is a fifth grader with low-level spina bifida. She can run, but she is slower than her peers and has a scissors gait. The class did a disability awareness unit and learned what Jane can and cannot do. Before each unit, the physical education teacher, Mr. Short, allows all students in the class (including Jane) to brainstorm appropriate adaptations for Jane. The softball unit is no exception. Jane bats, runs, and fields on her own. The only modifications are that Jane uses some physical assistance to bat and scores a run for every base she touches; thus if she runs to second base before being called out, she scores two runs. This simple rule modification is responsive to her mild disability. The kids are very accepting, and they fight over which team Jane will be on! Jane considers herself a good softball player and plans to join a summer league so she can continue to play the game.

▶ Jane is successfully included in the softball unit with some minor rule adaptations.

In many cases, rule modifications come naturally when keeping normalization theory in mind. For many students, inclusion in a game with traditional rules would be impossible, and physical educators must consider alternative rules to ensure inclusion of all students in general physical education.

Environmental Modifications

Environmental modifications may be needed to successfully include a child with a disability. Often, necessary modifications are not conceived of until a problem arises, and it is never too late to modify the environment to increase a person's success (Petersen & Piletic, 2006). Environmental modifications include decreasing distractions, increasing visual cues, limiting noise, changing lighting, and increasing accessibility of the playing area; modifications may also address access to facilities (Petersen & Piletic, 2006).

Environmental modifications can greatly increase the amount of involvement in physical education for students with disabilities (Menear & Davis, 2007). In the sidebar story about Charlie, swimming in the designated area was not possible or conducive to his learning. At the same time, changing the environment is not always as simple as it was in Charlie's case; oftentimes, the instructor must gain added permission or personnel (e.g., a lifeguard). Other examples of environmental manipulations include acquiring additional keys to lights, closing folding doors, covering windows that create glare, or minimizing decorations that might distract attention. In any case, the increased involvement of students with disabilities is the reward for all the extra work of changing the environment.

Environmental Modification Example

Charlie is a third grader who moved to a new district and a new elementary school at midyear. Charlie has autism and limited communication skills. The special educators in his new school read his IEP and found no goals related to physical education, even though adapted physical education was checked off on the front page of his IEP. They had no idea what Charlie could do or what he needed in terms of instruction. The physical education teacher, Mr. Wilkinson, wanted Charlie to receive his adapted physical education program in his general physical education class. The class was working on a 3-week swimming unit at the middle school pool. Charlie's mother had signed the permission form for swimming and checked off intermediate level. Mr. Wilkinson was happy about that and allowed Charlie's paraeducator, Ms. Brown, to go into the pool with him. There were 33 students in the class, and Mr. Wilkinson was busy with the other students. Charlie's immediate reaction to the pool was very negative. He screamed, kicked, and continuously tried to swim to the deep end. He would not calm down. He had no verbal communication skills, so the teachers were puzzled about what was wrong. His mother had said that he could swim well.

After 30 minutes of struggling to keep Charlie in the shallow end with the other students, Mr. Wilkinson and Ms. Brown gave up and let him swim to the deep end. This was the answer to the problem. Charlie's autism made him hypersensitive to noise and distractions, and he could not tolerate swimming in the shallow end with the other kids. But with a simple modification in the environment (using the deep end of the pool), Charlie swam and improved greatly during the 3-week unit. He even started using a trained peer tutor in the deep end, and this tutor became his friend throughout the school day.

Instructional Modification

Teachers have many variables that they can modify when teaching a lesson. In addition to equipment, rules, and environment, teachers can modify the way they instruct a class (including using small groups and individualized instruction). The following list presents teaching cues in a hierarchy from least invasive to most invasive. In some cases, these techniques need to be paired (e.g., verbal cueing and modeling); in others, a simple cue will elicit the desired behavior.

Teaching Cues

1. Verbal cues are used to explain in simple terms what you want the student to do; they should be
   - clear, specific, concise, and free of jargon and slang;
   - done in a mode of communication that the child understands;
   - repeated in a different way if the child does not understand the first time;
   - used with demonstration to ensure understanding if the child has usable vision; and
   - given in such a way as to allow appropriate time for the student to process.

2. Demonstration or modeling involves showing through actions or pictures what you want the student to do (Waugh, Bowers, & French, 2007); it should be done
   - in the child's field of vision;
   - by someone as close as possible to the student's size and ability, and
   - in a whole-part-whole manner when possible (i.e., you should demonstrate the whole skill, then the task-analyzed parts, then the whole skill again).

3. Physical assistance or guidance involves physically helping the student through the desired skill or movement; it should be
   - documented in terms of where you physically assisted, how much assistance you gave, and for how long;
   - preceded by telling the child you are going to touch him or her; and
   - decreased to "normal" touch cues when possible.

4. Tactile modeling involves allowing the learner to feel a peer or instructor executing a skill or movement that was difficult to learn when using the three previous approaches (Lieberman & Cowart, 1996; O'Connell, Lieberman, & Petersen, 2006); it should be
   - preceded by telling the child where and when to feel you or a peer executing the skill;
   - documented as to when and where the child touched you or a peer, and why;
   - repeated as many times as necessary to ensure understanding; and
   - combined with other teaching methods to increase understanding.

Teachers can also modify their teaching approach; some common approaches include the following:

1. Direct instruction. The teacher directs the class by telling students what to do and how to do it, then actively oversees the learners and provides feedback.
2. Task teaching. This style can involve using a series of task cards (which may be brailled or rendered in pictures) that progressively lead to the achievement of an instructional objective. The task style also allows different students to practice different tasks at the same time. This approach is also known as practicing station teaching or using learning centers.

3. Guided discovery. Using a series of questions or short statements, the teacher guides students in a progressive series of steps resulting in the discovery of a movement solution that meets the criteria intended by the teacher.

4. Problem solving. As with guided discovery, the problem-solving style emphasizes the development of multiple solutions to a given problem posed by the teacher.

These teaching approaches should be varied depending on task demands and intended outcomes.

Teachers can also consider class organization, which can take any of the following forms:

- Whole group
- Small groups (squads)
- Stations
- Pairs or dyads
- Individual work

Before employing any of these modifications, it is important for the instructor to consider the following questions:

1. Is the adaptation safe?
2. Does the modification maintain the concept of the game?

Summary

This chapter has provided ideas for adapting activities to include students with disabilities in general physical education classes. The principles for adapting activities are based on the literature of adaptation theory, normalization theory, empowerment theory, and self-determination theory. Another basis is the use of Universal Design for Learning, which stresses preplanning. The areas of adaptation highlighted in this chapter include equipment, rules, environment, and instruction. The adaptation strategies presented here can be used to allow students with disabilities to achieve their IEP goals and objectives in inclusive settings. By facilitating success in physical education, teachers can help empower students with disabilities to consistently involve themselves in physical activities, sports, and recreation with their friends and family.

CHAPTER 6

Support Service: Making Inclusion a Reality

Amanda is a fourth grader who is visually impaired because of retinopathy of prematurity. She has just started at Katie Stanton Elementary School; previously, she attended a state school for the blind that was located outside her district and thus necessitated a 1-hour bus ride each way. Her parents decided that she should attend school in her home district, and the district supported their decision. Amanda has limited vision and needs a cane to walk independently. Her full-time paraeducator, Mrs. Dudak, accompanied her to physical education class periodically (i.e., if she was not preparing for other academic lessons). Amanda's physical education teacher, Mr. Aiello, had created a wonderful adapted curriculum for her and welcomed her into his physical education class. When Mrs. Dudak came to class with Amanda, Mr. Aiello noticed that when he told the class to get a partner, Amanda was always left with no partner or would partner up with Mrs. Dudak. Amanda began to feel very isolated and told her parents that she did not want to go to school anymore. This was her first year with her new peers, and by October she had withdrawn herself and stopped talking to her peers altogether.

Amanda's parents spoke with her teachers. For physical education, Mr. Aiello and Mrs. Dudak talked about how they could make Amanda feel more welcomed in the class. Mr. Aiello decided to create a disability awareness unit to increase her classmates' understanding of visual impairments. In fact, he began to create disability awareness activities for each new unit he taught so that the children would have a better understanding of individual differences. In addition, Mrs. Dudak implemented ideas she had learned from an in-service about how to facilitate more social interactions between Amanda and her peers. She took the time to train three peers to tutor Amanda in physical education. The students' understanding and empathy for Amanda increased, and her classmates began to play with her at recess, sit with her at lunch, and ask to be her partner in physical education. Amanda was even invited to her first sleepover during the February break!

The purpose of this chapter is to help readers

- ▪ be able to determine what types of support personnel are needed to help individualize instruction in an inclusive physical education class;
- ▪ understand the positive attributes of using peer tutors, paraeducators, grandparents, and professional preparation students; and
- ▪ be able to plan and implement training programs for support personnel.

Today more than ever, general physical educators are expected to teach heterogeneous classes that may include students with a variety of disabilities. In order for these classes to be effective, trained support personnel must be involved on a daily basis to help individualize instruction and ensure successful inclusion.

Peer Tutors

In the opening scenario, Mr. Aiello used a disability awareness unit to help sensitize peers to their new classmate who had a visual impairment. While this approach is both worthwhile and highly encouraged, the use of peer tutoring programs can also help to facilitate acceptance. The concept of peer tutoring in physical education is not new. Project PEOPEL, started in 1980 (Long, Irmer, Burkett, Glasenapp, & Odenkirk, 1980), included a training protocol and specific guidelines for implementation. There are several key reasons that physical educators are encouraged to think about implementing a peer tutor program in physical education (see figure 6.1).

The most important reason, of course, is that it allows for individualized instruction. Peer tutoring gives students with disabilities time in class to work on developmental skills vital to their involvement in physical activity in the future. It allows a student with a disability to receive instruction, increased practice time, increased

---

FIGURE 6.1

Reasons for Using a Peer Tutor Program

1. Students with disabilities need smaller ratios for learning than do students without disabilities.
2. One-to-one instruction increases academic learning time (DePaepe, 1985; Webster 1987; Wiskochil, Lieberman, Houston-Wilson, & Petersen, 2007).
3. Tutors learn skills better than they would have if not teaching them (Briggs, 1975).
4. Peer tutoring increases leadership experience among tutors (Rink, 1998).
5. Peer tutoring stimulates socialization among peers (Ernst & Byra, 1998).
6. Cooperative learning experiences promote more interpersonal attraction between students with and without disabilities, higher self-esteem, and greater empathy on the part of all the students.
7. Participating together as partners and equals encourages positive relationships (Sinibaldi, 2001).

---

reinforcement, and continuous feedback on progress by a tutor on a one-to-one basis (Delquadri, Greenwood, Whorton, Carta, & Hall, 1986). For example, not only could Amanda benefit from having a peer tutor guide her in the locomotor skills unit, but also she would automatically have a partner when the class paired up for activities.

Peer tutoring is an appropriate and effective way to set up meaningful activity that includes opportunity for high rates of motor-appropriate practice. Many researchers agree that implementing a peer tutor program can improve the level of skills and socialization for students with disabilities (Copeland et al., 2002; d'Arripe-Longueville et al., 2002; Hughes et al., 2004). When students are inconsistent or do not perform skills correctly, they fail to appropriately learn the skills and may even learn them incorrectly; peer tutors, however, can help students with disabilities learn skills and practice them correctly. In addition, peer tutoring offers an inexpensive way to help students with disabilities succeed in the general physical education class in terms of both motor abilities and fitness (Barfield, Hannigan-Downs, & Lieberman, 1998; Block, 2007; Houston-Wilson, Lieberman, Horton, & Kasser, 1997). Finally, Ernst and Byra (1998) found that working with a peer was a positive experience and enhanced much-needed social interaction between students.

Types of Peer Tutor Programs

It is important to distinguish between peer interaction and peer tutoring. The term *peer interaction* refers to a relationship where the peers receive no formal training, whereas the term *peer tutoring* is used if appropriate training is provided. The person doing the tutoring is known as the *tutor*, and the person being tutored is known as the *tutee*. Types of peer tutor programs include unidirectional, bidirectional (or reciprocal), classwide, same-age, and cross-age.

▶ These students are involved in unidirectional peer tutoring because the trained peer tutor takes on the role of teacher, and the partner remains the student.

1. **Unidirectional peer tutoring.** In this approach, the trained peer tutor teaches the entire time, and the student with a disability remains the tutee in the pair. This method is effective when working with students who have more severe disabilities, such as severe autism, mental retardation, visual impairment, or cerebral palsy. The benefits of this option are that the tutor and tutee always know their roles and that the peer tutor carries the responsibility throughout the entire program. Its weakness is that the tutee never gets to take on a leadership role and may at some point come to resent being constantly tutored.

2. **Bidirectional or reciprocal peer tutoring.** In this model, a student with a disability and a student without a disability form a dyad, or pair. Each student takes turns at being the tutor while the other serves as tutee. Roles can be switched by the skill, class, week, or unit. This method is most effective with students who have mild disabilities. The main benefit of this approach is that each student has an opportunity to practice leadership while serving as the tutor.

3. **Classwide peer tutoring.** This strategy involves breaking the entire class into dyads or small groups. Each student participates in reciprocal peer tutoring by providing his or her partner(s) with prompts, error correction, and feedback (Greenwood, Carta, & Hall, 1988). Classwide peer tutoring is unique in that all students are given task cards to keep them focused on the objectives of the lesson (though task cards can be used any time, not exclusively for peer tutoring). The tutor uses task cards to keep track of skills mastered by the tutee. This method is most effective with students who have mild disabilities. Its main benefit is that it involves the entire class in the tutoring activity, which means that no students are singled out because of disability. Johnson and Ward (2001) revealed that classwide peer tutoring was effective for both low- and high-skilled students and for both boys and girls. In their study, low-skilled boys and girls made improvements similar to those of their average and high-skilled counterparts.

4. **Same-age peer tutoring.** In this approach, students who are of similar age or grade tutor each other. This form of tutoring can be done in both the unidirectional and bidirectional models. Benefits are that peers get to know each other well and they are in the same class. This method is less effective when the children are young (under second grade) or have a severe disability.

5. **Cross-age peer tutoring.** This strategy involves an older student being chosen to tutor a younger student. It works best when the peer tutor is interested in working with students with disabilities. A cross-age peer tutor is more effective than a same-age peer tutor when the student with a disability is very young (i.e., below second grade) or the disability is more serious (such as severe cerebral palsy, mental retardation, or autism) (Houston-Wilson, Lieberman, Horton, & Kasser, 1997; Lieberman, Newcomer, McCubbin, & Dalrymple, 1997). The cross-age peer tutor can be chosen according to willingness, physical skills, and availability. The main benefit of this approach is that the tutor gains valuable teaching experience while the tutee receives effective individualized instruction and feedback.

It is important to note here that students with behavioral or learning disabilities can serve as effective cross-age peer tutors (Friend, 2005), and providing these students with the chance to take responsibility for another individual (especially one who is younger or has more severe disabilities) helps to foster leadership, confidence, and the feeling of being needed. Characteristics of a good peer tutor are listed in figure 6.2.

The Peer Tutor Training Program

Experts believe that training tutors is essential to the success of the program (Houston-Wilson, Dunn, van der Mars, & McCubbin, 1997; Lieberman, Dunn, van der Mars, & McCubbin, 2000; Wiskochil, Lieberman, Houston-Wilson, & Petersen, 2007). The peer tutor training program can take an hour or more, depending on the age of the tutor, the student's disability, and the unit of instruction. A peer tutor training handout is included on the accompanying CD-ROM. For example, if a hearing student is in a reciprocal peer tutor program with a deaf child, he or she will need to go through the basic training program and spend additional time learning important signs. If a student is in a unidirectional peer tutor program and is tutoring a student with autism during a dance unit, then the tutor will first need to understand the dance steps before attempting to teach them. In these cases,

▶ Cross-age peer tutoring allows for increased instruction and feedback.

FIGURE 6.2

Characteristics of a Good Peer Tutor

Interest in tutoring

Same gender as student being tutored (if the tutor prefers)

Average or above-average skill performance (d'Arripe-Longueville, Gernigon, Huet, Cadopi, & Winnykamen, 2002)

Well behaved and reliable (Ward & Lee, 2005)

Experienced with younger siblings (with or without disabilities)

Enthusiastic and positive

Patient

Experienced in working with students with disabilities

Experienced in living with learning or behavioral disabilities (may need additional guidance)

Adapted from L.J. Lieberman, C. Houston-Wilson, and R. Aiello, 2001, *Developing and implementing a peer tutor program.* Presentation at the American Alliance for Health, Physical Education, Recreation and Dance National Conference, Cincinnati, Ohio.

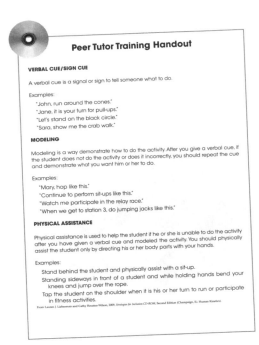

Peer Tutor Training Handout

VERBAL CUE/SIGN CUE

A verbal cue is a signal or sign to tell someone what to do.

Examples:

"John, run around the cones."
"Jane, it is your turn for pull-ups."
"Let's stand on the black circle."
"Sara, show me the crab walk."

MODELING

Modeling is a way demonstrate how to do the activity. After you give a verbal cue, if the student does not do the activity or does it incorrectly, you should repeat the cue and demonstrate what you want him or her to do.

Examples:

"Mary, hop like this."
"Continue to perform sit-ups like this."
"Watch me participate in the relay race."
"When we get to station 3, do jumping jacks like this."

PHYSICAL ASSISTANCE

Physical assistance is used to help the student if he or she is unable to do the activity after you have given a verbal cue and modeled the activity. You should physically assist the student only by directing his or her body parts with your hands.

Examples:

Stand behind the student and physically assist with a sit-up.
Standing sideways in front of a student and while holding hands bend your knees and jump over the rope.
Tap the student on the shoulder when it is his or her turn to run or participate in fitness activities.

From Lauren J. Lieberman and Cathy Houston-Wilson, 2009, *Strategies for Inclusion CD-ROM, Second Edition* (Champaign, IL: Human Kinetics).

the tutor would require more time in training. Training typically occurs before school, after school, during lunch, during recess, as part of a physical education class, or, if possible, on a staff development day with tutors choosing to participate on their day off.

The basic peer tutor training program may take about 1 hour, possibly broken into shorter sessions. Training time would be increased by adding information about treatment of disability, the unit of instruction, or program goals. The training time should be short (15 to 30 minutes) but within a close time frame (one to two weeks). If peer tutors can be trained within a 2-week period, they will be better able to retain and use the information. Beyond the training and in-class tutoring, peer tutors and tutees should periodically arrive at class a few minutes early to discuss the lesson for the day. This meeting allows the peer tutor to plan instructional strategies and address questions free from interruption and distraction.

Here are some recommendations for establishing an effective training program. First, when possible, include the student with the disability in the training. This approach ensures that the tutor and tutee are in agreement with all the instructional techniques taught and that the tutor will know and better understand the student with the disability. Second, make sure the training includes scenarios, so that the dyad has the opportunity to practice instruction and feedback with an upcoming unit before it happens. Last, and most important, since the tutor is just learning how to teach, that student will need oversight and feedback from the instructor. As when using any form of support personnel, it is ultimately the teacher's responsibility to ensure that learning is occurring for all parties involved.

Setting up the peer tutor training program is not difficult. Our model incorporates all necessary steps that should be considered when planning and implementing a peer tutor training program. Feel free to add your own components as you find necessary.

Step 1: Develop an Application Procedure   One rule of thumb when setting up peer tutoring programs is that tutors should *want* to participate; in addition, we believe the desire to tutor should be intrinsic, which in turn means that very little extrinsic reward should be offered. It's fine to give buttons, stickers, or certificates at the end of the program, but higher grades or monetary rewards would be inappropriate. Some programs throw an ice cream or pizza party at the end of the year, which is acceptable since such parties allow students to celebrate the year's accomplishments. To ensure intrinsic motivation and strong desire, many schools choose to have tutors apply for positions just as they would apply for a job. You can find an example of a peer tutor application on the CD-ROM.

Byra and Marks (1993) have proposed allowing students to self-select based on friendships, if possible, since students who considered themselves friends gave feedback at higher rates.

In any case, it is recommended that you choose three peer tutors for each student with a disability so that the tutors have the opportunity to rotate. In addition, if one is absent, moves, or develops bad feelings toward the tutee, there are still several trained peers to choose from. It is important to rotate the peer tutors equally so that they remain in practice and maintain their interest in the work. Along the same lines, if a peer tutor wants a unit "off" from tutoring to participate uninhibitedly in a favorite unit, this wish should be accommodated.

Application to Be a Trained Peer Tutor

Name: _____
Grade: _____
Name(s) of teacher(s): _____
Periods free to tutor:
1st choice _____
2nd choice _____
3rd choice _____

AVAILABILITY FOR TRAINING

(Minimum of 2 hours; may involve four 30-minute periods, six 20-minute periods, or one staff development day where the student chooses to participate on his or her day off.)

____ Recess	Time _____
____ Before school	Time _____
____ After school	Time _____
____ During lunch	Time _____
____ Staff development day	Time _____
____ Study halls	Time _____
____ Portion of physical	Time _____
education class	
____ Other time	Time _____ (Be specific)

Experience in working with students with disabilities:

_____
_____
_____
_____

Please describe briefly why you want to be a peer tutor and indicate whether you have a specific friend you would like to tutor.

_____
_____

From Lauren J. Lieberman and Cathy Houston-Wilson, 2009, *Strategies for Inclusion CD-ROM, Second Edition* (Champaign, IL: Human Kinetics).

Step 2: Obtain Permission   In many cases, if the formal program is part of the physical education program and involves out-of-class-training, it is necessary to obtain permission from parents, the tutor, the student with disabilities (if appropriate), and administrators. A sample Parental Permission Slip is included on the CD-ROM.

If the entire class is part of the tutoring program, there is no need for permissions. In some cases, however, the administration might worry that this program will replace instruction by the teacher, so it is a good idea to assure administrators that the peer tutoring program can enhance the instruction given by the physical educator. Without peer tutors, the physical educator's efforts must be spread much more thinly, and as a result he or she may be less effective for everyone involved.

Step 3: Develop Disability Awareness Activities   An effective training program for peer tutors must ensure that the tutors understand the disability affecting the student with whom they will work. It can be difficult to describe a disability in language that students understand, and we have provided simple descriptions of many disabilities in appendix A. Instructors are also encouraged to review the information about disability awareness levels in chapter 7.

Step 4: Develop Communication Techniques   The next step in the training program is to teach about modes of communication. For example, if a peer tutor is working with a student with limited language, the tutor should be taught the difference between expressive and receptive language. *Expressive communication* refers to words or concepts that are spoken *by* the student, and *receptive communication* indicates information or cues received *by* the student. Children with deafness, hardness of hearing, autism, or any of various other severe disabilities may have unique forms of communication. Whereas communicating with deaf persons involves signs, communicating with students who have autism may require the use of picture boards. Students with some severe disabilities may use augmentative devices that relay computer-generated words when prompted to do so by the user. Whatever the communication method, it is essential that time be spent on this important component of the training program.

Step 5: Teach Instructional Techniques   Training peers to teach students with disabilities requires a good understanding of a teaching process known as the *system of least prompts* (Dunn, Morehouse, & Fredericks, 1986). The goal is to allow individuals to perform skills as independently as possible. The least prompt would be a verbal cue; a more intensive prompt would be a model or demonstration, and one still more intensive would be physical assistance. These skills are taught to the tutor through the use of scenarios. For example, if the tutor provides a verbal cue asking the tutee to throw a ball and the skill is executed incorrectly, the tutor should then model the skill appropriately to facilitate understanding before asking again. If the combination of cue and model proves unsuccessful, the final prompt would be to add physical assistance. This type of prompt should be used only when working with students with severe disabilities who need physical assistance to complete tasks or with a compliant tutee who is just not grasping the concept of a certain skill.

Tutors should also be taught how to give feedback about skill performance. Verbal feedback consists of positive general statements, positive specific statements, and corrective statements. Nonverbal feedback can involve such things as a high five or a thumbs-up. Positive feedback is given after the student executes a skill correctly, and corrective feedback is given after the student executes a skill incorrectly.

■ Trained peer tutors are more effective than nontrained peer tutors.

▶ Encourage peers to provide positive, instructional feedback to one another.

Step 6: Use Scenarios to Aid in Teaching During the tutor training program, it is essential that the instructor use real-life scenarios to check for understanding (Houston-Wilson, Lieberman, Horton, & Kasser, 1997). For example, if, in a given scenario, the peer tutor is teaching a throwing skill and the tutee is either unresponsive or does the skill incorrectly, the instructor should ask the tutor, "What should you do now?" The tutor would need to state—or state and model—the task. If the tutee then exhibits the appropriate behavior, the peer tutor should give appropriate feedback. By practicing such techniques, tutors will become confident in their abilities and will perform more effectively. The instructor should provide at least 5 to 10 different scenarios to make sure that the peer tutor understands what he or she is being asked to do within the parameters of the program. If the tutor participates in the scenario incorrectly, the instructor should go over the concept again until the tutor fully understands what is expected.

Step 7: Test for Understanding The training program can include a peer tutor test (Houston-Wilson, Dunn, van der mars, & McCubbin, 1997), which might address any information directly relevant to the particular program. Things to consider include (1) the type of disability (e.g., use of signs for a child who is deaf or techniques for giving physical assistance to a child with cerebral palsy), (2) the unit of instruction (e.g., cooperative games, basketball, swimming), and (3) the goals of the program (e.g., teamwork, improvement of skills, improvement of fitness, socialization). Instructors should decide what skills tutors must be able to articulate, then develop written or oral exams to test their knowledge of these skills. A tutor should be able to score at least 90 percent in order to continue in the peer tutor program. If the child does not meet this standard, then he or she should be instructed in the weak areas and given the test again. The CD-ROM contains an example of a peer tutor test.

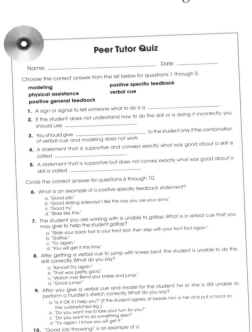

Step 8: Monitor Progress   It is important to document the progress of all students, including those involved in the peer tutor program. Just as an instructor makes use of assessment data, a peer tutor can also learn how to collect data. It is an acceptable practice for students to collect performance data about other students; the process has, in fact, been deemed legal through a Supreme Court ruling, and Batista and Pittman (2005) summarized the findings by noting that records are not considered private information until the data are recorded in the instructor's record book. After data are collected, the instructor should check on progress and observe the tutors periodically to make sure data are being collected accurately.

Peer tutors can collect data in several ways. The first is through the use of a *process checklist,* which contains a breakdown of skills into component parts; such a breakdown is also known as a task analysis (see the CD-ROM for a sample process checklist for basketball). The peer tutor can observe the tutee executing the skill and check off the components that were done correctly. The second way to collect data is through the use of *rubrics* (see chapter 2); the peer tutor can mark off which level the student reaches during each class period. A third way to collect data is by simply *tallying opportunities.* Any discrete skill can be tallied, including such activities as doing push-ups, kicking a ball, walking across a beam, moving through an obstacle course, or running laps around the gymnasium. Each time the tutee accomplishes a task that can be tallied, the tutor makes a check mark. This system allows instructors to note how often the student is engaged in activity. For those skills that cannot be tallied, tracking *time on task,* or how long the student is engaged in the activity, is another way to collect data. Butler and Hodge (2001) reported that peer assessment yielded the following benefits: enhanced feedback, increased trust, and increased time on task. Research has also shown that well-trained students from third grade through high school can assess their peers reliably (70 to 96 percent agreement with researchers) (Johnson & Ward, 2001; Ward & Lee, 2005).

It is also important to monitor the progress of the peer tutors themselves. This can be done informally throughout the experience—before, during, or after class. The process can also be conducted more formally by using a peer tutor evaluation form (a sample is included on the CD-ROM). This form can be filled out during the program, at the end of the program, or at both times in order to give the tutor feedback on his or her performance.

Step 9: Use Behavior Programs (If Necessary)   Peer tutors should also be aware of any behavior plans that are in place for the child they are tutoring. The peer tutor, however, should not be responsible for implementing the behavior plan. It is up to the teacher or assigned paraeducator or support staff to handle any behavior problems that may occur during the class.

Using peer tutors is one way to improve instruction and feedback. Incorporating paraeducators is an additional method that can benefit everyone in the class.

Paraeducators

It has been 50 years since "teacher aides" were introduced into our nation's schools to enable teachers to spend more time planning and implementing instructional activities. Initially, the duties assigned to aides were primarily routine and included clerical tasks, monitoring students in nonacademic learning environments, duplicating instructional material, and reinforcing lessons introduced by teachers.

Teacher aides are now also referred to as paraprofessionals, paraeducators, educational assistants, teaching assistants (TAs), and support personnel. The term *paraeducator* derives from the concept that these professionals work along with the teacher in much the same way as a paralegal works with a lawyer and a paramedic works with a physician. Research has determined that in today's schools most paraeducators spend part or all of their time assisting teachers and other licensed practitioners in various phases of the instructional process, including the delivery of direct services to learners and their parents (Downing, Ryndak, & Clark, 2000; Killoran, Templeman, Peters, & Udell, 2001; Riggs & Mueller, 2001). The professional organization for support personnel refers to them as *paraeducators*, and this is the term that will be used to refer respectfully to these valuable colleagues throughout this chapter.

Purpose of Paraeducators

Like peer tutors, paraeducators are there to facilitate a more successful inclusive environment (French, 2003; Piletic, Davis, & Aschemeier, 2005). Because some students with disabilities benefit from one-to-one instruction, these individuals are important in appropriate inclusive environments. Some paraeducators may expect to have the period of physical education serve as a break or planning period, but this is not acceptable (Block, 2007). If a class or a child needs a paraeducator in the classroom, it is likely that the support will be even more needed in physical education. Common duties assigned to paraeducators include the following:

1. Implement teacher-created lessons in small groups or in one-to-one fashion in the gymnasium or in the community.
2. Carry out behavior management and disciplinary plans created by the teacher.
3. Assist the teacher with assessment activities.
4. Assist with activity modifications as necessary.
5. Document and provide the teacher with objective information about learner performance to aid in planning.
6. Assist teachers with organizing and maintaining supportive, safe learning environments.
7. Assist teachers with involving parents and other caregivers in the child's education.
8. Shadow the child with a disability and the child's peer tutor, giving feedback and support to each.
9. Help related service personnel (e.g., nurses, physical therapists, occupational therapists, and speech-language pathologists) provide, implement, and generalize services.
10. Physically support the instructor in tasks such as helping students with toileting, changing clothes, and adjusting adapted materials and mobility.
11. Participate in the development and implementation of the IEP or 504 plan.

12. Share ideas with the teacher to enhance learning opportunities (Davis, Kotecki, Harvey, & Oliver, 2007; Horton, 2001; Lieberman, 2007; Mach, 2000; Picket, 2002; Piletic et al., 2005; Wallace, Shin, Bartholomay, & Stahl, 2001).

While this list is not comprehensive, it makes it easy to see that paraeducators juggle multiple responsibilities, and, as with peer tutors, they need training in order to be effective. Davis, Kotecki, et al. (2007) found that the training areas most sought after by paraeducators for physical education were activity modifications, attributes of students with disabilities, and knowledge of motor skill development.

When paraeducators are working one to one with students with disabilities, they should encourage social interactions with other students in the class. Block (1998) recommends that students with disabilities who are assigned a one-to-one paraeducator be provided with as many social interactions with other students as possible, because the one-to-one relationship can be a limiting factor in social interactions in physical education. Giangreco, Edelman, Luiselli, and MacFarland (1997) determined that one of the biggest problems with the use of paraeducator support is that unnecessarily close proximity can have unintended negative social effects for the students with disabilities (Broer, Doyle, & Giangreco, 2005). Classmates tend to avoid those students who have a paraeducator with them on a regular basis. Here are a few examples where paraeducator proximity may hinder social interactions between peers (Causton-Theoharis & Mamgren, 2005):

■ Maintaining physical contact with the student
■ Sitting directly next to the student
■ Allowing the student to sit on the paraeducator's lap
■ Accompanying the student everywhere in the school setting
■ Speaking for the student

It is also important to keep in mind that student-to-student interactions are considered a critical component of learning (Cullinan, Sabornie, & Crossland, 1992; Folsom-Meek & Aiello, 2007; Ward & Ayvazo, 2006). As general physical education placements are becoming more common, educators are seeking out innovative and effective ways to support students with disabilities who are placed in classrooms alongside their typically developing peers (Causton-Theoharis & Mamgren, 2005). Figure 6.3 presents strategies that can be employed to help foster student-to-student interactions.

In addition to helping improve social interaction, the paraeducator is also part of the multidisciplinary team charged with improving behavior. It is very important for the teacher and the paraeducator to be clear on the roles that each one plays in the development and implementation of the behavior management plan. Table 6.1 summarizes the distribution of duties between teachers and paraeducators in this area.

Teachers who work with paraeducators should be clear about their expectations and give appropriate direction and guidance so that the support is useful (French, 2003; Trautman, 2004). According to Mach (2000), it is helpful if support personnel receive training in emergency procedures and participate in an orientation session addressing the physical education program in which they will be working. Failure to make expectations clear can lead to frustration for the teacher and the paraeducator (Hauge & Babkie, 2006). Until recently, there was no clarity about who would train paraeducators for physical education or how they would be trained. Now, however, thanks to support from the Adapted Physical Activity Council (APAC) of the American Association for Physical Activity and Recreation (AAPAR) and from the American

■ Trained paraeducators increase the entire class' opportunities for successful academic learning time.

FIGURE 6.3

Strategies to Promote Student-to-Student Interaction

1. Ensure that students with disabilities are placed in rich social environments.
2. Highlight the similarities rather than the differences between students with disabilities and typically developing peers.
3. Redirect student conversation to include the student with a disability. (Some able-bodied peers tend to talk around or over the individual with a disability.)
4. Directly teach and practice interaction skills in appropriate natural settings (i.e., during games, waiting time, transition time, or on the sideline).
5. Use instructional strategies that promote interaction (e.g., small groups, pairs, guided discovery, task-style learning).
6. Teach others (peer tutors) how to interact with students with a disability.
7. Reward behavior that is social in nature (e.g., interactive games, partner activities, helping with attendance). All students who increase socialization at appropriate times can get stickers, for example, or preferred activity or free time at the end of class.
8. Give the student responsibilities that allow for interaction with peers (e.g., squad leader, equipment manager).
9. Systematically fade out any direct support.
10. Make interdependence a goal for the student (e.g., using assistance from peers rather than help from the paraeducator).

Adapted from J. Causton-Theoharis and K. Mamgren, 2005, "Building bridges: Strategies to help paraprofessionals promote peer interaction," *Teaching Exceptional Children* July/August, 20.

TABLE 6.1

Teacher and Paraeducator Roles in Behavior Management

Roles in planning and implementation	Paraeducator	Teacher
Establish classroom rules.		X
Establish class schedules and activities.		X
Observe student behavior.	X	X
Design behavior management plans.		X
Establish objectives for student behavior.		X
Select appropriate reinforcers.		X
Record and chart student behavior.	X	X
Provide consequences according to the behavior plan.	X	X
Provide praise to the student.	X	X
Evaluate intervention effectiveness.		X
Provide feedback according to appropriate behavior.	X	X

Alliance for Health, Physical Education, Recreation and Dance (AAHPERD), there is a training manual for paraeducators which can be used to assist them in working with students with disabilities in physical education (Lieberman, 2007). Here is a summary of this training program.

Training Paraeducators

The paraeducator training program is broken down into eight categories of instruction. Each is explained below.

1. Define physical education. This part of the training reviews the purpose of physical education and addresses the National Association for Sport & Physical Education (NASPE) standards as well as state standards. Common terminology is clarified, and attention is paid to teaching styles, lesson plan format, and the teacher's pedagogical philosophy.

2. Define roles. The various roles of the paraeducator and the teacher are reviewed here and made specific to the age, type of disability, class size, and needs of the learner. Roles may vary as units change, as more paraeducators enter the classroom, and during assessment.

3. Review disabilities. Although the paraeducator usually knows the student(s) better than the physical educator does, it is important to reserve a part of the training for reviewing the disabilities of the students in the class. Both the teacher and the paraeducator can share information about the etiology (cause) of a disability, characteristics of persons who have that type of disability, behaviors of the student, functional ability of the student, IEP goals for physical education, and any contraindicated activities (i.e., activities that should be avoided). This information is crucial for both the physical educator and the paraeducator.

4. Discuss inclusion strategies. The teacher may use a variety of inclusion strategies, and these should be shared with the paraeducator. Inclusion strategies to review might include the following: peer tutors, as discussed earlier in this chapter; activity modifications; equipment modifications; rule modifications; instructional techniques such as cueing, prompting, modeling, and providing physical assistance; teaching styles such as command, task, guided discovery, and exploration; and provision of feedback on both skill and behavior.

5. Discuss assessment strategies. Assessment is a critical component of instructing all students in physical education. It helps to determine what to teach, how students are progressing, and whether learning has occurred. The instructor will need assistance in setting up the gymnasium for assessment, collecting assessment data, documenting performance, and

▶ The teacher and paraeducator must work together to collect information about the student's abilities and skill level.

entering data into the computer. The communication of specific expectations regarding assessment ensures an accurate, smooth, and enjoyable assessment experience for everyone.

6. Review behavior management plans. Each child has individual strengths and weaknesses regarding behavior in physical education. It is imperative that the teacher and paraeducator use the same behavior management techniques with the student. In many cases, the behavior program will be developed by a multidisciplinary team and implemented throughout the student's school day. In some instances, the training time gives the paraeducator the opportunity to share the plan with the physical educator. In any case, it is imperative that the management plan be discussed and clarified before implementation.

7. Discuss conflict resolution strategies. Even the most well-meaning, hardworking teachers and paraeducators occasionally possess differing ideas on how to handle a situation, and conflicts can arise even with the best staff. Therefore, a complete training program should define the hierarchy of command, as well as the protocol to follow regarding conflicts. The authors of this book suggest that teachers and paraeducators set an open-door policy related to issues in physical education. In other words, each party should feel comfortable sharing their opinions, issues, or problems with the other in a nonbiased, safe space. This way, conflicts are resolved quickly, honestly, and positively, thus creating a win-win situation for everyone, especially the students involved. Ultimately, however, it is the teacher's responsibility to ensure that best practices are being followed.

8. Share resources. The last part of the training should involve a sharing of resources. The paraeducator can share resources that he or she is aware of which may be useful in physical education, and the physical education teacher can share resources that may be helpful in understanding physical education more fully. These resources might include books, CDs, Web sites, and journals.

When possible, this training program should be presented at the beginning of the year so that all parties are on the same page. The training could occupy a day, a half day, or a regularly scheduled slot (e.g., Friday afternoons). In any case, many variables change throughout the school year, and good communication is a must between the physical educator and the paraeducator. Mauerer (2004) found that communication was seen as one of the biggest barriers to the success of the paraeducator in physical education. When asked the best way to communicate new information to each other, physical educators and paraeducators shared the following approaches (Mauerer, 2004):

- E-mail
- Short meetings before or after class
- Meetings before school
- Meetings after school
- Sharing of lesson plans in mailboxes
- A whiteboard or blackboard in the gymnasium with specific instructions from the teacher or specific feedback from the paraeducator
- Meetings during lunch or planning times

Even the most well-trained and dedicated paraeducators can often be overheard telling someone, "I am only a para." This feeling of inadequacy or lack of importance can lead to apathy, absenteeism, and inappropriate instruction. Paraeducators must feel like the dedicated, committed, invaluable professionals they are. Without this feeling of importance, the very person the paraeducator is supposed to help will be the one who suffers most. Here are some ideas for increasing paraeducators' sense of being a valued member of the team:

- *Name on door:* The door to the gymnasium has the name of the physical educators. Adding the paraeducators' names gives them a better sense of identity and belonging in the gymnasium and in physical education.

- *Introduction:* When doing introductions at the beginning of the school year, teachers can introduce paraeducators as assistant teachers and make them feel as important as they are to the success of the class. In addition, teachers can address them as Mr., Ms., or Mrs. to suggest the same respect given to teachers.

- *Whiteboard or blackboard:* Posting a whiteboard or blackboard on the wall provides a means of communication between teacher and paraeducator.

- *Equipment assistance:* When ordering equipment, taking time to get input from the paraeducator will give a more accurate idea of what is needed and will also help the paraeducator feel a true ownership stake in the program.

- *Modification ideas:* The paraeducator can help make modifications in equipment, rules, instruction, and environment at the start of each unit. Asking the paraeducator's opinion will help ensure that the lesson meets the students' needs and increases the paraeducator's sense of self-value in helping implement the lesson.

- *Locker:* In many instances, paraeducators may not come to school prepared for the physical education environment. Providing them with lockers where they can keep comfortable shoes or clothes helps them be more prepared for physical education and more effective while there.

- *Refreshing drink or protein bar:* In addition to a locker and changing area, giving paraeducators a healthy snack before or after a strenuous unit will replenish their system, in addition to letting them know that you want them to do well. This small gesture can go a long way in giving them a positive perspective on your classes and their participation.

- *Recognition:* It often takes great energy and effort to teach students with disabilities who participate in physical education, and their success cannot be achieved without the dedication and commitment of the paraeducator. Recognizing individual students' accomplishments and at the same time giving credit to their paraeducators as primary instructors can be accomplished during IEP meetings and staff meetings, through school or physical education newsletters, and on physical education bulletin boards.

- *Thank-you:* A genuine thank-you can be expressed in various forms, such as homemade cookies, a plant, a card, or a balloon. A small gesture can go a long way in ensuring that the paraeducator never feels like she or he is "only a para" in physical education.

Adapted, by permission, from R. Lytle, L.J. Lieberman, and R. Aiello, 2007, "Motivating paraeducators to be actively involved in physical education programs," *Journal of Physical Education, Recreation, and Dance* 78: 26-30, 50.

These relatively simple tasks will help create a strong and dedicated instruction team.

Senior Citizens

As mentioned earlier in this chapter, instruction for individuals with disabilities is best when done on a one-to-one basis. Many schools have limited resources for employing paraeducators, which leaves the instructor with the responsibility of teaching all students—both with and without disabilities—and, perhaps, the feeling that no one's needs are being fully met. One often-overlooked resource is senior citizens. More and more people today are retiring with plenty of energy and enthusiasm left to contribute to society. Whether or not they have experience in working with students with disabilities, these citizens are readily available to assist the physical educator in a variety of ways. They can contribute in many of the same ways mentioned earlier regarding paraeducators, and they can also be trained in much the same way as peer tutors. They can help create and adapt equipment, improve time on task, give feedback, and perform evaluations. In fact, senior citizens who are former teachers may need very little training and may welcome the opportunity to share their expertise on a less demanding schedule.

You can find senior citizens to assist in physical education by sending letters home with the students, recruiting on open school night, making phone calls to follow up on suggestions from parents, and putting up notices at senior centers. Any way you look at it, this is a win-win situation for everyone involved, especially for students with disabilities!

College Students

University or community college students are another resource that is not tapped into often enough. Most university programs in special education, physical education, adapted physical education, and counseling have practicum requirements for their students. When these educators in training serve as support personnel, students with disabilities benefit from the individualized instruction, the college student benefits by gaining more experience in teaching, and the instructor benefits by having additional hands in the gym. College students can be used and trained in the same way as peer tutors or paraeducators. Some may even offer teaching methods that they have learned in class and are eager to try out with real students.

You can find university students to assist in physical education by calling or writing letters to relevant departments at local universities. The physical education teacher will need to find out the requirement for each specific university department and create a proposal that would allow the university student to meet his or her requirement. The physical educator could ask for the student's class syllabus to ensure that the student is meeting class objectives through his or her work in the physical education class. This approach encourages the college or university to send students to the school as student teachers, who typically teach on a full-time basis. Again, this is a win-win situation.

Summary

Today more than ever, as students with disabilities are increasingly being fully included in general education, teachers need additional support to facilitate the learning of all students. This chapter has presented strategies for working with support personnel such as peer tutors, paraeducators, senior citizens, and college students. Training these individuals to assist within the physical education class is a necessary component of the program. Using the ideas and training methods presented in this chapter may at first seem time consuming, but the benefits reaped from such a program are well worth the effort.

CHAPTER 7

Creating an Atmosphere for Achievement

Dylan is a sixth grader who loves to be involved in physical activity. He was born with spina bifida, a congenital birth defect in which the neural tube fails to close completely during the first four weeks of fetal development. The result is an opening in the spinal column which typically results in some degree of paralysis. Dylan generally uses a walker to get around but also uses a wheelchair when he is involved in activities that require a great deal of walking. Over the years, Dylan has had a very restricted physical education program, consisting of either a separate class or a small group of students with a variety of disabilities. When, in the fifth grade, Dylan was finally permitted to receive his adapted physical education program in his general physical education class, his teacher, Mrs. Buckley, relegated Dylan to a corner of the gym where he practiced ball skills with his paraeducator. Mrs. Buckley did not want Dylan to do any activities that moved too quickly, for she feared that Dylan could hurt himself or the other children in the class. As a result, even though Dylan played tee ball (with help from a pinch runner) at recess and often played four square (he was good at bouncing and catching the ball because that is what he did most of the time in physical education), he never thought he could be truly included in his physical education classes.

When Dylan moved up to middle school, however, he had a new physical education teacher named Mrs. Ellis, who was creative, enthusiastic, and committed to including all students in physical education. She made sure that Dylan was cleared to fully participate in physical education by connecting with Dylan's parents and doctors. The only precaution for Dylan was that, due to an allergy, he was not to use equipment made of latex. To facilitate the inclusion process, Mrs. Ellis first set up a disability awareness program with Dylan's permission. She brought in a video about Jean Driscoll, a famous wheelchair athlete who won the Boston Marathon eight times. Seeing a person with spina bifida accomplish such lofty goals was extremely impressive to Dylan, his classmates, and his parents. Next, the students learned about myelomeningocele, the type of spina bifida that Dylan has, and practiced getting around the school and the gymnasium with a walker and a wheelchair. Then, still using the walker or wheelchair, they tried to play a few activities such as soccer and ultimate Frisbee. As a result of these experiences, their understanding of Dylan's needs, and their acceptance of him, improved greatly. It would sometimes get to a point where his classmates would argue over who would be Dylan's partner. Mrs. Ellis continued to creatively include Dylan in all of her units of instruction, and during the aquatics unit Dylan really excelled. He joined his local YMCA's swim team and began competing regularly. Dylan even used his wheelchair to join his classmates in their roller hockey games. Mrs. Ellis showed Dylan and his peers that, with some creativity and forethought, a child with spina bifida can be successfully included in any activity.

The purpose of this chapter is to help readers

- understand various disabilities and their effect on physical education,
- develop a communication protocol for promoting inclusion in physical education,
- develop methods for facilitating inclusion, and
- incorporate strategies for supplementing instruction.

Understanding Disabilities

People with disabilities have gone through various periods of oppression, separation, and discrimination over the years. An era of acceptance is now a possibility, yet many misconceptions, myths, and prejudices linger about individuals with disabilities. Some folks believe that people with disabilities are second-class citizens, that all people with disabilities have intellectual disabilities, are unemployed, have no physical relationships, and do not contribute to society—just to name a few. In addition, in some instances when a person with a disability performs well, he or she is treated as a superhero just for performing everyday skills, as if it is rare for a person with a disability to get something done.

While it is essential that we respect and treat students with disabilities as equals, there are disabling conditions that teachers of physical education should know about (Pangrazi, 2007). Current federal legislation identifies 13 disability populations who require specific accommodations to meet unique needs in physical education and other academic areas through the use of an IEP. The relevant disability categories are autism, deafness, deafblindness, emotional disturbance, hearing impairment, learning disability, mental retardation, multiple disabilities, orthopedic impairment, speech or language impairment, traumatic brain injury, visual impairment, and other health impairment. Other conditions that may affect educational performance are accommodated through the use of a 504 plan, which helps ensure that students with disabilities are being provided with appropriate curricular programming and support.

Appendix A provides an overview of these various disabilities, as well as modified terminology that can be used to explain these conditions to children in a simple manner. If everyone has an understanding of a disability, it is easier to make necessary adjustments in the curriculum and in class activities. Teachers are urged to seek out resources and learn as much as they can about the conditions of students included in their classes in order to prevent doing contraindicated activities and to facilitate activities that can be beneficial.

Another source of assistance is the medical field. In the past, students with disabilities were routinely excused from physical education due solely to their disability; in fact, without clear understanding of physical education content, medical personnel often provided medical excuses that restricted participation in physical education. Today, however, the medical field is promoting physical activity to overcome the obesity epidemic, and teachers who work as partners with people in the medical field can help physicians gain an understanding of the "new PE." In turn, students with disabilities are not excluded from participation; rather, appropriate accommodations are made from the start to ensure success and full participation.

Communication Protocol

Many students, both with and without disabilities, cannot be fairly included in general physical education due to blanket medical excuses from a physician. In many of these cases, the student's physical or medical problems can in fact be safely accommodated in general or adapted physical education. However, if the student's physician does not believe, or has not been made aware, that the child can safely participate in physical education, then he or she will continue to write blanket medical excuses. Physicians simply may not understand the current nature of physical education (it is not dodgeball and regulation games), and they may not be aware of the supports and modifications that can be provided to enable students to participate safely and successfully in physical education. Unfortunately, an initial physician's recommendations sometimes cause a child's parents and physical education teacher to fear involving the child in general physical education classes. Parents may believe they are doing what is best for their child simply because they are unaware of alternatives such as adaptations, partial participation, and small group work. One caveat here: Physical education teachers should never defy a physician's order. Even though they may disagree with it, they must adhere to an order for "no physical education" until such time as the physician can be persuaded to alter the order. It is never acceptable to ignore a doctor's order.

Overcoming Blanket Medical Excuses

While physicians are well meaning when it comes to making medical decisions, parents and educators must realize that most physicians simply do not know what modern-day physical education entails. Physicians may picture physical education as 11v11 soccer games, 5v5 basketball games, or even mass dodgeball games. In

■ Educate physicians about the "new PE" to promote inclusion.

reality, of course, most physical education programs are much more developmentally appropriate and individualized. In addition, physicians may not be aware of the numerous types of modifications that can be used to make physical education safe—for example, lighter, softer equipment; smaller groups; modified rules; and the use of paraeducators. Physical educators, parents, and even children themselves need to take a more proactive approach in order to educate physicians who want to excuse students with disabilities from physical education. The key is to explain to the physician that the student with disabilities should and can be involved in an ongoing, high-quality physical education program that is safe, beneficial, and responsive to his or her unique needs.

Lieberman and Cruz (2001) noted that the key to providing such programs is found in open lines of communication between physical education teachers (general and adapted) and the student's special education teacher, parents, nurses, and physician. They also identified three major steps to take when attempting to overcome blanket medical excuses:

1. Become familiar with the disability to determine possible modifications.
2. Communicate these modifications to the physician to procure permission for participation.
3. Implement the modified program and reevaluate.

Become Familiar With the Disability   Disabilities come in many forms and can involve complications and contraindications. Table 7.1 provides a brief overview of some common contraindicating conditions that lead to exclusion of students with disabilities from physical education, as well as suggested appropriate modifications to promote inclusion. It is difficult, however, to know every condition and contraindicated activity, so it is important to confer with other members of the child's IEP team (e.g., parents, special education teacher, physical therapist, school nurse, or the student him- or herself) and to make use of reliable resources on the Internet or in print. With such information in hand, it is possible to explain to a child's parents and physician the areas of capability that can be worked on (e.g., fitness, gait, leisure skills), the type of program (general or adapted), and the modifications that will be made to ensure safety.

Another source of information that teachers should have access to is a list of students who have allergies, health problems, medications, and contraindicated activities. These lists are typically generated by the nurse's office and should be distributed to all physical education teachers at the beginning of the school year. Unfortunately, this list often provides just a name and a health condition. However, the physical educator, nurse, and physician can be proactive and add a third column identifying potential modifications for physical education. Table 7.2 provides an example of a list of students with medical issues and suggested modifications.

Communicate Directly With the Physician   Most physical educators and physicians are busy people, and it is often difficult to contact the physician and even more difficult to get a timely response. It is important, however, that the physician be apprised of the physical educator's familiarity with the student's condition and the suggested modifications. The CD-ROM includes a

▶ To become familiar with a student's skill level, it is best to assess the student during the activity, as shown here during a beep baseball unit.

TABLE 7.1

Common Contraindicating Conditions and Appropriate Modifications

Disability	Contraindicated activities	Modifications
Atlantoaxial instability: instability in the neck region	Head-jerking activities Forward rolls (jerking of the neck) Neck rolls Heading a soccer ball Diving	Avoid head-jarring activities. Acceptable activities include: Log rolls Forward head rolls Catching the soccer ball Jumping in the pool
Asthma: compromised breathing	Extrinsic factors (e.g., pollen, dust, grass) Continuous vigorous activity	Make sure inhaler/medication is readily available. Avoid freshly mowed fields. Permit breaks as needed.
Cystic fibrosis: excessive excretion of mucus	Continuous vigorous activity	Make sure medication is readily available. Permit breaks as needed.
Juvenile rheumatoid arthritis: swollen joints and stiffness	Running, jumping Heavy weight training Continuous vigorous activity	Include flexibility activities. Permit breaks as needed. Other good activities: Walking and low-impact activities Mild strengthening activities Water activities (warm water when possible)
Osteogenesis imperfecta: brittle bones	Repetitive activities Heavy weight training Contact sports Continuous vigorous activity	Permit breaks as needed. Good activities include: Walking and low-impact activities Use of modified/light equipment Noncontact sports
Seizures: abnormal electrical activity in the brain, resulting in various levels of unconsciousness	High balance beam, climbing ropes Deepwater diving Prolonged holding of breath	Make sure medication is readily available. Permit activity at heights with appropriate support, or when condition is under control. Permit surface dives or jumps into the pool. Use a buddy system in the pool.
Shunt: device used to drain excess fluid from the brain	Head-jerking activities Forward rolls (jerking of the neck) Neck rolls Heading a soccer ball Diving	Avoid head-jarring activities. Acceptable activities include: Log rolls Forward head rolls Catching the soccer ball Jumping in the pool

TABLE 7.2

List of Students With Medical Issues and Modifications

Student name*	Medical issue	Modification
Marcus Anderson	Atlantoaxial instability	Can do log rolls, jump in the pool, catch the soccer ball (no heading), use Nerf/soft balls; do forward head stretches only.
Jennifer Chandler	Asthma (pollen, dust, grass, mold)	Avoid extrinsic factors, use warm-up at all times, utilize prescribed medication, take breaks when necessary.
Gary Clinton	Attention-deficit/ hyperactivity disorder	Use prescribed medication (e.g., Ritalin), decrease distraction within the gymnasium, use task cards.
Sarah Evans	Exercise-induced asthma	Emphasize relaxation, use warm-up at all times, use prescribed medication, allow student to take breaks when necessary, monitor breathing.
Valerie Kingsly	Retinal detachment	Can play noncontact positions in games, use softer balls (Nerf or beach balls), participate in activities that do not jerk head (e.g., log roll), catch ball with hands, and jump in the pool.
Eric Smith	Latex allergy	Avoid contact with equipment or gloves coated with latex.
Jonathan Rutherford	Profoundly deaf	Use signs, interpreter, visual cues; face him when speaking.
Michelle Timms	Seizures (grand mal)	Avoid heights, avoid being underwater for lengths of time, utilize peer tutor.

*All names are fictitious.

Adapted, by permission, from L.J. Lieberman and L. Cruz, 2001, "Blanket medical excuses from Physical Education: Possible Solutions," *Teaching Elementary Physical Education* July, 27-31.

sample one-page form that can be presented to the student's physician by the child's parents. Approval of the suggested modifications by the physician is vital to inclusion of the student in physical education. Here are some suggestions to help you get this approval form filled out and signed by the physician.

1. **Physical educator empowers parents to act as advocates.** Because parents are seen as consumers, it often behooves the physical educator to empower them to deliver the form and discuss proposed adaptations with the physician. The physical education teacher must meet with the parents and educate them about all the options for each physical education unit discussed. The parents can then contact or meet with the physician to discuss the options. After this initial contact by parents, it may be easier for the physical educator to communicate with the physician directly (e.g., in person or via e-mail, fax, or phone).

2. **Physical educator meets with school nurse.** The school nurse is often more accessible and very willing to meet and discuss possible modifications for physical education. Parents can attend this meeting, and if all three parties agree, they can expedite acquisition of the physician's permission and implementation of the plan. After an initial

meeting, the school nurse can contact the physician for consent. The advantage of contact through the nurse is that he or she may already have a positive, professional working relationship with the physician.

   3. **Physical educator sets up a meeting with the physician.** After obtaining permission from the child's parents, the physical educator can set up a direct meeting with the physician, whether in person, through e-mail, or by phone. Such contact allows the physical education teacher to directly explain the units in the curriculum and the adaptations planned to ensure safe participation. The physical educator is likely to gain good insight into the student's disability and medical condition even as she or he educates the physician about physical education and possible modifications and adaptations. Although time consuming at first, this approach can save the educator a lot of time that would otherwise be spent later in explaining and making corrections. After this initial contact, it may be easier to send faxes or e-mails back and forth.

Implement the Program   Once approval has been obtained, the instructor can feel comfortable implementing the program. It is imperative that only the activities approved by the physician are implemented. Also, professional courtesy dictates that the physical education teacher share with the physician the early results of the student's success in physical education. This sharing might take the form of a simple note or e-mail. If a paraeducator or nurse works specifically with the student, the instructor must provide appropriate and continuous training in the modifications to this individual to make sure that he or she is implementing the program as prescribed. Finally, the physical educator should conduct ongoing assessment of the program to ascertain the comfort level and success of the student, to ensure that contraindicated activities are avoided, and to check whether the student is meeting the intended objectives of the unit and the individualized education plan. This ongoing assessment can be shared with the student's parents and physician in the form of a quarterly progress report (Block, 2007).

   Physical educators should be prepared to deal with well-intentioned physicians who give blanket medical excuses to students with disabilities (Kasser & Lytle, 2005). Too often, students with even relatively mild disabilities are being unnecessarily excluded from physical education because physicians perceive that physical education is not safe. This practice can have detrimental lifelong effects on students with disabilities who have limited motor, fitness, and leisure skills and may already be inclined toward a sedentary lifestyle. The three-step approach we have provided here should give the instructor a way to combat unnecessary exclusion from physical education (Lieberman & Cruz, 2001).

Facilitating Inclusion

Teachers can also help to overcome misconceptions and misunderstandings of disability through the use of awareness programs that address disability and ability (Colette, 2005; Schuldberg, 2005; Wilson & Lieberman, 2000).

Disability Awareness

Disability awareness programs have been proven to improve attitudes of typically developing students toward students with disabilities (Campbell, 2007; Chadsey & Gun Han, 2005; Loovis & Loovis, 1997; Mpofu, 2003). Unfortunately, simply placing students with disabilities in environments with students without disabilities does

FIGURE 7.1

Basic Principles of Disability and Ability Awareness Programs

1. Discuss the proposed program with students with disabilities in the class to ensure their comfort with and understanding of the activities.

2. Inform students' parents of any sensitivity activities planned throughout the year.

3. Always use person-first terminology when discussing individuals with disabilities; in other words, put the person before the disability, as in the phrase "individuals with disabilities" (rather than "disabled persons").

4. Do not promote pity. Individuals with disabilities do not want pity; they want people to understand who they are and what they can do as people. Promote the idea of ability over disability. Show students what people with disabilities can do.

5. Disability and ability awareness activities should not be a 1-week or 1-month unit. Awareness activities should be ongoing throughout the school year and throughout the students' schooling. This will show students that disabilities do not go away, that they are lifelong and need to be considered in every unit and in every place they go.

6. The goal of all these activities is to bring all students to awareness level III, the level of ownership.

Strategies: Disability awareness physical education (13(6): 12), pages 29-33 (2000) reprinted with permission from the National Association for Sport and Physical Education (NASPE), 1900 Association Drive, Reston, VA 20191-1599.

not guarantee social acceptance; therefore, disability and ability awareness activities should be among the first things presented to a class that includes a student with a disability (Blinde & McCallister, 1998; Block, 2003a, b; Fittipaldi-Wert & Brock, 2007; Johnson, 2006; Tripp, French, & Sherrill, 1995). Figure 7.1 lists basic principles for implementing a disability awareness program. If followed, these principles can prove helpful in achieving understanding and success for everyone involved.

Levels of Awareness

People can go through three levels of awareness in their understanding of disabilities (Wilson & Lieberman, 2000). Level I is centered on exposure, level II on experience, and level III on ownership. When worked with in a sensitive, deliberate, and matter-of-fact way, these levels can be used to foster understanding and acceptance. The goal of the program is to have all students achieve level III, or ownership.

Level I: Exposure   At this level of awareness, students are exposed to individuals with disabilities through various methods. A good starting method is to simply describe the disability itself. Appendix A provides definitions of disabilities as well as ways to describe the conditions in "kid terms," which can be used to enhance level I awareness. This is a great resource for giving students an understanding of disabilities without leaving them feeling overwhelmed or scared. The descriptions define disabilities and emphasize what is similar about the student with the disability rather than just focusing on differences between students.

Level I Disability Awareness Methods

Invite speakers who have disabilities.

Read and distribute newspaper articles, books, and literature about people with disabilities.

Watch videos about people with disabilities. YouTube is a great resource.

Visit Web sites about people with disabilities.

Experiences at this level of awareness help typically developing students realize that they share characteristics with those who have a disability. Such realizations help students examine situations from a different perspective and see the bigger picture. They also help students understand their own feelings related to disabilities and learn how to handle interactions, solve problems, overcome challenges, and be sensitive to the needs of others. Through being exposed to people with disabilities and vicariously experiencing their struggles, typically developing students can come to a better understanding and acceptance of others (Andrews, 1998; Campbell, 2007; Chadsey & Gun Han, 2005; Mpofu, 2003).

Level II: Experience   At this level, students are given opportunities to experience a constructed disability for a short or long period of time. Level II activities might include having students ambulate in a wheelchair or with a walker, participate in activities with a forced visual impairment, try to follow instructions with their hearing limited, or play a game using a scissors gait. The key is the teacher's attitude toward the activities.

The teacher must introduce the activities so that a positive, comfortable environment is created. The atmosphere is considered positive when the teacher introduces the material in a nonthreatening, nonpitying, matter-of-fact, informative way. If the teacher answers all questions in a positive way, with no negative emotion or regrets, the atmosphere remains positive. This type of atmosphere allows all participants to ask questions, express concerns, and become sensitive to obstacles that individuals with disabilities may face on a daily basis. Appendix B addresses specific experiential activities that teachers can implement with their classes.

Level III: Ownership   At this final level of awareness, students—both with and without disabilities—become advocates for individuals with disabilities. They take it upon themselves to help ensure that people with disabilities are being treated fairly and equally by society and that they have financial stability, access, independence, and recognition. In fact, it is not unusual to find students taking on teaching roles at this level of awareness. They may choose to make peers or community groups aware through fundraisers or through advocacy for, say, sighted guides and wheelchair categories at running events or interpreters during concerts. They may even be found picketing a building that is inaccessible to persons with disabilities. Ultimately, the goal is for all students to reach this level of awareness. More examples for level III can be found in appendix B.

Integrating disability awareness into your curriculum will increase typically developing students' understanding and acceptance of students with disabilities. It should also be noted here that disability awareness activities can be infused into the general curriculum using disability-specific sports such as sitting volleyball; wheelchair basketball; and goal ball, a sport played by persons with visual impairments in which teams of three athletes (all wearing blindfolds) try to roll an audible ball past their opponents (Foley, Tindall, Lieberman, & Kim, 2007; Siedentop, Hastie, & van der mars, 2004). Only when a child is accepted will he or she have the chance to enjoy equal relationships with peers and perhaps even experience leadership opportunities.

Creating Leadership Opportunities

The word *leadership* comes from the Anglo-Saxon *laedan* (for *go*) and means guiding, conducting, preceding, or being foremost among (Sherrill, 1988). Experiencing leadership can improve a student's self-esteem, self-confidence, and self-perception (Sherrill, 2004), and leadership experiences are important for all students, including those with disabilities. However, students with disabilities are often put in the position of being followers and may have little exposure to formal opportunities to practice and experience leadership (Lieberman, Arndt, & Daggett, 2007). Leadership opportunities can be provided by teachers and other professionals in a variety of ways, including asking a student to read aloud, choosing a student to serve on safety patrol, or choosing a student to be trained in conflict resolution and encouraging him or her to resolve conflicts between peers.

Leadership opportunities can also be provided during physical education classes, and in this section we discuss concrete ideas for promoting leadership in physical education in the K–12 setting, particularly for students with disabilities. As mentioned earlier in this chapter, students with and without disabilities may have attributes that perpetuate experiences as a follower. For example, Damian is hard of hearing, and in order to make sure he knows what is happening he consistently waits for his peers to start an activity before he begins. This habit ensures that he is continually following his peers as opposed to leading activities. Physical education has built-in opportunities for all students to experience leadership, and it is extremely important that the teacher take the time and energy to provide the same leadership experiences for all students. Here is a short list of some leadership opportunities that can easily be implemented in physical education for everyone (Lieberman, Arndt, & Daggett, 2007):

▶ To increase peers' understanding of visual impairments, use activities such as goal ball during a disability awareness unit.

- Ask a student to be a squad leader.
- Ask a student to demonstrate the skill being taught.
- Set up a reciprocal peer tutor program (see chapter 6 for more on this topic).
- Have students take turns setting up and cleaning up equipment.
- Have students help you or the paraeducator in taking attendance.
- Choose students with disabilities as captains of preselected teams.
- Set up personal improvement goals as opposed to competition (Macdonald & Block, 2005).
- Have students take turns leading warm-up stretches at the start of class or cool-down stretches at the end of class.
- Use the sport education model curricular approach to ensure that each child has opportunities to be a referee, coach, timer, or team owner (Foley et al., 2007).
- Use the Project Adventure model to encourage students to take turns leading adventure challenge activities.

Through the use of both disability awareness programs and leadership opportunities, teachers are creating positive atmospheres for achievement in physical education. The final strategy used to foster success in physical education for students with disabilities relates to supplemental instruction.

▶ Provide frequent opportunities for students to demonstrate leadership, such as allowing a peer to lead a demonstration.

Supplementing Instruction

Students with disabilities can benefit from additional practice in real-life motor settings and from one-to-one instruction. The more opportunities students are given to practice motor skills, the better they become at them. The better they become at them, the more likely they are to stay involved in physical activity throughout their lifetime. This section reviews several strategies for supporting the learning of motor skills by students with disabilities—specifically, the use of homework, community resources, technology, and role models.

Homework

Many students with disabilities exhibit delays as compared with their same-age peers in physical skills, fitness, and motor development. When the developmental delay or limited level of fitness becomes significant enough, it can be difficult for the student with a disability to keep up with his or her same-age peers. In this case, the typical scheduling of physical education two or three times per week will not be truly effective in meeting the student's educational objectives (Hart, 2001). In such a case, it is perfectly acceptable—in fact, preferred—to give the student (or the class) homework to improve skills or fitness level. The following list presents suggestions for setting up a homework program in physical education:

1. Establish a method of communicating with the family regarding physical education goals and objectives. One popular approach is to use notebooks or folders.

2. Send a copy of the class goals and objectives home at least monthly.

3. Provide individual skill rubrics or tasks that are easy to follow and can easily be implemented in the home. (See chapter 2 for more information on this topic.)

4. Be specific about the number of times the student is to complete the task and provide a specific due date for return to school. Include a place for a parent to sign off on completion of the assignment.

5. Report to the parents the student's accomplishments on a quarterly basis and explain any future goals you have for the student related to physical education objectives and IEP objectives.

6. If the student does not have the appropriate equipment at home (e.g., scarves for juggling, hula hoops, jump ropes, softball gloves, lacrosse sticks, in-line skates), allow the student to sign out equipment for a scheduled period of time. This policy facilitates appropriate practice and may provide the parents with guidance on buying age-appropriate and enjoyable equipment.

7. If the student shows a genuine interest in a certain activity and the family does not have the equipment at home, send a copy of an equipment catalog or the phone number or Web site of a company from which the item can be purchased.

8. In cases where families are unable to supply physical education equipment, seek donations from the athletic director, PTA, or special education department to facilitate the families' acquisition of items.

▪ Physical education skills are as important as other subject areas and should be practiced several days each week.

To sustain your efforts, give positive feedback to families who implement the homework by recognizing them in a newsletter or presenting a certificate of achievement to the student. Encourage them to continue what they have been doing and be sure to document the additional parental involvement in the IEP.

Community Resources

Use of community facilities is necessary to ensure a high quality of life after the school years. For individuals with and without disabilities, this practice does not have to wait until age 21. In fact, we are now seeing a trend toward including individuals with disabilities in general community recreation programs (Block, 2007; Conatser, Block, & Lepore, 2000; Lepore, Gayle, & Stevens, 2007; Petersen & Piletic, 2006). Using community facilities (e.g., pools, ice rinks, parks, health clubs, and climbing walls) can facilitate a variety of physical education and transition goals (Kasser & Lytle, 2005; Lepore et al.) that address such diverse areas as communication, socialization, daily living activities, physical activity, improved motor skills, and even banking and budgeting.

Minor barriers to community involvement may include attitudes of community personnel, transportation to and from school, and time missed from a core subject area. One major potential barrier is physical access to facilities (Petersen & Piletic, 2006); make sure all facilities are accessible before embarking on a community-based program. The benefits of community involvement far outweigh the required setup time and missed class time. In fact, many of the goals and objectives taught in core classes can be embedded into participation in community recreation programs. For example, students can meet speech and language goals by communicating with personnel at health clubs, they can meet physical therapy goals by participating in rock climbing, and they can meet math goals by calculating the distance of a hike.

By providing opportunities for students with disabilities to participate in community-based programs during school, you will help them learn the skills needed to access this environment on their own time.

Technology

In addition to teaching students with disabilities how to access and use community resources, teachers should also spend time instructing students on how to use technology to enhance physical activity levels. For example, teaching students how to use pedometers and heart rate monitors in class can provide carryover benefits in their daily lives. Research indicates that when students are able to see the gains they have made—for example, in number of steps taken per day or increased heart rates—they are more likely to sustain this form of active involvement (Lieberman, Stuart, Hand, & Robinson, 2006).

Other popular forms of technology include computer-based programs that students watch and follow to gain points. One such product that has become very popular is Dance Dance Revolution (DDR), in which students take turns following the moves of the arrow or dancer on the screen. The moves become increasingly difficult while simultaneously enhancing fitness levels. This activity can be modified for students with disabilities by slowing down the speed of the arrows, increasing the space in which to move, decreasing the number of arrows, or isolating the arrows (i.e., removing background music or other distractions). Another computer sport game, popular with individuals of all ages and abilities, is the Nintendo Wii. Again, by exposing students to such forms of technology in the classroom, you can increase the likelihood of continued involvement in physical activity.

▶ Participating in programs outside of school enhances social skills and integration into a larger community.

Role Models

It is also important to take advantage of role models in physical activity and sport. Typically developing students often have role models in sport, and they often want to emulate their hero's greatness in the arena or on the field. Until recently, however, students with disabilities rarely heard about outstanding athletes in disability sport; fortunately, this has changed, thanks in part to more media coverage of the Paralympics and other sporting events for persons with disabilities. There are now many role models—male and female—to choose from in dozens of sports. These figures can foster motivation, goal setting, and inspiration (Depauw & Gavron, 2005; Joukowsky & Rothstein, 2002).

For example, Jean Driscoll, an athlete with spina bifida, won the wheelchair marathon in the 2000 Paralympics in Sydney, Australia, with a time of 1 hour and 51 minutes! Rachel Scdoris, who is visually impaired, finished seventh among 20 rookies competing in the 2006 Iditarod. Jason McElwain, a high school student with autism, entered his first varsity basketball game and scored 20 points, including six three-pointers, in the last 4 minutes. Oscar Pistorius, both of whose legs were amputated below the knee when he was an infant, used prosthetics to run times that were fast enough to qualify for the 2008 Olympics in Beijing. These and other stories should be shared to provide athletic role models for persons who have disabilities. The sidebar offers various ways in which teachers can foster all students' learning regarding athletes with disabilities.

Teachers can also include inspirational stories of athletic accomplishments at the start of units on sports or activities in which athletes with disabilities have achieved greatness. Appendix I provides a list of relevant, inspirational books and resources that can be shared with students.

■ Individuals with disabilities can serve as valuable role models for all.

Role Model Learning

Posters on the wall

Interviews with role models

Newspaper articles about role models

Short videos about the success of a person with a disability

Field trips to competitions or tournaments

Guest speakers (either in class or during halftime of a sporting event)

A role model's participation with the class in a sport or activity

Summary

The responsibility for creating an atmosphere that promotes achievement rests primarily on the instructor. Gaining an understanding of disabilities and their medical implications does require additional work, but it is part of the instructional process involved in teaching students with disabilities. Teachers can work with parents, school-related personnel, and physicians to make sure that all parties share information about what the student can or should not do in physical education. They can also help the student's classmates gain understanding and awareness of disabilities.

Promoting disability awareness activities and advocacy projects on behalf of individuals with disabilities creates a sense of ownership among students in promoting the rights of individuals with disabilities. And allowing students with disabilities to take on leadership roles in class promotes ownership on the part of the student with the disability, so that he or she can become a self-advocate. Finally, the use of appropriate homework, community resources, and technology to support the learning of physical education and physical activity among students with disabilities can help them realize that they are able to accomplish great things, just like others with disabilities who have come before them.

Strategies for Inclusion

Part II will enable you to set up a challenging environment for students with disabilities who participate in an inclusive physical education class. You can use the support strategies of peer tutors; evaluate skills using current assessment tools; and adapt the rules, instruction, and environment to the needs of the students. Then you can use the rubric assessments when writing progress reports and IEP goals and objectives. More than 25 rubrics and 18 unit adaptations are provided; we encourage you to use these resources and to develop and create your own to include all students in physical education.

Part II provides ideas for adaptations, assessments through the use of rubrics, and specific ways to document individual performance. Keep in mind that part II consists only of selected ideas; it is not a total curriculum. The text offers examples as a starting point for developing more ideas. You will need to look at specific areas before starting: skills and abilities of children with disabilities, unit of instruction, and goals and objectives of the class.

The adaptation part of the curriculum is divided into four sections, each of which offers several variables. For example, in a unit on soccer, you might play keep-away or small-sided games and use specific adaptations and instructional modifications to meet the goals and objectives of the soccer unit for that age group. You can inform the students of the adaptations presented in this book so that the children know what variables are available. Children are more likely to be invested and motivated in each unit if they have some ownership of variable selection. If a student does not know what to do, you can choose from the variables presented and try a combination that may prove to be successful.

Rubrics make up the next part of this curriculum. Each unit offers at least one rubric that you can use as the basis for additional rubrics. For example, the soccer unit has only dribbling, passing, and game rubrics. You will need to create additional rubrics for defense and other game skills.

The rubrics fit into the assessment process by documenting the level at which each child performs. The elementary rubrics are divided into seven levels, each a different color of the rainbow. For the elementary section, the rubrics begin with red, the simplest, and move through the rainbow to violet, which is the most difficult. The sports, recreation, and fitness rubrics have distinct levels represented by colors used in martial arts: White is the simplest and black is the most difficult. The task descriptions are the skills or games that the student is asked to execute for authentic assessment. The scale components are what the child is being evaluated on during the lesson.

Regardless of the complexity of the units or students' level of ability, any child can participate in this assessment process. You are encouraged to create your own rubrics and add to the existing list of adaptation variables when necessary. With careful planning and preparation, all your students will maintain a lifelong passion for physical activity!

CHAPTER 8

Basic Skills

Purpose: The importance of fundamental motor skills cannot be overlooked in elementary physical education. These are the prerequisites for participation in more advanced movement skills, sports, and recreational activities. Introduction of these skills at the appropriate developmental level is essential for successful performance in middle and high school.

Unit adaptations: There are many ways of adapting the curriculum for students with disabilities, and it is imperative that the modifications for each student be specific to his or her needs. For example, if a student has athetoid cerebral palsy and moves more slowly than his or her peers do, the instructor can slow down the activity, use a different teaching style to focus on individual movement, or use a technique that would slow down the movement of the student's peers.

Assessment options: In this section, each unit includes at least one rubric for evaluating the process or product of movements; you might also create your own rubrics. Instructors can also create checklists and rating scales and have students keep journals, all of which can be included in student portfolios (see chapter 2).

Here are some ideas that can be used in teaching various physical activities; they involve equipment that can be used, rules that can be modified, environments that can be altered, and instructions that can be varied. Instructors can check off those that apply to the learner or those that the learner can accomplish.

Potential Modifications and Adaptations

Equipment	Rules	Environment	Instruction
☐ High beam	☐ Wall for support	☐ Balance stations	☐ Verbal cues
☐ Low beam	☐ Holding hands, walk forward	☐ Sequence centers	☐ Demonstration/model
☐ Narrow beam	☐ Holding hands, walk sideways	☐ Small space	☐ Physical assistance
☐ Wide beam	☐ Holding hands, walk backward	☐ Large space	☐ Peer tutor
☐ Balance board/tilt board	☐ Holding hands, step over object	☐ Obstacle course	☐ Paraeducator
☐ Jump ropes on the ground	☐ Holding hands, step in object (hoop)		☐ Task cards (enlarged if needed)
☐ Tires	☐ Holding hands, step out of object		☐ Pictures
☐ Steps	☐ Hands free, walk forward		☐ Tactile modeling
☐ Hula hoops	☐ Hands free, walk sideways		☐ Guided discovery
☐ Thin to thick mats	☐ Hands free, walk backward		☐ Problem solving
☐ Lines on the floor	☐ Hands free, step over object		☐ Task analysis
☐ Low trampoline	☐ Hands free, step in object		☐ Proximity (instructor stands close to student with disability)
☐ Bench	☐ Hands free, step out of object		☐ Interpreter
☐ Beanbags			☐ Individualized instruction (one-to-one)
			☐ Sign language
			☐ Feedback

Balance Beam

Task	Student will walk forward and backward on balance beam.
Scale components	(a) Assistance, (b) height of beam
Rubric level and color	**Rubric descriptors**
1. Red	Student balances with assistance on low beam (____ inches [centimeters] high from floor).
2. Orange	Student walks sideways with assistance on low beam.
3. Yellow	Student walks forward with assistance on low beam.
4. Green	Student walks backward with assistance on low beam.
5. Blue	Student walks forward without assistance on low beam.
6. Indigo	Student walks backward without assistance on low beam.
7. Violet	Student balances with assistance on high beam (____ inches [centimeters] high from floor).
8. Black	Student walks sideways with assistance on high beam.
9. White	Student walks forward with assistance on high beam.
10. Bronze	Student walks backward with assistance on high beam.
11. Silver	Student walks forward without assistance on high beam.
12. Gold	Student walks backward without assistance on high beam.

Potential Modifications and Adaptations

Equipment	Rules	Environment	Instruction
☐ Shorter rope	☐ Roll over rope	☐ Rope laid on floor	☐ Verbal cues
☐ Longer rope	☐ Crawl over rope	☐ Rope suspended from cones	☐ Demonstration/model
☐ Heavier rope	☐ Step over rope	☐ Rope tied across chairs	☐ Physical assistance
☐ Bright rope	☐ Leap over rope	☐ Poly spots on ground for jumping on	☐ Peer tutor
☐ Handled rope	☐ Jump forward over rope	☐ Poly spots on ground for jumping over	☐ Paraeducator
☐ Cloth rope	☐ Jump sideways over rope	☐ Slant rope to jump over at various heights	☐ Task cards (enlarged if needed)
☐ Plastic rope	☐ Swing rope and step over	☐ Hoops for jumping in and out of	☐ Pictures
☐ Beaded rope	☐ Swing rope and jump over once, then repeat		☐ Tactile modeling
☐ Bells on rope	☐ Swing rope and jump consecutively		☐ Guided discovery
☐ Rope cut in half for turning with hands (no jumping)	☐ Jump over as rope is turned slowly		☐ Problem solving
☐ Velcro glove to keep rope held	☐ Jump over rope while swinging it with arms		☐ Task analysis
☐ Glove for hand padding	☐ Double Dutch		☐ Proximity (instructor stands close to student with disability)
			☐ Sign language
			☐ Feedback

Jump Rope

Task description	Student can perform the act of rolling, walking, hopping, or jumping over a rope at any height.
Scale components	(a) Number of jumps, (b) direction of jumps
Rubric level and color	**Rubric descriptors**
1. Red	Student crawls, rolls, walks, or jumps over a rope placed up to 1 foot (0.3 meter) off the ground.
2. Orange	Student steps or jumps forward over a rope placed 1 foot off the ground (either stationary or swinging).
3. Yellow	Student brings rope over head with arms and steps or rolls over rope once.
4. Green	Student brings rope over head with arms and steps or rolls over rope 2 to 20 times.
5. Blue	Student jumps rope, swinging rope over head backward, 1 to 20 times.
6. Indigo	Student jumps rope to music in a mixture of forward, backward, and crisscross jumps for 1 to 5 minutes.
7. Violet	Student jumps rope to music, either alone or with a partner, for 6 to 20 minutes.

Potential Modifications and Adaptations

Equipment	Rules	Environment	Instruction
☐ Cones	☐ Move in own space	☐ Concrete boundaries	☐ Verbal cues
☐ Directional arrows	☐ Move at own speed	☐ Small space	☐ Demonstration/model
☐ Poly footprints	☐ Use no time restriction	☐ Large space	☐ Physical assistance
☐ Poly spots	☐ Follow leader/peer	☐ Ropes taped on floor	☐ Peer tutor
☐ Ropes	☐ Start/stop with music	☐ Indoor gym/ multipurpose room	☐ Paraeducator
☐ Hoops	☐ Do animal walk	☐ Outdoor fields	☐ Task cards (enlarged if needed)
☐ Tires		☐ Outdoor track	☐ Pictures
☐ Mats		☐ Mirrors on wall	☐ Tactile modeling
☐ Tunnel			☐ Guided discovery
☐ Stairs			☐ Problem solving
☐ Rails			☐ Task analysis
☐ Guide wire			☐ Proximity (instructor stands close to student with disability)
☐ Ramps			☐ Interpreter
☐ Scooters			☐ Sign language
☐ Walker			☐ Feedback
☐ Wheelchair			
☐ Sound source			
☐ Carpet squares			

Running

Task description	Student will run from one side of the gymnasium to the other (50 feet, or 15 meters) with best form.
Scale components	(a) Flight phase, (b) arm opposition, (c) 90-degree back leg bend, (d) heel-to-toe placement
Rubric level and color	**Rubric descriptors**
1. Red	Student runs from one end of gymnasium to cone 50 feet away.
2. Orange	Student runs from one end of gymnasium to cone 50 feet away, with flight phase during at least 4 rotations.
3. Yellow	Student runs with flight phase and arm opposition during at least 4 rotations.
4. Green	Student runs with flight phase, arm opposition, and back leg bent at least 90 degrees during at least 4 rotations.
5. Blue	Student runs with flight phase, arm opposition, back leg bent at least 90 degrees, and feet landing heel-to-toe, during at least 4 rotations.
6. Indigo	Student runs with flight phase, arm opposition, back leg bent at least 90 degrees, and feet landing heel-to-toe, a distance of 50 feet, 3 out of 5 times.
7. Violet	Student runs with proper form consistently for 50 feet.

Potential Modifications and Adaptations

Equipment	Rules	Environment	Instruction
☐ Large ball	☐ Varied distance	☐ Reduced stimuli	☐ Verbal cues
☐ Small ball	☐ Varied points	☐ Stations/sequence centers	☐ Demonstration/model
☐ Auditory ball	☐ Varied time	☐ Concrete boundaries	☐ Physical assistance
☐ Yarn ball	☐ Start/stop with music	☐ Small space	☐ Peer tutor
☐ Wiffle ball	☐ Follow peer/leader	☐ Large space	☐ Paraeducator
☐ Tactile ball	☐ Against a wall	☐ Ropes taped on floor	☐ Task cards (enlarged if needed)
☐ Heavy ball	☐ At a target	☐ Indoor gym/ multipurpose room	☐ Pictures
☐ Light ball	☐ Dominant hand	☐ Outdoor fields	☐ Tactile modeling
☐ Bright ball	☐ Nondominant hand	☐ Outdoor track	☐ Guided discovery
☐ Beach ball	☐ Dominant foot	☐ Mirrors on wall	☐ Problem solving
☐ Balloon	☐ Nondominant foot	☐ Music	☐ Task analysis
☐ Deflated ball	☐ Stationary	☐ No music	☐ Proximity (instructor stands close to student with disability)
☐ Nerf ball	☐ Traveling	☐ Mat panels used as a wall to reduce distractions	☐ Interpreter
☐ Velcro ball		☐ Secluded	☐ Sign language
☐ Sponge ball		☐ Flat surface	☐ Feedback
☐ Foam ball		☐ Railing for assistance	☐ Give-and-get (reciprocal actions)
☐ Ball on rope		☐ Wide goals	
☐ Regulation ball		☐ Narrow goals	
☐ Short racket		☐ Lower target	
☐ Long racket		☐ Closer target	
☐ Short foam racket			
☐ Long foam racket			
☐ Paddle			
☐ Fat bat			
☐ Short bat			
☐ Wiffle bat			
☐ Bat (wooden or aluminum)			
☐ Batting tee			
☐ Velcro mitt			
☐ Gloves			
☐ Softball glove			
☐ Auditory bases			
☐ Bases			
☐ Baskets/buckets (laundry, garbage)			
☐ Lower baskets			
☐ Wide-rimmed baskets			
☐ Rim attachment on basketball rim that allows the ball to roll directly back to the shooter			
☐ Cones			

(continued)

Example 1: Kicking

Task description	Student can kick a stationary ball.
Scale components	(a) Three-step approach, (b) trunk inclined backward during contact, (c) forward swing of opposite arm, (d) follow-through
Rubric level and color	**Rubric descriptors**
1. Red	Student kicks stationary ball with any form.
2. Orange	Student kicks stationary ball with a three-step approach, walking or running during most kicks.
3. Yellow	Student kicks stationary ball with a three-step approach and trunk inclined backward during contact during most kicks.
4. Green	Student kicks stationary ball with a three-step approach, trunk inclined backward during contact, and forward swing of opposite arm during most kicks.
5. Blue	Student kicks stationary ball with a three-step approach, trunk inclined backward during contact, and forward swing of opposite arm during 3 out of 5 kicks.
6. Indigo	Student kicks stationary ball with a three-step approach, trunk inclined backward during contact, forward swing of opposite arm, and follow-through, propelling the ball 30 feet (9 meters).
7. Violet	Student kicks stationary ball with a three-step approach, trunk inclined backward during contact, forward swing of opposite arm, and follow-through, propelling the ball 60 feet (18 meters).

Example 2: Underhand Roll

Task description	Student will roll underhand to peer.
Scale components	(a) Step with opposite foot, (b) release in front, (c) shift weight forward, (d) follow through.
Rubric level and color	**Rubric descriptors**
1. Red	Student attempts to roll a ball underhand to a peer standing 10 feet (3 meters) away.
2. Orange	Student rolls a ball underhand, stepping with the opposite foot most of the time.
3. Yellow	Student rolls a ball underhand, stepping with the opposite foot and releasing in front of the body most of the time.
4. Green	Student rolls a ball underhand, stepping with the opposite foot, releasing in front of the body, and shifting weight forward during the throw most of the time.
5. Blue	Student rolls a ball underhand, stepping with the opposite foot, releasing in front of the body, shifting weight forward during the throw, and following through most of the time.
6. Indigo	Student rolls a ball underhand, stepping with the opposite foot, releasing in front of the body, shifting weight forward during the throw, and following through, to a partner 10 feet away.
7. Violet	Student rolls a ball underhand, stepping with the opposite foot, releasing in front of the body, shifting weight forward during the throw, and following through to hit an 8-foot-square (2.4-meter-square) target, 15 feet (4.6 meters) away, 3 out of 5 times.

Potential Modifications and Adaptations

Equipment	Rules	Environment	Instruction
☐ Large parachute ☐ Small parachute ☐ Towel ☐ Sheet ☐ Straps on chute ☐ Ace bandage around hand ☐ Bells on chute ☐ Bright parachute ☐ Tactile parachute ☐ Wrist straps on chute ☐ Music ☐ Poly spots ☐ Assorted balls for activities ☐ Auditory balls for activities	☐ Decrease number of shakes ☐ Increase number of shakes ☐ Limit range of motion ☐ Increase range of motion ☐ Parachute chair height ☐ Two hands on parachute ☐ One hand on parachute ☐ Walk ☐ Movement in own space ☐ Big waves ☐ Small waves ☐ Holding a panel of a different color using different locomotor skills or in pairs ☐ Name game, change places ☐ Animal movements, change places	☐ Indoors ☐ Outdoors ☐ Smooth surface ☐ Grass ☐ Mats ☐ Circle marked on floor ☐ Large space ☐ Small space ☐ Tactile boundaries ☐ Roped boundaries	☐ Verbal cues ☐ Demonstration/model ☐ Physical assistance ☐ Peer tutor ☐ Paraeducator ☐ Task cards (enlarged if needed) ☐ Pictures ☐ Tactile modeling ☐ Guided discovery ☐ Problem solving ☐ Task analysis ☐ Proximity (instructor stands close to student with disability) ☐ Interpreter ☐ Individualized instruction (one-to-one) ☐ Sign language ☐ Feedback

Example 1: Parachute

Task description	Student will progress from maintaining one level to being able to change levels to a rhythm.
Scale components	Able to change levels at any time from low to medium to high, according to the rhythm.
Rubric level and color	**Rubric descriptors**
1. Red	Student is able to hold onto a parachute at a medium level using any grip (with or without assistance).
2. Orange	Student is able to hold onto a parachute at a medium level using an overhand grip.
3. Yellow	Student is able to hold onto a parachute at a medium level, using an overhand grip, and take his or her part of the parachute to a low level and back to a medium level.
4. Green	Student is able to hold onto a parachute at a medium level, using an overhand grip, and take his or her part of the parachute to a high level and back to a medium level.
5. Blue	Student is able to hold onto a parachute at a medium level, using an overhand grip, and take his or her part of the parachute to any level, on cue.
6. Indigo	Student is able to hold onto a parachute at a medium level using an overhand grip, and take his or her part of the parachute to any level, in rhythm and on cue.
7. Violet	Student is able to hold onto parachute at a medium level, using an overhand grip, and take his or her part of the parachute to any level, in rhythm and on cue, for the duration of a song.

Sport Skills and Teamwork

Purpose: The importance of sports and teamwork cannot be overestimated in secondary physical education. The framework of good sporting behavior, basic skill, and problem solving will help students not only in class but also in the world of work. Introduction of these skills at the appropriate developmental level is essential for successful performance in adulthood.

Unit adaptations: There are many ways of adapting the curriculum for children with disabilities, and it is imperative that the modifications for each child be specific to his or her needs. For example, if a child has spina bifida and uses a wheelchair, adaptations might include allowing more bounces in tennis or more hits in volleyball, or using a bigger ball for soccer or modified rules for badminton.

Assessment options: In this section, each unit includes at least one rubric for evaluating the process or product of movements; you might also create your own rubrics. Instructors can also create checklists and rating scales and have students keep journals, all of which can be included in student portfolios (see chapter 2).

Here are some ideas that can be used in teaching various physical activities; they involve equipment that can be used, rules that can be modified, environments that can be altered, and instructions that can be varied. Instructors can check off those that apply to the learner or those that the learner can accomplish.

Potential Modifications and Adaptations

Equipment	Rules	Environment	Instruction
☐ Beeper ball	☐ Hit off of tee	☐ Ropes leading to bases	☐ Verbal cues
☐ Auditory ball	☐ Hit off of ground	☐ Guide rails	☐ Demonstration/model
☐ Bell ball	☐ Hit hanging ball	☐ Chalk lines to bases	☐ Physical assistance
☐ Tactile ball	☐ All bat before switching	☐ Tactile lines	☐ Peer tutor
☐ Bright ball	☐ Vary number of strikes	☐ Auditory lines	☐ Paraeducator
☐ Nerf ball	☐ Time limitations	☐ Bright lines	☐ Task cards (enlarged if needed)
☐ Wiffle ball	☐ Vary number of people in the outfield	☐ Cones next to bases	☐ Pictures
☐ Softball	☐ Vary number of people in the infield	☐ Clap behind bases to add auditory cue for those who need one	☐ Tactile modeling
☐ Velcro ball	☐ Two bases only	☐ On field	☐ Guided discovery
☐ Bigger ball	☐ Point for each base	☐ On pavement	☐ Problem solving
☐ Lighter ball	☐ Boundary limitations	☐ In gymnasium	☐ Task analysis
☐ Colored ball	☐ No tag-outs	☐ Shorter base distance	☐ Proximity (instructor stands close to student with disability)
☐ Buzzer on bases	☐ Tag-outs on bases (you can tag the base to get someone out)	☐ Shorter pitching distance	☐ Task-analyze skills
☐ Flat bases	☐ Peer runner/guide		☐ Individualized instruction
☐ Thick bases	☐ No score		☐ Sign language
☐ Bigger bases	☐ No double play		☐ Feedback
☐ Safety base	☐ Rotate positions		
☐ Wiffle bats	☐ Two extra tosses to field players (add a rule that the ball must be thrown to two people in the field before they can attempt an out)		
☐ Fat bats			
☐ Short-handled bats			
☐ Long-handled bats	☐ Ground pass		
☐ Regulation bats	☐ Out in air or on bounce		
☐ Batting tee	☐ Throw ball to make an out to a base before the runner gets there		
☐ Gloves and catcher's mitt different sizes and textures			
☐ Helmet			
☐ Pinnies to distinguish teams			

Example 1: Throwing

Task description	Student will throw the ball from shortstop to first base.
Scale components	(a) Form of throw, (b) distance, (c) accuracy
Rubric level and color	**Rubric descriptors**
1. White	Student can throw ball from shortstop position to second base most of the time.
2. Yellow	Student can throw ball with opposite-foot step, weight shift, hip rotation, and a follow-through across the body, from shortstop position to second base, most of the time.
3. Orange	Student can throw a ball, with proper form, from shortstop position to second base, 75 percent of the time.
4. Green	Student can throw a ball, with proper form, from shortstop position to first base, 75 percent of the time.
5. Blue	Student can throw a ball, with proper form, from shortstop position to first base, 85 percent of the time.
6. Brown	Student can throw a ball, with proper form, from shortstop position to first base, so first base player can catch the ball, 85 percent of the time.
7. Black	Student can throw a ball, with proper form, from shortstop position to first base, so first base player can catch the ball, 95 percent of the time.

Example 2: Fielding

Task description	Student will show proper form and skill in fielding the ball.
Scale components	(a) Proper form, (b) percentage of stopped balls
Rubric level and color	**Rubric descriptors**
1. White	Student knows ready position in the field and can show this 100 percent of the time.
2. Yellow	Student keeps knees bent and eyes on the ball most of the time when the ball is hit to him or her.
3. Orange	Student keeps knees bent, eyes on the ball, and glove down on the ground, most of the time when the ball is hit to him or her.
4. Green	Student keeps knees bent, eyes on the ball, glove down on the ground, body behind the ball, and non-glove hand covering the ball, most of the time when the ball is hit to him or her.
5. Blue	Student uses proper form for fielding a ball and slides right or left to field any ball hit near him or her most of the time.
6. Brown	Student uses proper form for fielding a ball, slides right or left to field any ball near him or her 75 percent of the time, and stops at least 50 percent of the balls that come near.
7. Black	Student uses proper form for fielding a ball, slides right or left to field any ball near him or her 95 percent of the time, and stops at least 95 percent of the balls that come near.

(continued)

Example 3: Batting

Task description	Student will bat a ball from a tee or when pitched to him or her.
Scale components	(a) Form, (b) hitting percentage
Rubric level and color	**Rubric descriptors**
1. White	Student can hit a ball off of a tee, with shoulder to outfield and nondominant foot forward, most of the time.
2. Yellow	Student can hit a ball off of a tee, with shoulder to outfield, nondominant foot forward, and weight shift to front foot, most of the time.
3. Orange	Student can hit a ball off of a tee, with shoulder to outfield, nondominant foot forward, weight shift to front foot, ball contact in front of front foot, and follow-through with the bat, most of the time.
4. Green	Student can hit a ball off a tee, with shoulder to outfield, nondominant foot forward, weight shift to front foot, ball contact in front of front foot, and follow-through with the bat, 90 percent of the time.
5. Blue	Student can bat a ball, with proper form, from a pitch, contacting the ball 50 percent of the time.
6. Brown	Student can bat a ball, with proper form, from a pitch, contacting the ball 75 percent of the time.
7. Black	Student can bat a ball, with proper form, from a pitch, contacting the ball 75 percent of the time, and hit it in desired direction 50 percent of the time.

Potential Modifications and Adaptations

Equipment	Rules	Environment	Instruction
☐ Basketball	☐ Increase number of fouls allowed	☐ Cones as boundaries	☐ Verbal cues
☐ Large ball	☐ No 3-second rule	☐ Bright boundaries	☐ Demonstration/model
☐ Small ball	☐ No double-dribble rule	☐ Ropes as boundaries	☐ Physical assistance
☐ Bright ball	☐ Can walk with ball without dribbling	☐ Beeper/auditory boundaries	☐ Peer tutor
☐ Textured ball	☐ Different points awarded for baskets	☐ Visual shooting line	☐ Paraeducator
☐ Heavy ball	☐ Extra step on lay-up	☐ Smooth surface	☐ Task cards (enlarged if needed)
☐ Light ball	☐ Undefended	☐ Modify court size	☐ Pictures
☐ Foam ball	☐ No defense for X number of seconds	☐ Stations	☐ Tactile modeling
☐ Nerf ball	☐ Free shooting (no defense)		☐ Guided discovery
☐ Beach ball	☐ Everyone touches ball before a shot is attempted		☐ Problem solving
☐ Deflated ball	☐ Pass X number of times before a shot is attempted		☐ Task analysis
☐ Auditory ball	☐ Vary playing times		☐ Proximity (instructor stands close to student with disability)
☐ Buzzer basket	☐ Limit boundaries		☐ Interpreter
☐ High basket	☐ Small-sided games (e.g., 3v3)		☐ Individualized instruction (one-to-one)
☐ Low basket	☐ Increase number of players		☐ Sign language
☐ Bright basket			☐ Feedback
☐ Wide basket			

(continued)

Example 1: Dribbling

Task description	Student will dribble a basketball around cones and inactive defensive players.
Scale components	(a) Form, (b) control
Rubric level and color	**Rubric descriptors**
1. White	Student dribbles in place, using fingertips at waist height, with ball contacting floor in front of (or to the outside of) the foot on the same side as the dribbling hand, most of the time.
2. Yellow	Student dribbles while walking around eight cones placed 5 feet (1.5 meters) apart, using fingertips at waist height, with ball contacting floor in front of (or to the outside of) the foot on the same side as the dribbling hand, most of the time.
3. Orange	Student dribbles with proper form, while walking around eight cones placed 5 feet apart, controlling the ball 50 percent of the time.
4. Green	Student dribbles with proper form, while jogging around eight cones placed 5 feet apart, controlling the ball 50 percent of the time.
5. Blue	Student dribbles with proper form, while jogging around eight cones placed 5 feet apart, controlling the ball 75 percent of the time.
6. Brown	Student dribbles with proper form, while jogging around eight cones placed 5 feet apart, controlling the ball 75 percent of the time with dominant hand and 50 percent of the time with nondominant hand.
7. Black	Student dribbles with proper form, while jogging around eight stationary defenders placed 5 feet apart, controlling the ball 75 percent of the time with dominant hand and 50 percent of the time with nondominant hand.

Example 2: Foul Shot

Task description	Student will shoot foul shots from the foul line.
Scale components	(a) Form, (b) accuracy
Rubric level and color	**Rubric descriptors**
1. White	Student attempts to shoot foul shot from 5 feet (1.5 meters) in front of the foul line.
2. Yellow	Student faces the basket from 5 feet in front of the foul line with knees bent, dominant hand palm-up under ball, and nondominant hand supporting ball from side, most of the time.
3. Orange	Student faces the basket from 5 feet in front of the foul line, with knees bent, dominant hand palm-up under ball, nondominant hand supporting ball from side, and with knee and arm extension during the shot, most of the time.
4. Green	Student shoots foul shot with proper form from the foul line.
5. Blue	Student shoots foul shot, with proper form, from the foul line, and hits the rim most of the time.
6. Brown	Student shoots foul shot, with proper form, from the foul line, and makes 7 out of 10 shots.
7. Black	Student shoots foul shot, with proper form, from the foul line, and makes at least 8 out of 10 shots.

Example 3: Game Play

Task description	Student will be evaluated on offensive skills during game play.
Scale components	(a) Use of passes, dribbling, and shooting, (b) ability to retain ball on offensive side or to score
Rubric level and color	**Rubric descriptors**
1. White	Student properly uses bounce pass and chest pass during game play.
2. Yellow	Student properly uses the triple threat by obtaining possession and then dribbling, passing, or shooting, according to the appropriate option, 50 percent of the time.
3. Orange	Student uses the triple threat by obtaining possession and then dribbling, passing, or shooting, according to the appropriate option, 75 percent of the time.
4. Green	Student dribbles around defenders and retains possession, completes passes, and shoots accurately (i.e., hits basket rim or backboard, or makes the shot), 50 percent of the time.
5. Blue	Student dribbles around defenders and retains possession, completes passes, and shoots accurately, 75 percent of the time.
6. Brown	Student assists others in shooting by passing to an open teammate 75 percent of the time.
7. Black	Student properly uses triple threat and displays appropriate skills 95 percent of the time, with accuracy in passing, shooting, and dribbling at least 50 percent of the time.

Potential Modifications and Adaptations

Equipment	Rules	Environment	Instruction
☐ Soccer ball	☐ Hands used for protection	☐ Cones as boundaries	☐ Verbal cues
☐ Large ball	☐ No heading	☐ Bright boundaries	☐ Demonstration/model
☐ Small ball	☐ Walk with ball	☐ Ropes as boundaries	☐ Physical assistance
☐ Bright ball	☐ Stay in assigned area	☐ Visual shooting line	☐ Peer tutor
☐ Textured ball	☐ Peer places ball on ground for kicking	☐ Beeper/ auditory boundaries	☐ Paraeducator
☐ Heavy ball	☐ Undefended	☐ Smooth surface	☐ Task cards (enlarged if needed)
☐ Light ball	☐ No defense for X number of seconds	☐ Modified field size	☐ Pictures
☐ Foam ball	☐ Free shooting (no defense)	☐ Stations	☐ Tactile modeling
☐ Nerf ball	☐ Everyone touches ball before shots on goal		☐ Guided discovery
☐ Beach ball	☐ Pass X number of times before shots on goal		☐ Problem solving
☐ Deflated ball	☐ Vary playing times		☐ Task analysis
☐ Auditory ball	☐ Limit boundaries		☐ Proximity (instructor stands close to student with disability)
☐ Bell ball	☐ Lane soccer		☐ Interpreter
☐ Ball on string	☐ Small-sided games		☐ Individualized instruction (one-to-one)
☐ Front bumper on chair			☐ Sign language
☐ Bells on net			☐ Feedback
☐ Buzzer on net			
☐ Wider goal			
☐ Smaller goal			
☐ Bright goal			
☐ Flags			
☐ Cones			
☐ Shin guards			
☐ Mouth guards			

Example 1: Dribbling

Task description	Student can dribble using both inside and outside of foot against a defender.
Scale components	(a) Form, (b) velocity of performance, (c) radius of direction change, (d) number of defenders
Rubric level and color	**Rubric descriptors**
1. White	Student attempts to dribble with dominant foot and nondominant foot.
2. Yellow	Student dribbles with inside of each foot through 10 cones located 7 feet (2.1 meters) apart, up and back, without losing the ball.
3. Orange	Student dribbles fast, with outside of each foot, through 10 cones located 7 feet apart, up and back, without losing the ball.
4. Green	Student dribbles fast, with inside and outside of each foot, through 10 cones located 5 feet (1.5 meters) apart, up and back, without losing the ball.
5. Blue	Student dribbles against a defender, with inside and outside of foot, for 30 yards (27.4 meters).
6. Brown	Student dribbles against a defender through 10 cones located 5 feet apart, up the field without losing the ball.
7. Black	Student dribbles against two defenders, for 30 seconds, within a 20-yard (18.3-meter) radius, using the inside and outside dribble, without losing the ball.

Example 2: Passing

Task description	Student can perform an exact pass, using the inside or outside of the foot, to a standing or moving partner.
Scale components	(a) Form, (b) number of performances, (c) motion
Rubric level and color	**Rubric descriptors**
1. White	Student attempts to pass with dominant foot and nondominant foot.
2. Yellow	Student passes with inside of the foot to a partner standing 10 feet (3 meters) away, using each foot 10 times.
3. Orange	Student passes with outside of the foot to a partner standing 10 feet away, using each foot 10 times.
4. Green	Student passes with inside or outside of the foot, to a partner standing 20 feet (6.1 meters) away, using each foot 10 times (5 with the inside foot and 5 with the outside foot).
5. Blue	Student passes, using only the inside of the foot, to a partner moving up and down the field, without losing control.
6. Brown	Student passes, using only the outside of the foot, to a partner moving up and down the field, without losing control.
7. Black	Student passes to a partner 20 yards upfield, leading the receiver on the run, keeping ball within 5 feet (1.5 meters) of the receiver's foot, 8 out of 10 times.

(continued)

Example 3: Game Play

Task description	Student can play and be an active participant in a soccer game.
Scale components	(a) Dribbling, (b) passing, (c) defense, (d) shooting (all performed consistently during a scrimmage or game situation)
Rubric level and color	**Rubric descriptors**
1. White	Student participates in a 3v3 game, demonstrates a dribble and a pass when on offense, and shows knowledge of defense when his or her team is on defense.
2. Yellow	Student participates in a 3v3 game, consistently demonstrates a dribble and a pass when on offense, and consistently shows knowledge of defense when team is on defense.
3. Orange	Student participates in a 5v5 scrimmage, consistently demonstrates a dribble and a pass when on offense, and consistently shows knowledge of defense when team is on defense.
4. Green	Student demonstrates all previous skills, cuts for a pass, and shoots on goal when a shot is available.
5. Blue	Student demonstrates all previous skills, consistently cuts for a pass, and consistently shoots on goal when a shot is available.
6. Brown	Student participates in a full-field soccer game, with consistent offensive and defensive skills, for at least 10 minutes.
7. Black	Student participates in a full-field soccer game, with consistent offensive and defensive skills, for at least 15 minutes.

Potential Modifications and Adaptations

Equipment	Rules	Environment	Instruction
☐ Tennis ball ☐ Large ball ☐ Bright ball ☐ Heavy ball ☐ Light ball ☐ Foam ball ☐ Nerf ball ☐ Beach ball ☐ Auditory ball ☐ Wiffle ball ☐ Tetherball ☐ Larger racket ☐ Smaller racket ☐ Wider racket ☐ Shorter racket ☐ Foam racket ☐ Strap for racket ☐ No net ☐ Lower net	☐ Hit off of tee for serve ☐ Bounce serve ☐ Two-step serve ☐ Unlimited steps for serve ☐ More than one bounce ☐ Vary points awarded ☐ Bounce the ball and hit it with a racquet to specific areas on opposite side for points	☐ Play against wall ☐ Extended boundaries ☐ Limited boundaries ☐ Cones as boundaries ☐ Bright boundaries ☐ Ropes as boundaries ☐ Beeper/auditory boundaries ☐ Varied playing surface (e.g., dirt, smooth, grass)	☐ Verbal cues ☐ Demonstration/model ☐ Physical assistance ☐ Peer tutor ☐ Paraeducator ☐ Task cards (enlarged if needed) ☐ Pictures ☐ Tactile modeling ☐ Guided discovery ☐ Problem solving ☐ Task analysis ☐ Proximity (instructor stands close to student with disability) ☐ Interpreter ☐ Individualized instruction (one-to-one) ☐ Sign language ☐ Feedback

Example 1: Forehand

Task description	Student will hit a forehand shot in a tennis game.
Scale components	(a) Form, (b) number of performances, (c) placement
Rubric level and color	**Rubric descriptors**
1. White	Student hits a tennis ball, thrown with a bounce from 6 feet (1.8 meters) away, with a forehand shot.
2. Yellow	Student hits a ball thrown with a bounce, with body turned sideways, making contact in front of body, most of the time.
3. Orange	Student hits a ball thrown with a bounce, with body turned sideways, making contact in front of body and distinctly shifting weight forward, most of the time.
4. Green	Student hits a thrown ball, with body turned sideways, making contact in front of body, shifting weight forward, and following through, most of the time.
5. Blue	Student hits a forehand, with proper form, from a toss, and gets ball over the net 8 out of 10 times.
6. Brown	Student hits a forehand, with proper form, during a game situation, and gets ball over the net 7 out of 10 times.
7. Black	Student hits a forehand, with proper form, during a game situation, and gets ball over the net 9 out of 10 times.

(continued)

Example 2: Serve

Task description	Student will hit a serve in a tennis game.
Scale components	(a) Form, (b) number of performances, (c) success
Rubric level and color	**Rubric descriptors**
1. White	Student serves the tennis ball from half-court (the back of the service boundary line).
2. Yellow	Student serves the ball from half-court with shoulder facing the net, makes proper toss above head, and makes contact out in front of the body, most of the time.
3. Orange	Student serves the ball from half-court with shoulder facing the net, makes proper toss above head, makes contact out in front of the body, shifts weight, and follows through, most of the time.
4. Green	Student serves the ball from half-court with shoulder facing the net, makes proper toss above head, makes contact out in front of the body, shifts weight, follows through, and gets ball over the net 5 out of 10 times.
5. Blue	Student serves the ball from half-court, with proper form, and gets ball over the net 8 out of 10 times.
6. Brown	Student serves the ball from the service line with proper form during a game situation and gets the ball over the net 7 out of 10 times.
7. Black	Student serves the ball from the service line, with proper form during a game situation, getting the ball over the net 9 out of 10 times and in the proper service box 5 out of 10 times.

Example 3: Game Play

Task description	Student will participate in a game of tennis.
Scale components	(a) Choice of shots, (b) percentage of successful shots
Rubric level and color	**Rubric descriptors**
1. White	Student participates in a game of tennis, using the forehand and backhand shots correctly 50 percent of the time.
2. Yellow	Student participates in a game of tennis, using the forehand, backhand, drop shot, and overhand smash shot correctly 50 percent of the time.
3. Orange	Student participates in a game of tennis, using the forehand, backhand, drop shot, and overhand smash shot correctly 75 percent of the time.
4. Green	Student participates in a game of tennis, using the forehand, backhand, drop shot, and overhand smash shot correctly 75 percent of the time and getting the ball over the net 50 percent of the time.
5. Blue	Student participates in a game of tennis, using the forehand, backhand, drop shot, and overhand smash shot correctly 75 percent of the time and getting the ball over the net 75 percent of the time.
6. Brown	Student participates in a game of tennis, using the forehand, backhand, drop shot, and overhand smash shot correctly 90 percent of the time and placing the ball in the desired spot 50 percent of the time.
7. Black	Student participates in a game of tennis, using the forehand, backhand, drop shot, and overhand smash shot correctly 95 percent of the time and placing the ball in the desired spot 75 percent of the time.

CHAPTER 10

Health and Fitness

Purpose: The importance of fitness skills and activities cannot be overlooked at any age. A basic fitness level is vital to enjoyment of physical activity and sport. In addition, possessing adequate fitness helps ward off heart disease, high cholesterol, the potential for diabetes, and obesity. Introduction of fitness skills at the appropriate developmental level is essential for successful performance throughout life.

Unit adaptations: There are many ways of adapting the fitness curriculum for children with disabilities. It is imperative that the modifications for each child be specific to his or her current fitness needs. For example, if a child is blind, he or she may use a guide wire or a guide with a tether when running, a tandem bike when riding, and a long pole with a ball on the end (a "bonker") to indicate the end of a lane when swimming.

Assessment options: In this section, each unit includes at least one rubric for evaluating the process or product of movements. The instructor can also use the Brockport Physical Fitness Test (see chapter 2).

Here are some ideas that can be used in teaching various physical activities; they involve equipment that can be used, rules that can be modified, environments that can be altered, and instructions that can be varied. Instructors can check off those that apply to the learner or those that the learner can accomplish.

Potential Modifications and Adaptations

Equipment	Rules	Environment	Instruction
☐ Stereo	☐ No music to start	☐ Accessible	☐ Verbal cues
☐ Music	☐ Go at own pace	☐ Indoors	☐ Demonstration/model
☐ Television or video	☐ Create own dance	☐ Outdoors	☐ Physical assistance
☐ Lines on floor	☐ Modify movements	☐ Flat surface	☐ Peer tutor
☐ Poly spots	☐ Dance while sitting	☐ Matted surface	☐ Paraeducator
☐ Ribbon	☐ Shadow partner	☐ Spacing from peers adequate for movement	☐ Task cards (enlarged if needed)
☐ Scarves	☐ Work with partner	☐ Bright and clear boundaries	☐ Pictures
☐ Stretch bands	☐ Work in groups	☐ Spots mark places	☐ Tactile modeling
☐ Mats	☐ Repeat moves	☐ Steps by the wall (so the wall can be used for balance)	☐ Guided discovery
☐ No mats	☐ Slower tempo	☐ Blinking lights to time with the beat	☐ Problem solving
☐ Mirrors	☐ Low impact		☐ Task analysis
☐ Lights	☐ Modify time		☐ Proximity (instructor stands close to student with disability)
☐ Bar for balance			☐ Interpreter
☐ Lower steps			☐ Individual instruction
☐ Light weights			☐ Sign language
☐ Modified weights			☐ Feedback
			☐ Heart rate check

Basic Aerobic Workout

Task description	Student will participate in a 30- to 45-minute aerobics class.
Scale components	(a) Ability to execute the skill that is demonstrated, (b) keeping up a 1/8 beat, (c) duration of continuous exercise
Rubric level and color	**Rubric descriptors**
1. White	Student is able to execute 3 or 4 aerobic moves with no music, as demonstrated by the instructor.
2. Yellow	Student is able to execute 5 to 8 aerobic moves with no music, as demonstrated by the instructor.
3. Orange	Student is able to execute at least 8 aerobic moves with music, as demonstrated by the instructor, to a 1/4 count, for 10 minutes continuously.
4. Green	Student is able to execute at least 10 aerobic moves with music, as demonstrated by the instructor, to a 1/4 count, for 15 minutes continuously.
5. Blue	Student is able to execute at least 10 aerobic moves with music, as demonstrated by the instructor, to a 1/8 count, for 20 minutes continuously.
6. Brown	Student is able to execute any number of moves with music, as demonstrated by the instructor, to a 1/8 count, for 20 to 30 minutes continuously.
7. Black	Student is able to execute any number of moves with music, as demonstrated by the instructor, to a 1/8 count, for 30 to 45 minutes continuously. Optional: Student could lead all or part of the workout.

Potential Modifications and Adaptations

Equipment	Rules	Environment	Instruction
☐ Chair lift	☐ Stop on first whistle	☐ Warm water	☐ Verbal cues
☐ Mats	☐ Exit for two whistles in case of emergency	☐ Visual boundaries	☐ Demonstration/model
☐ Lane lines	☐ Buddy system	☐ Mark off shallow end	☐ Physical assistance
☐ Buoys	☐ No rough play	☐ Mark off deep end	☐ Peer tutor
☐ Personal flotation	☐ Walk on deck	☐ Dry deck	☐ Paraeducator
☐ Water wings	☐ Appropriate spacing		☐ Task cards (enlarged if needed)
☐ Kickboard	☐ Permit approximations of skills		☐ Pictures
☐ Tube	☐ Swim for time, not distance		☐ Tactile modeling
☐ Waist float	☐ Modify distance		☐ Guided discovery
☐ Raft	☐ Respect others		☐ Problem solving
☐ Extension pole with tennis ball at the end for tapping individuals with visual impairments as a signal before they touch the wall			☐ Task analysis
☐ Whistle			☐ Proximity (instructor stands close to student with disability)
☐ Goggles			☐ Interpreter
☐ Nose plug			☐ Individual instruction
☐ Fins			☐ Sign language
☐ Flippers			☐ Feedback
☐ Deck rings			☐ Teach in progressions, such as: water adjustment, pre-swim skills, swim skills, lifesaving skills
☐ Hula hoop			
☐ Beach ball			
☐ Bright ball			
☐ Bell ball			
☐ Sinking objects			
☐ Aqua gloves			
☐ Aqua jogger			
☐ Snorkels			
☐ Aqua socks			
☐ Noodles			
☐ Rescue tube			
☐ Safety devices			

For aquatics assessment, please see appendix C and the CD-ROM.

(continued)

Distance Swim

Task description	Student will swim and increase distance as much as possible.
Scale components	(a) Distance, (b) timing (optional)
Rubric level and color	**Rubric descriptors**
1. White	Student swims 200 yards (183 meters) with any stroke, stopping when necessary.
2. Yellow	Student swims 250 yards (229 meters) with any stroke, stopping when necessary.
3. Orange	Student swims 300 yards (274 meters) with any stroke, stopping when necessary.
4. Green	Student swims 350 yards (320 meters) with any stroke, stopping when necessary.
5. Blue	Student swims 400 yards (366 meters) with any stroke, stopping when necessary.
6. Brown	Student swims 450 yards (411 meters) with any stroke, stopping when necessary.
7. Black	Student swims at least 500 yards (457 meters) with any stroke, stopping when necessary. Optional: Time decreases with practice for distance of 500 yards.

Potential Modifications and Adaptations

Equipment	Rules	Environment	Instruction
☐ Bars and weights	☐ No max weight	☐ Accessible	☐ Verbal cues
☐ Wooden weights	☐ Put equipment back where you got it (for safety)	☐ Music	☐ Demonstration/model
☐ Light weights		☐ Video on proper technique	☐ Physical assistance
☐ Rubber weights	☐ Warm up	☐ Bright atmosphere	☐ Peer tutor
☐ Modified bars	☐ Breathe properly	☐ Positive feedback	☐ Paraeducator
☐ Ankle weights	☐ Follow individual program	☐ Padding on floor	☐ Task cards (enlarged if needed)
☐ Bright weights		☐ Wheelchair access	
☐ Barbell without weights	☐ Spotter	☐ Acceptance	☐ Pictures
☐ Hand grips	☐ Proper form	☐ Posters	☐ Tactile modeling
☐ Weight belt	☐ Stretch	☐ Visuals of muscles used	☐ Guided discovery
☐ Velcro straps around hands and hand grip	☐ Learn names and function of muscles as they go	☐ Cushioned areas	☐ Problem solving
		☐ Texture of walls can change for different areas (i.e., stretching areas, free weights, etc.)	☐ Task analysis
☐ Straps			☐ Proximity (instructor stands close to student with disability)
☐ Task cards	☐ Isometric		
☐ Towel	☐ Isotonic		
☐ Sneakers	☐ Isokinetic	☐ Large area	☐ Interpreter
☐ Stretch bands	☐ Own pace	☐ Minimal distractions	☐ Individualized instruction (one-to-one)
☐ Gloves	☐ Half sets	☐ Take turns	
☐ Shorter benches	☐ Always with partners	☐ Indoors or outdoors	☐ Sign language
☐ Smaller machines	☐ Stop if it hurts	☐ Respect others	☐ Feedback
☐ Carpets	☐ Personal space	☐ Encourage everyone	
☐ Fitness machines	☐ Cool down		
☐ Everyday objects (e.g., cans, jugs)			

Bench Press

Task description	Student will lift the weight bar during a bench press, increasing the maximum amount of weight on the bench press by percentage of initial pretest maximum.
Scale components	Weight increase
Rubric level and color	**Rubric descriptors**
1. White	Student lifts weight equal to pretest maximum.
2. Yellow	Student lifts weight 1 to 3 percent heavier than pretest maximum.
3. Orange	Student lifts weight 4 to 6 percent heavier than pretest maximum.
4. Green	Student lifts weight 7 to 9 percent heavier than pretest maximum.
5. Blue	Student lifts weight 10 to 12 percent heavier than pretest maximum.
6. Brown	Student lifts weight 13 to 15 percent heavier than pretest maximum.
7. Black	Student lifts weight more than 15 percent heavier than pretest maximum.

CHAPTER 11

Recreation and Life Skills

Purpose: The importance of recreation skills cannot be overlooked at any age. Recreation and the ability to participate in enjoyable leisure-time activities are crucial to enjoying a high quality of life at school age and beyond.

Unit adaptations: There are many ways of adapting the recreation curriculum for children with disabilities. It is imperative that the recreation modifications for each child be specific to his or her needs. For example, a 13-year-old child with an intellectual disability was going to an in-line skating party. He had never done in-line skating before, but with some physical assistance from his physical educator, he was able to use teaching cues to work through slow, small steps and become proficient enough to be independent at the birthday party!

Assessment options: In this section, each unit includes at least one rubric for evaluating the process or product of movements. Instructors can also create checklists and rating scales and have students keep journals, all of which can be included in student portfolios.

Here are some ideas that can be used in teaching various recreation activities; they involve equipment that can be used, rules that can be modified, environments that can be altered, and instructions that can be varied. Instructors can check off those that apply to the learner or those that the learner can accomplish.

Potential Modifications and Adaptations

Equipment	Rules	Environment	Instruction
☐ Smaller bags	☐ Stay with group	☐ Nature	☐ Verbal cues
☐ Lighter packs	☐ Use buddy system	☐ Fields	☐ Demonstration/model
☐ Water bottle	☐ Stay on path	☐ Gym	☐ Physical assistance
☐ Walking stick	☐ No alternative trails	☐ Smaller hills	☐ Peer tutor
☐ Rails on side of path	☐ Know environment	☐ Smooth walking path	☐ Paraeducator
☐ Bright trail markers	☐ No running	☐ Groomed trails	☐ Task cards (enlarged if needed)
☐ Large trail markers	☐ Modify pace	☐ Accessible trails	☐ Pictures
☐ Bright flag markers	☐ Shorter trails	☐ Daytime hours	☐ Tactile modeling
☐ Color-coded maps	☐ Identify poison ivy	☐ Marked boundaries	☐ Guided discovery
☐ Large compasses	☐ Don't touch plants	☐ Sun not in eyes	☐ Problem solving
☐ Ropes for tethering or guiding	☐ Don't eat anything		☐ Task analysis
☐ Proper footwear	☐ Drink or rest when needed		☐ Proximity (instructor stays close to student with disability)
☐ Proper clothing	☐ Know basic first aid		☐ Interpreter
☐ Change of clothes	☐ Know what to do when lost		☐ Individual instruction
☐ Water	☐ No littering		☐ Sign language
☐ Nourishment	☐ Keep hands free		☐ Use the buddy for support
☐ Camp gear			☐ Feedback
☐ First-aid kit			
☐ Whistle			
☐ Toilet paper			

Backpacking and Hiking

Task description	Student will hike with or without a pack.
Scale components	(a) Distance, (b) terrain, (c) weight of and distance with a pack (optional)
Rubric level and color	**Rubric descriptors**
1. White	Student walks on a flat trail in the woods with few roots and rocks for 0.5 mile (0.8 kilometer).
2. Yellow	Student walks on a flat trail in the woods with few roots and rocks for 1 mile (1.6 kilometers).
3. Orange	Student walks moderate hills with some roots and rocks for 1 mile.
4. Green	Student walks moderate hills with some roots and rocks for 2 miles (3.2 kilometers).
5. Blue	Student walks terrain with 250- to 500-foot (76- to 152-meter) elevation with some roots and rocks for 2 miles.
6. Brown	Student walks terrain with 250- to 500-foot elevation with some roots and rocks for 3 miles (4.8 kilometers) or more. Optional: Carry 10- to 25-pound (about 4.5- to 11-kilogram) pack.
7. Black	Student walks terrain with 250- to 1000-foot (76- to 305-meter) elevation with abundant roots and rocks for 3 or more miles. Optional: Carry 20- to 40-pound (about 9- to 18-kilogram) pack.

Potential Modifications and Adaptations

Equipment	Rules	Environment	Instruction
☐ Plastic ball ☐ Playground ball ☐ Lighter ball ☐ Brighter ball ☐ Smaller ball ☐ Snap-handle ball (bowling ball with handle that snaps back in after the throw) ☐ Ramp ☐ Floor markings ☐ Bumpers ☐ Rails ☐ Colored pins ☐ Lighter pins	☐ Two hands if needed ☐ More than two turns at a time ☐ Stand at line ☐ One-step approach ☐ Any number of steps ☐ Can cross line ☐ Spare equals strike ☐ Tutor recovers ball	☐ Directional arrows ☐ Guide rails ☐ Shorter distance ☐ Shorter lanes ☐ Wider lanes ☐ Sloped lanes ☐ More pins ☐ Fewer pins ☐ Have only one ball in ball return rack ☐ One person bowls at a time ☐ Indoors or outdoors ☐ Machine keeps score automatically ☐ Use Nintendo Wii bowling	☐ Verbal cues ☐ Demonstration/model ☐ Physical assistance ☐ Peer tutor ☐ Paraeducator ☐ Task cards (enlarged if needed) ☐ Pictures ☐ Tactile modeling ☐ Guided discovery ☐ Problem solving ☐ Task analysis ☐ Proximity (instructor stands close to student with disability) ☐ Interpreter ☐ Individualized instruction (one-to-one) ☐ Sign language ☐ Feedback

Bowling

Task description	Student will bowl a bowling ball in a game.
Scale components	(a) Form, (b) accuracy
Rubric level and color	**Rubric descriptors**
1. White	Student attempts to roll the bowling ball.
2. Yellow	Student uses 3-step approach and steps with opposite foot most of the time.
3. Orange	Student uses 3-step approach, swings ball from back to front, and steps with opposite foot most of the time.
4. Green	Student uses 3-step approach, swings ball from back to front, steps with the opposite foot, and releases ball out front with a smooth transition most of the time.
5. Blue	Student uses proper form, with a smooth release, and hits the pins, without rolling the ball into the gutter, 5 out of 10 times.
6. Brown	Student uses proper form, with a smooth release, and hits the pins, without rolling the ball into the gutter, 8 out of 10 times.
7. Black	Student uses proper form and hits at least 3 pins in 8 out of 10 tries.

Potential Modifications and Adaptations

Equipment	Rules	Environment	Instruction
☐ Bamboo pole ☐ Short pole ☐ Longer pole ☐ Pole holder in belt ☐ Holder for pole ☐ Auto-cast on pole ☐ Blunt hook ☐ Velcro glove for holding pole ☐ Life jacket	☐ From sitting position ☐ No-cast ☐ Multiple tries for cast ☐ From boat with fixed chair ☐ No time limit ☐ Assistance with cast	☐ Calm water ☐ No ledge to water ☐ Stocked pond ☐ Few distractions	☐ Verbal cues ☐ Demonstration/model ☐ Physical assistance ☐ Peer tutor ☐ Paraeducator ☐ Task cards (enlarged if needed) ☐ Pictures ☐ Tactile modeling ☐ Guided discovery ☐ Problem solving ☐ Task analysis ☐ Proximity (instructor stands close to student with disability) ☐ Interpreter ☐ Sign language ☐ Feedback

Casting

Task description	Student will cast the fishing line with bait.
Scale components	(a) Skills, (b) independence, (c) distance of the cast
Rubric level and color	**Rubric descriptors**
1. White	Student baits own hook with verbal prompting and some physical assistance.
2. Yellow	Student baits own hook independently and can bring rod back and cast forward without allowing reel to release.
3. Orange	Student releases the reel and gets the line out by bringing rod across the body, most of the time.
4. Green	Student releases the reel, casts the line from behind the shoulder, and follows through out front, with line and bait casting at least 10 feet (3 meters), some of the time.
5. Blue	Student releases the reel, casts the line from behind the shoulder, and follows through out front, with line and bait casting at least 10 feet, most of the time.
6. Brown	Student releases the reel, casts the line from behind the shoulder, and follows through out front, with line and bait casting at least 10 feet, 8 out of 10 times.
7. Black	Student releases the reel, casts the line from behind the shoulder, and follows through out front, with line and bait casting at least 15 feet (4.6 meters), 8 out of 10 times.

Potential Modifications and Adaptations

Equipment	Rules	Environment	Instruction
☐ Rock wall	☐ Safety first	☐ Indoor wall	☐ Verbal cues
☐ Helmets	☐ Trust your leader	☐ Outdoor wall	☐ Demonstration/model
☐ Ropes	☐ Challenge by choice (the child can choose a more difficult part of the wall if desired)	☐ Mountain	☐ Physical assistance
☐ Safety lines		☐ Wheelchair accessible	☐ Peer tutor
☐ Carabiners		☐ More handholds	☐ Paraeducator
☐ Harness		☐ Sloped walls	☐ Task cards (enlarged if needed)
☐ Tandem belt	☐ Go at own pace	☐ Texture of rocks	☐ Pictures
☐ Belay	☐ Positively encourage	☐ Sun not in eyes	☐ Tactile modeling
☐ Cargo net	☐ Listen		☐ Guided discovery
☐ Ladder	☐ Communicate (one person gives instructions at a time)		☐ Problem solving
☐ Stall bars			☐ Task analysis
☐ Hand chalk	☐ Proper commands (specific to the climb and needs of the child)		☐ Proximity (instructor stays close to student with disability)
☐ Climbing shoes			
☐ Gloves	☐ Lower climbs		☐ Interpreter
☐ High ropes course	☐ Unlimited time		☐ Individual instruction
☐ Low ropes course	☐ Climb across, not up		☐ Sign language
☐ Whistle	☐ Climb side by side		☐ Feedback
☐ Red flags as boundaries	☐ One person climbs at a time		☐ Progress with height
	☐ Rocks close together and simply placed		☐ Small groups
☐ Cowbell at various locations			☐ Proper technique
	☐ Adjustable surface		☐ Review safety
	☐ Belayer takes most of weight		☐ Lesson on chalkboard or white board
	☐ Always have buddy		
	☐ Spotters		

Basic Rock Climbing

Task description	Student will climb a 30-foot (9.1-meter) rock wall with harness and helmet.
Scale components	(a) Preparation, (b) attempts at climbing, (c) descent
Rubric level and color	**Rubric descriptors**
1. White	Student puts on harness and helmet with assistance.
2. Yellow	Student puts on harness and helmet and understands the safety terminology sufficiently to begin climbing.
3. Orange	Student attempts to pull body up with both hands, up to 10 feet (3 meters), and climbs down.
4. Green	Student attempts to pull body up with both hands and feet, up to 10 feet, and climbs down.
5. Blue	Student uses both hands and feet, climbs 10 to 20 feet (about 3 to 6 meters), and attempts the backward fall (the skill needed to walk down the wall).
6. Brown	Student uses both hands and feet, climbs 10 to 20 feet, and properly executes the backward fall.
7. Black	Student uses both hands and feet, climbs 20 to 30 feet (about 6 to 9 meters), and properly executes the backward fall.

Potential Modifications and Adaptations

Equipment	Rules	Environment	Instruction
☐ Velcro skates ☐ Brakes (front and back) ☐ Wrist and knee pads ☐ Helmet ☐ Trash cans on wheels for support ☐ Shopping cart for support ☐ Walker on wheels for support ☐ Tether (short rope between guide and person with a visual impairment) ☐ Bar held by peer ☐ Hula hoop held by peer	☐ Skate slowly ☐ Skate forward ☐ Skate backward ☐ Skate in a circle ☐ Skate with partner ☐ Obstacle course ☐ Skate for distance ☐ Skate for time ☐ Skate and dance ☐ Roller hockey ☐ Skate for transportation	☐ Smooth surface ☐ Soft surface ☐ Inclined surface ☐ Limited space ☐ Larger space ☐ Visual boundaries ☐ Auditory boundaries ☐ Challenge using obstacles ☐ Limited number of people in the way	☐ Verbal cues ☐ Demonstration/model ☐ Physical assistance ☐ Peer tutor ☐ Paraeducator ☐ Task cards (enlarged if needed) ☐ Pictures ☐ Tactile modeling ☐ Guided discovery ☐ Problem solving ☐ Task analysis ☐ Proximity (instructor stays close to student with disability) ☐ Interpreter ☐ Individual instruction ☐ Sign language ☐ Feedback ☐ Use the wall for support

Skating and In-Line Skating

Task description	Student will skate or in-line skate in various directions, maintaining control.
Scale components	(a) Skill ability, (b) balance and control, (c) task complexity
Rubric level and color	**Rubric descriptors**
1. White	Student skates forward, close to railing or wall, without falling, for 5 minutes.
2. Yellow	Student brakes, using the brake at will, 4 out of 5 times at specific marks or cones on the floor.
3. Orange	Student skates forward on one foot (right, then left, then right) for 20 feet (about 6 meters) without losing balance, 4 out of 5 times.
4. Green	Student skates in a circle 10 to 20 feet (about 3 to 6 meters) in diameter, clockwise and counterclockwise.
5. Blue	Student skates backward for 20 feet without losing balance.
6. Brown	Student skates backward in a 10- to 20-foot circle, once.
7. Black	Student skates forward and changes to backward while moving, in a straight line and in a circle, and stops on command without losing balance, 4 out of 5 times.

Disabilities in Kid Terms

This section contains definitions of many disabilities in terms easily understood by children. Each definition includes a description of the disability, some common characteristics that kids may see in a child with the disability, and what kids can do to make sure that child feels included in his or her educational setting.

It is important to note that instructors should emphasize similarities as well as differences. Instructors can easily think of similarities, but the following example demonstrates the presentation of similarities for each child.

The instructor might tell students, "You can make sure your friend is included in games and activities in your neighborhood or on the playground by adapting the equipment, the playing area, or the rules. He is just like you in many ways. He likes to play with his friends, eat ice cream, go to games, and be included in a group. You can help him feel good about himself by understanding who he is and what he needs. He will do the same for you if you give him a chance."

ARTHROGRYPOSIS

- Children with arthrogryposis have a difficult time bending their arms and legs.

- They were born with very stiff joints. Their knees, wrists, elbows, ankles, and shoulders are very stiff in everything they do.

- They have a hard time walking, moving, eating, dressing, and playing.

- Some kids may walk with crutches or a walker or use a wheelchair.

- They may be able to push their own chairs, or they may need help pushing the chair or use an electric wheelchair.

- Most of the time, these kids are able to think and talk just like anyone else.

- Sometimes you may need to be patient when they talk so that you can understand them.

Inclusion Ideas

- You can help kids with arthrogryposis by pushing their chairs if they need you to, waiting for them if they walk a little slowly, or helping them put their coats on if they need you to.

- You may need to help them get things they can't get for themselves, write down what they are thinking if they can't, or assist them in playing volleyball by helping their hands hit the ball.

- Other kids may look at them funny or tease them because of the way they look, but it is important to let others know that they are just like everyone else in more ways than not.

ASTHMA

- Children with asthma have a hard time breathing in certain situations. The difficulty breathing may occur after a stressful activity, such as running, or if they are scared or overly tired.

- It may also happen if the person is allergic to pollen, grass, perfume, smoke, or animals.

- Either way, the problem will start with shortness of breath and, if not taken care of, progress to wheezing, coughing, and perhaps even lack of air.

- Most people with asthma carry some type of inhaler, or breathing device, to help them when the problem starts so that it does not progress to a dangerous situation.

- This may be a very scary situation for the person who is having the attack.

- Students with asthma will not only have to temporarily leave the current activity; they may also feel embarrassed because they are different in this way and attention was focused on them.

Inclusion Ideas

- You can help kids with asthma by helping them remember to bring their inhaler or prescribed medication.

- You can also help by calming them if they do have an attack.

- Let them know that everything will be OK and it is not a big deal if they have to miss some of the class or game.

- You can put yourself in their situation and understand that it is hard to breathe and frustrating to have to sit out at any given moment.

- You can make sure the playing area is not too big if your friends have a hard time covering large areas.

- You can also make sure they get rest periods when they need them so that breathing does not get too difficult.

- It will also help if you and your friends have a signal for when a student with asthma feels as though he or she is in too much trouble with breathing and may need you to call the nurse, the teacher, or 911.

ATTENTION-DEFICIT/HYPERACTIVITY DISORDER (ADHD)

- Children with attention-deficit/hyperactivity disorder have a hard time paying attention in school, at home, and in social and play situations. This is just the way they were born, and they may take medication to help them pay attention better.
- They are distracted very easily and sometimes make mistakes because they are rushing through an assignment or chore.
- They are often restless, fidgety, or hyperactive, and they may even run away from you in the middle of a game.
- Sometimes they have a hard time organizing schoolwork, their desks, or their lockers. They may interrupt a conversation or talk out of turn. They may seem lazy, unreliable, or uncaring.

Inclusion Ideas

- You can help these classmates to be organized and pay attention to what they need to do.
- If they become distracted in the middle of a game, group assignment, or conversation, then remind them of what they were doing and help them finish if possible.
- If they choose not to finish what they were doing at that time, remind them at another time, and help them remember what they had to do.
- If they run away from a game at recess, know that they will come back and welcome them when they do.
- You can understand that they may have a hard time paying attention to one thing for a long time, and perhaps help them structure their days so that they do not have to remain in one place for too long.
- Do not look at what they did not have time to do; look at what they did, and let them know they are doing a good job.
- Know that they are still your friends even if it appears that they are ignoring you, or if they run away from you.

AUTISM

- Children with autism have a difficult time relating to people.
- They may be more interested in playing with an object or watching their hand than in talking to a person.
- They may play in a corner all by themselves or run around for no apparent reason.
- They may have very limited communication or no communication, and what they do say may not make very much sense.
- They may be very good at some things and not be able to do other things at all.

- They may react to touch, noise, or lights very differently. Sometimes a low noise will seem very loud to them, so much that they will cover their ears.
- They may cry from a soft touch or cover their eyes from a dim light.
- Other kids may appear deaf when there is a loud noise, may seek out deep pressure or textured feelings on their skin, or may look for very bright lights to stimulate themselves.
- Each person with autism is different, and you need to understand what he or she wants and needs in order to be able to cope with the environment.

Inclusion Ideas

- You can help classmates with autism by talking clearly and asking them only one or two things at a time.
- You can help them when they don't know what to do, redirect them when they are doing the wrong activity, and help other people understand what they are good at and what they need help with.
- You can learn what makes them mad, frustrated, and happy, and you can help convey these feelings to other classmates and the teacher.

BLINDNESS AND VISUAL IMPAIRMENT

- Children who are blind or visually impaired have difficulty seeing.
- They have this disability because of a birth accident, an accident after birth, or a sickness.
- Some kids can see a little bit and walk around by themselves; some kids can see a little bit but need some help getting around; and some kids cannot see anything and need help in getting around.
- With practice and a cane or a seeing-eye dog, kids may be able to walk around school and their neighborhood by themselves.
- These kids will eat by themselves and use the "clock system" for knowing where things are. You can tell them their milk is at 12:00, which means their milk is at the very top of the plate, and their fork is at 9:00, which means their fork is just to the left of the plate.
- These students can dress themselves, and they know which clothes are which color by reading brailled writing on the tag of the shirt.
- They find out what is happening in their environment, who is around them, and where they are going by having people tell them.
- Do not be afraid to use words like "see" or "look" in a sentence. Students with blindness or visual impairment will use these words, and you can, too.

Inclusion Ideas

- You can guide your classmates by allowing them to grab your elbow and walk one step behind you. This will allow them to let go if they want to.
- You can assist them in getting their food in the lunch line, and you can tell them where their food is on their plates.
- You can describe their environment to them, such as who is in the room, what the weather is like, and what equipment is located around the gym.
- You can answer their questions and make sure they are included in conversations.

- Do not ever leave a room without telling them you are leaving. They may want to talk to you and not know you are gone, and this is embarrassing.
- You can make sure they are included in games and activities in your neighborhood or on the playground by adapting the equipment, the playing area, or the rules.

CEREBRAL PALSY

- Children with cerebral palsy have a condition from birth that affects their arms and legs.
- They have this condition because their brains cannot tell their bodies what they want them to do.
- Their muscles contract and their body moves without control. This affects different kids in different ways.
- Sometimes they have difficulty walking, or they may look awkward when they walk.
- Children with cerebral palsy may walk with crutches or a walker or use a wheelchair.
- They may be able to push their own chairs, or they may need help pushing the chair or use an electric wheelchair.
- They may have difficulty with feeding themselves, getting dressed, or talking, and some kids with cerebral palsy communicate through a communication board or a voice synthesizer instead of with their voices.

Inclusion Ideas

- You can help your classmates who have cerebral palsy by pushing their chairs if they need a push or walking with them around school if they are a little slower so that they don't have to walk alone.
- You can go up the ramp or the elevator if they need to go a different way so that they do not have to go by themselves.
- You can be patient when they communicate with you and help others understand their wants and needs.

CONGENITAL HEART CONDITION

- Children with a heart condition have a hard time breathing or functioning in certain situations.
- The difficulty breathing may occur after a stressful activity like running or if they are scared, if they physically stress themselves, or if they are overly tired.
- The problem will start with shortness of breath and if not taken care of will progress to weakness and fatigue; the person may even faint.
- This situation may be very scary for the person who is having the attack. The person will not only have to temporarily leave the current activity but may also feel embarrassed because he or she is different in this way and has become the focus of attention.
- Most people with a congenital heart disorder participate in activity at a slower rate or for short periods.

Inclusion Ideas

■ You can help these kids by helping them remember to work at a slower pace and take rest periods.

■ You can also help by calming them if they do have an attack.

■ Let them know that everything will be OK and it is not a big deal if they have to miss some of the class or game.

■ You can put yourself in their situation and understand that it is hard to breathe and frustrating to have to sit out at any given moment.

■ You can also make sure they get rest periods when they need them so that effort and breathing do not get too difficult.

■ You can sit out with them when they are resting so that they do not have to sit out alone.

■ It will also help if you and your friends have a signal to use when a student with a congenital heart condition feels too much trouble with breathing and may need you to call the nurse, the teacher, or 911.

DEAFNESS AND HARDNESS OF HEARING

■ Children who are deaf or hard of hearing cannot hear like you and I can.

■ They hear much less than we do, and in some cases they cannot hear at all. Perhaps this is due to a fever their mother had during pregnancy, or perhaps their parents are deaf and their children became deaf also. They may have been premature at birth, had a sickness after birth, or become deaf from an accident.

■ Some kids wear hearing aids, cochlear implants, or other hearing devices to help them hear better.

■ Some kids with hearing difficulty can talk clearly; you can understand them, and they can read your lips.

■ Some kids communicate using hand gestures and sign language.

■ Some kids with hearing difficulty are not able to talk with their voices, and they may not be able to understand everything you say.

■ Some kids with hearing difficulty will prefer to talk mostly with other deaf kids; others will talk and make friends with anyone, hearing or deaf.

Inclusion Ideas

■ Because your classmates with hearing difficulty cannot hear, you can help them in many ways.

■ If they use their voices and read lips, you can help by making sure you are looking at each other when you talk.

■ You can tap them on the shoulder to get their attention if the teacher is talking, if there is a fire drill, or if someone wants to talk to them.

■ You can make sure they understand the instructions when you are in class, and you can answer any questions they have.

■ If your friends are totally deaf and use signs, you can learn some signs to aid in communication; if you don't know the signs, you can look at them when you are talking, and the interpreter will interpret what you say.

■ Many kids who are deaf feel lonely and left out, so it is important to try to include them in all activities, both in and out of school.

- It is also important that you do not make students with hearing difficulty feel bad if they do not understand something; instead, you can try to increase their understanding the best that you can.
- If you want to help students who are deaf or hard of hearing, always remember that you can make sure they are included in games and activities in your neighborhood or on the playground. Do this by communicating the rules, talking with them, and helping other kids understand them. They are just like you in many ways.

DWARFISM

- Children who have dwarfism are short in stature and may have shorter legs and arms than you have.
- For some kids, this happens at birth because of the way their bones are formed.
- Other kids are this way just because they did not grow as fast or as much as you.
- They may have a high voice and may have a hard time moving their arms and legs like you can.
- They may walk a little slower than you do and may have trouble moving their bodies in the ways you do.

Inclusion Ideas

- You can help kids with dwarfism by walking with them if they are at the end of the line so that they are not alone.
- You can help them reach something that is out of reach or assist them in doing an activity that may be difficult for them in class or on the playground.
- Other kids may give them funny looks or tease them because of the way they look, but it is important that you let others know that your friends are just like them in more ways than not.
- You can make sure they are included in games and activities in your neighborhood or on the playground by adapting the equipment, the playing area, or the rules.

EMOTIONAL DISABILITY/SERIOUS EMOTIONAL DISTURBANCE/ BEHAVIOR DISABILITY

- Children with one of these conditions may make physical or verbal attacks toward the teacher or other classmates.
- These attacks may include swearing, pushing, shoving, or destruction of property.
- Sometimes the teacher or teacher's aide may have to physically restrain the student or take him or her out of the room.
- This behavior often affects the student's performance in class, and he or she may be out of the classroom frequently because of this behavior. This is not anyone's fault—it just happens because of outside factors.
- These students do not try to have excessive misbehavior; it is part of who they are and may remain this way for a while until teachers, parents, and administrators can figure out how to help decrease the behaviors.

Inclusion Ideas

- You can help these kids by giving them positive feedback when they are exhibiting good behavior.
- You can talk to them about everyday things and get to know who they are.
- You can be their partners when others may not want to and try to accept them after they come back from a time-out.
- Other kids may give them funny looks or tease them because of the way they act, but it is important that you let others know that your friends are just like them in more ways than not.

LEARNING DISABILITY

- Children with learning disabilities have a difficult time in learning situations, with reading, or with comprehension. They are not stupid; their brains just have a hard time receiving information, processing information, or expressing or giving back information. This happens when they are born, and they look just like everyone else.
- These kids might also have problems with writing letters and numbers.
- These kids may have a hard time running the same way you do or playing a game in some situations. For example, they may run more slowly or have a hard time catching a ball or doing things with their upper bodies.
- Many kids with learning disabilities also have attention-deficit/hyperactivity disorder (ADHD). If they also have ADHD, please see the description of that condition to learn the characteristics and how you can help the student.

Inclusion Ideas

- You can help your classmates with learning disabilities by showing them the right way to catch a ball or run, assisting them in expressing their thoughts, and checking their writing if they need it.
- You can praise them when they accomplish their goals and encourage them when they are struggling.
- Because some activities or skills are more difficult for these classmates, you will need to be very patient and supportive.
- You can make sure that they are included in games and activities in your neighborhood or on the playground by adapting the equipment, the playing area, or the rules.

MENTAL RETARDATION

- Children with intellectual disability may not be able to think the same way you do. This is because they had an accident before, during, or after they were born, involving their heads or the chemicals in their bodies.
- They will sometimes be able to understand parts of what you say but not everything. They may also react to what they are asked in an unusual way because of the lack of understanding.
- These classmates may also have trouble communicating with you, taking care of themselves (such as feeding themselves), or putting on their coats.

- They may walk away when you are talking to them or laugh for no reason. They may have trouble going out into the community on their own to do things, such as taking a bus or going shopping.
- Sometimes during the day, they may not know what they want to do, they may not be aware of danger in the environment, or they may need help to do class-work or recreational activities such as walking, riding a bike, or bowling.

Inclusion Ideas

- You can help these classmates by talking clearly and asking them only one or two things at a time.
- You can help them when they don't know what to do, redirect them when they are doing the wrong activity, and help other people understand what they are good at and how they can be helped.
- You can make sure they are included in groups, games, and activities by giving them clear instructions and demonstrations throughout the activity and praising them when they do something right.
- These kids have the same feelings you have. They are hurt when other kids don't want to play with them; just like you, they enjoy things like eating ice cream, watching cartoons, and being part of the game.

OBESITY

- Children who are obese may be this way for many reasons.
- They may be on medication, they may have a glandular problem, they may have inherited much of their body composition, or they may not have learned how to balance diet and exercise.
- Whatever the reason for the obesity, it makes movement difficult.
- They have a difficult time running, moving their bodies, and perhaps being involved in activities for a long period.
- They may be afraid or embarrassed to participate in certain activities, such as gymnastics, dancing, or swimming.
- It is important to keep in mind that they can be involved in any activity with some minor modifications.
- They may need more rest time, they may need to cover less area in a game, or they may need to be involved in the activity in a different way.
- They may also need to substitute for activities that make their bodies hurt—for example, walking instead of running, hopping, or jumping, and doing log rolls instead of forward rolls.
- Swimming is an excellent activity for children who are obese. Be sure to make them feel welcome and encourage them to swim to the best of their ability.
- Students who are obese do need to be involved in activities, so it is important to allow them to modify any activity but continue to be involved to the maximum extent possible.

Inclusion Ideas

- You can help these kids by helping them remember to work at a slower pace and take rest periods.

- You can help them by giving them some positive feedback when they participate actively in a game.
- When they do something that you know is hard for them, be sure to give them a high five or thumbs-up, or just say, "Great job!"
- You can put yourself in their situation and understand that it is hard to move and frustrating not to be able to do everything that other kids are doing.
- You can make sure the playing area is not too big if your friends have a hard time covering large areas.
- You can also make sure they get rest periods when they need them, so that effort, movement, and breathing do not get too difficult.
- It will also help if you and your friends have a signal to use when students with obesity feel as though they are in too much trouble with breathing and may need you to call the nurse, the teacher, or 911.

OSTEOGENESIS IMPERFECTA (BRITTLE BONES)

- Kids with this condition are born with very fragile bones that often break even when they are not doing anything. This is just the way their bones formed, and this will be their condition until they are teenagers.
- This condition can be very frustrating, because they always have to be careful when doing everything, and they spend a lot of time in the hospital or at home.
- They may walk with a waddling gait, with crutches, or with a walker, or they may use a wheelchair.
- They may push their own wheelchairs, need to be pushed, or use an electric wheelchair.
- They may also be overweight because they do not have the opportunity to exercise, run, and play.
- They are just as smart as other kids in your class, and they usually talk very clearly.
- It may be hard for them to reach things far away or move very fast.
- They may need to play very modified games, and they cannot participate in activities that will place them in danger of breaking more bones.

Inclusion Ideas

- You can help them by pushing them if they need a push, slowing down if they are slow walkers, walking with them in class, or going up the ramp or elevator with them.
- If something is out of reach for them, you can help by pushing it closer or getting it for them.
- You can help others understand how similar they are to you; they share your hopes and dreams for the future.

SPINAL CORD INJURY AND SPINA BIFIDA

- A spinal cord injury occurs at birth or results from an accident or disease after birth.

■ The part of the spine affected is either partially or totally severed, and children with such a condition have total or partial paralysis from that point down.

■ The children have little or no feeling in or control of their legs, abdominal area, or, in some cases, arms.

■ Spina bifida happens when a person is born and part of the spine does not close all the way.

■ Their spinal cord is often not covered by bone or tissue.

■ This is always corrected by surgery, but the children are most often left paralyzed, either totally or partially, from that area down.

■ These kids will walk with an awkward gait or use crutches, a walker, or a wheelchair.

■ They may push their own wheelchairs, need to be pushed, or use an electric wheelchair.

■ They may urinate through a tube into a bag, and they may also have braces on their legs.

■ They are just as smart as other kids in your class, and they usually talk very clearly.

■ They need to use ramps and elevators to go up or down steps and to other floors, and they will need a bigger restroom stall than kids without wheelchairs need.

■ Other than these few differences, these kids are just like you.

Inclusion Ideas

■ You can help these classmates by pushing them if they need a push, slowing down if they are slow walkers, walking with them in class, or going up the ramp or elevator with them.

■ If something is out of reach for them, you can help by pushing it closer or getting it for them.

■ You can help others understand how similar these children are to you; they share many of your hopes and dreams for the future.

TRAUMATIC BRAIN INJURY

■ Children with traumatic brain injury have experienced a bad accident or a blow to the head.

■ This causes them to have short-term memory loss; sometimes their speech is slurred, and they may say whatever is on their minds.

■ Because they may not remember what does or does not hurt others' feelings, they may say something that does not make sense or is mean.

■ They do not do these things intentionally; it just happens because they do not know what is appropriate.

■ They may look unbalanced when they walk, or they may use a cane, crutches, or a wheelchair.

■ They may push their own wheelchairs, need to be pushed, or use an electric wheelchair.

■ They may have a hard time doing simple, everyday tasks such as brushing their teeth, putting their coats on, or eating. This is because they have difficulty in controlling their muscles. As a result, they may become frustrated with whatever they are doing.

■ It is important for you to realize that they are not mad at you but frustrated with the situation, because they could do these simple things before but cannot do them now.

Inclusion Ideas

■ You can help these classmates by being patient when they try to talk and by listening and responding. You can also help other classmates listen and understand.

■ You can push them if they need a push or walk with them if they walk slowly so that they don't have to walk alone.

■ You can offer them your hand if it looks as though they will lose their balance.

■ You can assist them in their daily activities until they can do them independently.

■ You can show them how to do the things they forget. You can remind them of the things they forget and applaud the things they remember.

■ Because some activities or skills are more difficult for this classmate, you will need to be very patient and supportive.

Disability Awareness Program

This appendix offers a compilation of ideas for disability awareness activities for children. The list includes only selected ideas and should assist the instructor in creating additional disability awareness activities at each level. These activities should be informative, fun, and memorable for the participants. Remember the rules of thumb for disability awareness activities from chapter 7.

Level I: Exposure

Videos about individuals with disabilities

Newspaper or magazine articles about individuals with disabilities

Speakers with disabilities

Web sites

Level II: Experience

TUNNEL VISION TOSS AND CATCH

Grade level
K–6

Disabilities
Retinitis pigmentosa or any visual impairment that results in tunnel vision

Materials needed
Safety goggles, masking tape, balls, paper, pens, bats

Time allotted
30 to 40 minutes

Space needed

Gymnasium or large classroom

Description of activity

First, discuss what tunnel vision is and why people have it. Next, have students put on goggles with peripheral vision blocked out. Then divide the class into pairs (you can have them do the activity simultaneously or one at a time). Students need to kick, bat, or toss and catch a ball while simulating tunnel vision. If you have limited space, you could also have students write sentences on paper while wearing the goggles.

Safety considerations

Place students in stations or in static positions to avoid collisions. Have students complete skills in the same direction.

Variations

Vary the size of the holes on the goggles (e.g., 1/4 inch, hole-punch size, pinhole). Add another disability, such as wheelchair use or cerebral palsy (see separate entries).

Questions the teacher can ask:

1. Can you see the sides?
2. Is it easy to see the target?
3. What would it be like to see this way all the time?
4. Is it easier to throw the ball or to catch it?
5. Which skills were harder?
6. How could you help a peer who has tunnel vision?
7. What other skills might be hard?

Created by Rodney Allen and Tim Eustice, Brockport, NY.

TAG GAMES

Grade level

K–5

Disability

Autism

Materials needed

Wool sweaters, burlap bags, audio recording with loud sounds (everyday sounds), bright lights, strobe lights, tape, heavy jacket

Time allotted

30 to 40 minutes

Space needed

Gymnasium

Description of activity

Describe autism, its common characteristics, and what you might expect to see with a student who has autism. Explain that these modifications are meant to suggest the sensory overload that a person with autism might experience. Then have students play various tag games wearing a wool sweater, burlap bag, or heavy coat. Music or noise is played very loudly, and bright light shines at the children. You could also wrap tape around the children's wrists to simulate a watch, or around the ankles to simulate socks.

Safety considerations

Use football flags or one hand to avoid excess contact. Use other safety considerations that are regularly in force for tag games.

Variations

Use various types of irritating material. Put tape or Velcro on children's arms so that it will catch on their clothes as they run.

Questions the teacher can ask:

1. How did the wool sweater make your skin feel?
2. Did the bright lights bother you?
3. How did the loud noises affect your concentration?
4. How did it feel to have your arms catch on your clothes?
5. Were you frustrated? Why?
6. What could you do to help a child with autism feel more comfortable in the classroom?

ALL THUMBS

Grade level

K–5

Disabilities

Muscular dystrophy, cerebral palsy, learning disability, juvenile rheumatoid arthritis

Materials needed

Gloves, mittens, Velcro, tape (enough for half the class)

Time allotted

20 to 25 minutes

Space needed

Classroom or small gymnasium

Description of activity

Describe a disability in which children have fine motor difficulties and let the class know that this simulation will help them understand how those kids feel every day. During the simulation, all the kids try to tie their shoes, button their shirts, zip their pants, and braid shoelaces or hair with gloves, mittens, or other materials hindering their hands.

Safety considerations

Common sense. Be sure kids do not run with shoes untied. Clean gloves between classes. Be aware of frustration or misbehavior.

Variations

Have kids try to type at a computer, open a door with a key, brush their hair, open a lunch bag and milk carton, or do other activities (anything involving fine motor skill).

Questions the teacher can ask:

1. What was hard about this exercise?

2. What was easy?

3. How did you feel?

4. How could you help a child with a fine motor challenge?

5. What would you do if you had to go through your entire life with this disability? What sorts of adaptations would you make?

MARSHMALLOW MADNESS

Grade level
K–6

Disabilities
Cerebral palsy, Down syndrome, speech disorder

Materials needed
Bags of marshmallows (four to six for each child), three notecards containing short sentences

Time allotted
20 to 30 minutes

Space needed
Classroom or small gymnasium

Description of activity
Describe when and why some children have speech problems; go over characteristics and common problems. Then have each child pair up with a partner. One partner at a time puts four to six marshmallows in his or her mouth and tries to say a phrase or sentence written on a notecard provided by the teacher. The other student tries to understand what the speaker is saying. After two or three tries, the partners switch.

Safety considerations
Make sure that participants don't eat too many marshmallows. Don't continue if they are laughing too hard.

Variations
Allow participants to make up phrases or sentences. Switch partners. Prevent the listener from looking at the speaker.

Questions the teacher can ask:

1. What did you feel like when you were trying to talk and it was hard?

2. What did you feel like when you were trying to listen and it was hard to understand?

3. Were you clear about the phrase or sentence?

4. What would it feel like to talk like this every day?

5. What could you do to help a student with this problem?

6. What other effective ways of communicating can you think of?

Created by Dr. Georgia Frey, Indiana University.

SHOW ME THE SIGN

Grade level
K–12

Disabilities
Deafness, hardness of hearing

Materials needed
Sign book or teacher who knows sign language

Time allotted
10 to 15 minutes

Space needed
Classroom or small gymnasium

Description of activity
Describe the culture shared by many people who are deaf or hard of hearing, then talk about etiology and common characteristics of these disabilities. Next, sign for one to five sentences and see if any of the kids understand. This is very similar to a situation in which a deaf child is sitting in a classroom, the teacher is talking, and there is no interpreter or other means of ensuring that communication is clear.

Safety considerations
None

Variations
Turn on a TV with no volume and try to guess what is happening. Or tell some of the kids, but not all, what is being signed, thus enabling those not told to know what it is like to feel left out of the conversation. Tell a joke in sign and let some of the kids know; when they laugh, it will be frustrating for the others, just as it is for kids who are deaf.

Questions the teacher can ask:
1. How did you feel when you did not know what I was saying?
2. What would you do if you were in this situation?
3. What would you do if you were in this situation all the time?
4. How can you help a child who is deaf feel better in your classroom?
5. What would it feel like if all the kids in your school spoke sign and you were the only person who could speak aloud and hear?

Community Awareness Activities

ACCESSIBLE TRANSPORTATION

Disability
Need for wheelchair use

Description
Go to your local bus stop in a wheelchair and wait for a bus that is wheelchair-accessible.

Questions:

1. How many buses are accessible to people who use a wheelchair, and how many are not?
2. What is the average time a person who uses a wheelchair has to wait for a bus?
3. What is the average time a person who does not use a wheelchair has to wait for a bus?
4. Did the bus driver know how to use the wheelchair lift? Did he or she treat you the same as if you did not use a wheelchair?
5. Does a person in a wheelchair have to pay the same price for the ride as a person not in a wheelchair pays?
6. Would you think this was a fair system if you used a wheelchair for your primary means of getting around?
7. What recommendations do you have for the local bus company?
8. If this were a perfect world, what else would you ask for?
9. Other questions or reactions

Reaction to the project:

_____

_____

_____

TELECOMMUNICATION DEVICES FOR THE DEAF (TDD OR TTY)

Disability

Deafness

Directions

According to current legislation, all hotels are supposed to own a "telecommunication device for the deaf" (TDD) and make it available 24 hours a day for people who are deaf or who need to speak with someone who is deaf. You and a friend are to go to three local hotels and ask to use the TDD. Ask the clerk to teach you how.

Questions:

1. Do they have a TDD?
2. If so, is it available for you to use immediately?
3. Does the clerk know how to use it?
4. Do you feel you could call a person who is deaf?
5. If the hotel did not have one, what was their excuse?
6. Do you think you could teach a peer how to use a TDD?
7. If you were deaf, how might you feel you had been treated in each hotel?
8. What would you suggest for each hotel?
9. Other questions or reactions

Reaction to the project:

_____

_____

_____

ROOM FOR INDIVIDUALS WITH DISABILITIES

Disability
Any

Description
Go to three local hotels and ask to see a room for people with disabilities. Then ask to see a room for guests without disabilities. Notice what is similar and what is different.

Questions:
1. What was different on the front door of the room for people with a disability?
2. What was different in the bedroom (bed, bureau, mirrors)?
3. What was different about the bathroom (toilet, shower, bathtub, towel rack, sink, mirror, closet)?
4. Was closed-captioning available on the television?
5. What about doorways? Were they wider or narrower than in the room for people without disabilities?
6. How many rooms were available for people with disabilities?
7. Does a room for people with disabilities cost the same as a room for people without disabilities?
8. Ask the clerks if they would have the time to help a person with a disability get into his or her room if necessary. If so, have they ever helped a person with a disability?
9. What about the room might be difficult for a person using a wheelchair? What might be easier?
10. Other questions or reactions

Reaction to the project:

_____

_____

_____

_____

LOCAL YMCA OR HEALTH CLUB

Disability
Any

Description
Go to a local YMCA or health club and ask the following questions:

1. Do you have special programs for people with disabilities? If so, what are they? How are the people who run these programs qualified?
2. If there are no special programs, can people with disabilities—such as a visual impairment, cerebral palsy (necessitating use of a wheelchair), deafness, or amputations join your activities (e.g., swimming, basketball, judo, weight training, gymnastics, dance, aerobics)?
3. If there are special programs, what specific accommodations do you make? Are these accommodations successful? Why or why not?
4. Where do people with disabilities go if they have an interest in physical activity yet cannot be included in your program?
5. Do you feel that your facility is or is not meeting the needs of people with disabilities? Why or why not?
6. What can you do to improve your current program? Would this be difficult to implement? Why or why not?
7. Is it the responsibility of the individual with a disability to make his or her own accommodations to be included in the local health club? Why or why not?
8. Other questions or reactions

Reaction to the project:

_____

_____

_____

CARS OR VANS FOR INDIVIDUALS WITH DISABILITIES

Disability
Spinal cord injury, dwarfism, spina bifida

Description
Go to a local automobile or van dealer and ask to see a car or van that is adapted to be accessible for people with spinal cord injuries, dwarfism, or spina bifida. If the dealer does not have one, ask where you might find one. When you do find one, answer the following questions.

Questions:
1. Who was the car or van adapted for?
2. What is different about the steering wheel?
3. What is different about the gas pedals?
4. Is the seat adapted? If so, how?
5. What is different about the back of the vehicle?

6. How is this car or van similar to one that is not equipped for transporting people with disabilities?

7. Would this car or van cost more than an unadapted one? Why or why not?

8. If the car or van costs more than the unadapted van, who pays for the adaptations?

9. Would you like this type of vehicle? Why or why not?

10. What did you learn from this project?

11. Other questions or reactions

Reaction to the project:

_____

_____

_____

Classroom Projects

CLASS BULLETIN BOARD

Disability
Any

Description
Class must collect information about athletes with disabilities and create an informative bulletin board to share with the school. Be sure to collect information about various disabilities and sports and about both males and females. Start with the Web site www.paralympics.org.

Questions:
1. What different types of disability are represented here?

2. How many males and how many females are featured?

3. What major topics are addressed about the featured athletes?

4. What particularly impresses you that you did not know before?

5. Was there anything you already knew?

6. Was anything missing that you thought your class would find in the newspapers or magazines?

7. How did your schoolmates react to the bulletin board? What was the most frequently heard comment?

8. What surprised you most about your schoolmates' reactions?

9. Other questions or reactions

Reaction to the project:

_____

_____

_____

SPEAKER WITH A DISABILITY

Disability
Any

Description
Invite a speaker with a disability to come in and talk about his or her life and about overcoming adversity.

Questions:
1. What was the speaker's disability?
2. How did the speaker come to have the disability (present at birth or acquired later)?
3. How does the disability affect the speaker's life now?
4. Is the speaker's home adapted?
5. Did his or her family have to adapt to the disability? If so, how?
6. What does the speaker do now?
7. How are everyday activities such as transportation, accessibility, or communication adapted for this individual?
8. What does he or she do for recreation or leisure? What barriers does he or she face in these activities, and how does he or she overcome them?
9. What advice does (or would) this person have for others with the same disability?
10. Other questions or reactions

Reaction to the project:

_____

_____

_____

Level III: Ownership

CLASS DISABILITY AWARENESS NIGHT
(OWNERSHIP EXPERIENCE FOR HIGH SCHOOL STUDENTS)

Disability
Any

Description
High school students organize a disability awareness night for the local middle school or elementary school. The students can send a preliminary questionnaire to the children who will participate, asking what they know and do not know about individuals with disabilities. The high school students are responsible for setting up and implementing a variety of disability awareness activities for the younger community. They must teach the children about the particular disability chosen, allow them to experience a simulation of that disability, and

conduct an activity to increase understanding and awareness of that disability. They could also teach basic sign language or bring in speakers who have disabilities. The questionnaires could be redistributed after the event to assess whether the participants learned what was intended.

Questions:
1. What was the general response to the preliminary questionnaire?
2. What were the common questions or comments on Disability Awareness Night?
3. What misconceptions or myths did you encounter about people with disabilities?
4. What effect did the experience have on the participants? Was it what you expected?
5. What did you learn from this experience?
6. What would you do differently if you were to do it again?
7. Other questions or reactions

Reaction to the project:

_____

_____

_____

CROSS-AGE PEER TUTORING
(OWNERSHIP EXPERIENCE FOR HIGH SCHOOL STUDENTS)

Disability
Any

Description
Students go through a 1- to 2-hour training session conducted by the physical education teacher on teaching, feedback, and evaluation. Students then serve as teachers and evaluators in designated physical education classes for younger students with disabilities (adapted physical education). This activity must be conducted for a specific period, such as a unit, quarter, or semester. It may work best if the adapted physical education class takes place at the same time as the high school students' study hall so they do not miss required classes.

Questions:
1. What disability did the student or students you worked with have?
2. How did you assist in the physical education class?
3. What teaching and feedback techniques worked best with the students?
4. What was difficult about this experience?
5. What was easy about this experience?
6. What would be difficult if you had the same disability?
7. What would you do differently if you were to participate in the same project again?
8. Other questions or reactions

Reaction to the project:

_____

_____

_____

WHEELCHAIR ROAD RACE
(OWNERSHIP EXPERIENCE FOR HIGH SCHOOL STUDENTS)

Disability

This race can benefit any person with a spinal cord injury or a person with limited use of the legs (due, for example, to cerebral palsy, spinal cord injury, spina bifida, multiple sclerosis, or muscular dystrophy).

Description

Students identify a local race and help organize an accompanying wheelchair race. The students are responsible for conducting advertising, arranging rewards for first, second, and third place for men and women, and handling recognition after the race. They must try to involve both men and women. It might be a good idea to interview potential participants about their previous experience in order to determine whether the race needs both open and amateur divisions. Students may need to go through the racecourse, by either using a wheelchair or going along with someone else who uses a wheelchair, to make sure that the course is safe. If it is not, they will of course need to alter it. Be sure to advertise before the race and recognize participants and winners after the race in local papers and on local radio and television stations.

Questions:

1. What did you learn about people who use wheelchairs?

2. What was the hardest part of this project?

3. What was the easiest part of this project?

4. Did you find the racecourse accessible? Why or why not?

5. Were the race organizers helpful in setting the parameters of the race? How or how not?

6. Were the police helpful? How or how not?

7. Other questions or reactions

Reaction to the project:

_____

_____

_____

BENEFIT WALKATHON
(OWNERSHIP EXPERIENCE FOR HIGH SCHOOL STUDENTS)

Disability
Whatever disability the students want to highlight (e.g., cystic fibrosis, diabetes, cancer, or multiple sclerosis)

Description
Students choose a particular disability and organize a walkathon to benefit persons affected by it. Students must first contact a local chapter of an organization addressing that disability (e.g., the local multiple sclerosis society) and ask whether the organization already stages a walkathon to raise money. If so, the students can help with the existing walk; if not, they can work with the organization to initiate one. The students must decide how far they want to walk (e.g., 5 kilometers [3.1 miles], 10 kilometers [6.2 miles]). Students must then help advertise and promote the walk; they should distribute sponsor sheets and encourage participants to target a certain amount of money to raise. They must also work with community leaders and local police to establish the walk route, and they will need to get local businesses to donate water, juice, food, and prizes (e.g., gift certificates) for participants who raise the most money. They may also get local businesses to donate money. After the walk, students will be responsible for collecting all the money from the participants and donating it to the local chapter of the chosen organization.

Questions:
1. What did you learn about the people for whom you raised money?
2. What was the hardest part of this project?
3. What was the easiest part of this project?
4. Were there any barriers on the course? If so, what were they, and how can you change that?
5. Were the people from the local organization helpful in setting up the walk? How or how not?
6. Were the police helpful? How or how not?
7. Other questions or reactions

Reaction to the project:

_____

_____

_____

FAIR OR FESTIVAL ACCESSIBILITY
(OWNERSHIP EXPERIENCE FOR HIGH SCHOOL STUDENTS)

Disability
Any

Description
Go to the planning committee for a local community fair or festival and ask the following questions:

1. Is the festival area accessible to people who use wheelchairs?
2. Are the restrooms accessible to people who use wheelchairs?
3. If the event includes live music or another type of performance, is the staging area accessible for wheelchairs?
4. Will interpreters be available to help attendees who are deaf for the duration of the fair?
5. If there is a live performance, will interpreters be provided?
6. Will guides be available to assist persons who are blind for the duration of the fair?
7. Is there a number to call to inform the committee that a person with a disability will participate in the fair?
8. Is the committee willing and prepared to make necessary accommodations for individuals with disabilities?
9. How much will they charge people with disabilities for admission?

Questions:
1. Is the fair accessible to people who use wheelchairs?
2. Is the fair accessible to people who are deaf?
3. Is the fair accessible to people who are blind?
4. Was the committee open to students' suggestions and help?
5. If the committee already accommodates people with disabilities, what new information or perspectives did you learn from meeting with them?
6. What suggestions did you make?
7. How can you help this committee in the future?
8. Other questions or reactions

Reaction to the project:

_____

_____

_____

Aquatic Skills Checklist

Cathy Houston-Wilson created an aquatic skills checklist that is hierarchical and based on level of independence. It should be used as a tool in evaluating initial swimming skills and in documenting progress on developing swimming skills. The full, printable checklist is available on the CD-ROM.

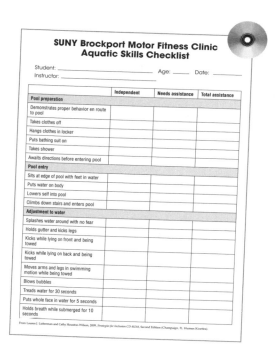

SUNY Brockport Motor Fitness Clinic Aquatic Skills Checklist			
Student: _____ Age: _____ Date: _____ Instructor: _____			
	Independent	Needs assistance	Total assistance
Pool preparation			
Demonstrates proper behavior en route to pool			
Takes clothes off			
Hangs clothes in locker			
Puts bathing suit on			
Takes shower			
Awaits directions before entering pool			
Pool entry			
Sits at edge of pool with feet in water			
Puts water on body			
Lowers self into pool			
Climbs down stairs and enters pool			
Adjustment to water			
Splashes water around with no fear			
Holds gutter and kicks legs			
Kicks while lying on front and being towed			
Kicks while lying on back and being towed			
Moves arms and legs in swimming motion while being towed			
Blows bubbles			
Treads water for 30 seconds			
Puts whole face in water for 5 seconds			
Holds breath while submerged for 10 seconds			

From Lauren J. Lieberman and Cathy Houston-Wilson, 2009, *Strategies for Inclusion CD-ROM, Second Edition* (Champaign, IL: Human Kinetics).

Disability Sport Organizations

These lists provide contact information for organizations working in adapted physical education and disability sport. Each should be used as a resource for gathering adaptation ideas, assisting the child in becoming involved in sport skills, informing parents, assisting coaches who have a child with a disability on their team, and increasing coaches' and physical educators' awareness. The first list arranges items in alphabetical order according to disability, whereas the second list is alphabetized by sport, and the third list (General Resources in Adapted Physical Education and Sport) is arranged in alphabetical order by organization name.

Disability Organizations

Australian Sports Commission
URL: **www.ausport.gov.au**

International Paralympic Committee
Adenauerallee 212-214
53113 Bonn
Germany
+49 228-2097-200
Fax: +49 228-2097-209
E-mail: **info@paralympic.org**
URL: **www.paralympic.org**

International Sports Organization for the Disabled
Idrottens Hus
Storforssplan 44
12387, Farsta
Sweden

U.S. Disabled Athletes Fund
BlazeSports
URL: **www.blazesports.com**

U.S. Les Autres Sports Association
Dave Stephenson, Executive Director
National Office
1475 West Gray Suite 165
Houston, TX 77019-4926
National Program Office
200 Harrison Avenue
Newport, RI 02840
401-848-2460

Asthma

American Lung Association (ALA)
1740 Broadway
New York, NY 10019
212-315-8700
URL: **www.lungusa.org**

Asthma and Allergy Foundation of America (AAFA)
1233 20th St. NW Suite 402
Washington, DC 20036
202-466-7643
800-7-ASTHMA
Fax: 202-466-8940
URL: **www.aafa.org**

Amputation

Amputee Information Network
URL: **www.amp-info.net**

Attention Deficit Disorder

*Children and Adults With Attention-Deficit/
Hyperactivity Disorder (CHADD)*
8181 Professional Place Suite 201
Landover, MD 20785
800-233-4050
301-306-7070
Fax: 301-306-7090
URL: **www.chadd.org**

*National Attention Deficit Disorder Association
(ADDA)*
1788 Second St. Suite 200
Highland Park, IL 60035
847-432-ADDA
Fax: 847-432-5874
URL: **www.add.org**
ADD on About.com
URL: **www.add.about.com**

Autism

Autism Resources
URL: **www.autism-resources.com**

Autism Society of America
7910 Woodmount Avenue Suite 300
Bethesda, MD 20814
800-3-AUTISM
URL: **www.autism-society.org**

Autistic Children's Activity Program
URL: **www.autismwebsite.com/acap**
For more information call 503-978-3989

Doug Flutie, Jr. Foundation for Autism
PO Box 767
233 Cochituate Road
Framingham, MA 01701
866-3AUTISM
508-270-8855
Fax: 508-270-8855
E-mail: **dougiesteam@yahoo.com**
URL: **www.dougflutiejrfoundation.org**

Blindness

American Council of the Blind
URL: **www.acb.org**

American Foundation for the Blind
11 Penn Plaza Suite 300
New York, NY 10001
800-232-5463
Fax: 212-502-7777
URL: **www.afb.org**

*Association for Education and Rehabilitation of the
Blind and Visually Impaired*
PO Box 22397
4600 Duke Street Suite 430
Alexandria, VA 22304
703-823-9690
Fax: 703-823-9695
URL: **www.aerbvi.org**

Blindness Resource Center
URL: **www.nyise.org/blind.htm**

Canadian Blind Sport Association
1600 James Naismith Drive
Gloucester, ON K1B 5N4, Canada
613-748-5609
URL: **www.canadianblindsports.ca**

International Blind Sports Federation
Hybratenveien No. 7C
Oslo 10, Norway
Enrique Sanz Jimenez, IBSA President
C/o Quevedo 1
28014 Madrid, Spain
+34 1-589-4537
URL: **www.ibsa.es**

Skating Association for the Blind and Handicapped
URL: **www.sabahinc.org**

Ski for Light
1455 West Lake Street
Minneapolis, MN 55408
612-827-3232
URL: **www.sfl.org**

United States Association for Blind Athletes
Charlie Huebner, Executive Director
33 North Institute Street
Colorado Springs, CO 80903
719-630-0422
Fax: 719-630-0616
E-mail: **usaba@usa.net**
URL: **www.usaba.org**

Cardiac Conditions

American Heart Association
URL: **www.aha.org**

University of Virginia Health System
URL: **www.healthsystem.virginia.edu/UVAHealth/
adult_cardiac/index.cfm**

Cerebral Palsy

American Academy for Cerebral Palsy and Developmental Medicine
6300 N. River Road Suite 727
Rosemont, IL 60018
847-698-1635
URL: **www.aacpdm.org/**

Brain Injury Association
1776 Massachusetts Avenue NW Suite 100
Washington, DC 20036-0190
202-296-6443

Canadian Cerebral Palsy Sports Association
1010 Ploytek St Unit 2 2nd Floor
Ottawa, ON K1J 9H9 Canada
613-748-1340
URL: **www.ccpsa.ca**

Cerebral Palsy Information Center
URL: **www.cerebralpalsy.com/links.html**

Cerebral Palsy International Sports and Recreation Association (CPISRA)
Miss Elizabeth Dendy, President
9 Kingswood Road
London, W4 5EU
United Kingdom
+44 181-994-4262
Fax: +44 181-994-4262
URL: **www.cpisra.org**
Trudie Rombouts
Secretariat CPISRA
6666 ZG HETEREN
The Netherlands
+31 26-47-22-593
Fax: +31 26-47-23-914

Easter Seals
230 West Monroe Street Suite 1800
Chicago, IL 60606
800-221-6827
URL: **www.easter-seals.org**

National Disability Sports Alliance
25 West Independence Way
Kingston, RI 02881
401-792-7130
401-792-7132
E-mail: **info@ndsaonline.org**
URL: **www.ndsaonline.org**

United Cerebral Palsy
1660 L Street NW Suite 700
Washington, DC 20036
800-872-5827
URL: **www.ucp.org**

Convulsive Disorder

Loyola University Medical Education Network
URL: **www.meddean.luc.edu/lumen/meded/ pedneuro/epilepsy.htm**

Cystic Fibrosis

Cystic Fibrosis Foundation
6931 Arlington Road
Bethesda, MD 20814
800-Fight CF
301-951-4422
Fax: 301-951-6378
E-mail: **info@cff.org**
URL: **www.cff.org**

Deafness and Hearing Impairments

Canadian Deaf Sports Association
4545 ave. Pierre-Du Coubertin
CP 1000 Succ. M
Montreal, Quebec H1V 3R2 Canada
800-855-0511
URL: **www.assc-cdsa.com**

National Association of the Deaf
URL: **www.nad.org**

National Information Center on Deafness
Gallaudet University
800 Florida Avenue NE
Washington, DC 20002-3625
202-651-5000

USA Deaf Sports Federation (USADSF)
102 North Krohn Place
Sioux Falls, SD 57103-1800
TTY: 605-367-5761
Voice: 605-367-5760
Fax: 605-782-8441
E-mail: **HomeOffice@usdeafsports.org**
URL: **www.usdeafsports.org**

Deafblindness

Helen Keller National Center for Deaf-Blind Youths and Adults
111 Middle Neck Road
Sands Point, NY 11050
516-944-8900
TTY: 516-944-8637
URL: **www.helenkeller.org/national**

National Consortium on Deaf-Blindness
URL: **http://nationaldb.org**

National Institute on Deafness and Other Communication Disorders
URL: **www.nidcd.nih.gov**

Diabetes

American Diabetes Association
1701 North Beauregard St.
Alexandria, VA 22311
800-DIABETES
800-342-2383
URL: **www.diabetes.org**

Children With Diabetes
URL: **www.childrenwithdiabetes.com**

Down Syndrome

National Association for Down Syndrome
PO Box 4542
Oak Brook, IL 60522
630-325-9112
URL: **www.nads.org**

National Down Syndrome Society
666 Broadway
New York, NY 10012
800-221-4602
212-460-9330 (local NY)
Fax: 212-979-2873
URL: **www.ndss.org**

Dwarfism

Dwarf Athletic Association of America
URL: **www.daaa.org**

Little People of America
National Headquarters
Box 745
Lubbock, TX 79408
1-888-LPA-2001
E-mail: **LPADataBase@juno.com**
URL: **www.lpaonline.org**

Juvenile Rheumatoid Arthritis

Arthritis Insight
URL: **jraworld.arthritisinsight.com**

Learning Disabilities

Council for Exceptional Children
1110 North Glebe Road Suite 300
Arlington, VA 22201
703-620-3660
TTY: 703-264-9446
URL: **www.cec.sped.org**

Council for Learning Disabilities
PO Box 40303
Overland Park, KS 66204
913-492-8755
URL: **www.cldinternational.org**

Learning Disabilities Association of America
4156 Library Road
Pittsburgh, PA 15234-1349
412-341-1515
Fax: 412-344-0224
URL: **www.ldanatl.org**

National Center for Learning Disabilities (NCLD)
381 Park Ave. South Suite 1401
New York, NY 10016
212-545-7510
Fax: 212-545-9665
Toll free: 888-575-7373
URL: **www.ncld.org**

Multiple Sclerosis

National Multiple Sclerosis Society
URL: **www.nationalmssociety.org**

Muscular Dystrophy/ Neuromuscular Diseases

Muscular Dystrophy Association–USA
National Headquarters
3300 East Sunrise Drive
Tucson, AZ 85718
800-572-1717
URL: **www.mdausa.org**

Intellectual Disability

American Association on Intellectual and Developmental Disabilities
444 North Capitol St. NW Suite 846
Washington, DC 20001-1512
800-424-3688
202-387-1968
Fax: 202-387-2193
URL: **www.aaidd.org**

Eunice Kennedy Shriver Center
200 Trapelo Road
Waltham, MA 02452-6319
781-642-0001
TTY: 800-764-0200
URL: **www.shriver.org**

International Sports Federation for Persons With Mental Handicap (INAS-FMH)
Bernard Atha, Executive Director
13-27 Brunswick Place
London N1 6DX
United Kingdom
+44 171-250-1100
Fax: +44 171-250-0110

Special Olympics International
Eunice Kennedy Shriver, Founder-Director
Timothy Shriver, CEO
Dr. Tom Songster, VP for Sports Policy and Research
1325 G Street, NW Suite 500
Washington, DC 20005-3104
202-628-3630
URL: **www.specialolympics.org**

Obesity

The Obesity Society
8630 Fenton Street, Suite 814
Silver Spring, MD 20910
301-563-6526
Fax: 301-563-9595
URL: **www.naaso.org**

Osteogenesis Imperfecta

Osteogenesis Imperfecta Foundation
URL: **www.oif.org**

Scoliosis

Scoliosis World
URL: **www.scoliosis-world.com**

Spina Bifida

Association for Spina Bifida and Hydrocephalus
URL: **www.asbah.org**

Spina Bifida Association
4590 MacArthur Blvd. NW Suite 250
Washington, DC 20007-4226
800-621-3141
202-944-3285
Fax: 202-944-3295
URL: **www.sbaa.org**

Canadian Wheelchair Sports Association
2460 Lancaster Road Suite 200
Ottawa, ON K1B 4S5 Canada
613-523-0004
Fax: 613-523-0149
E-mail: info@cwsa.ca
URL: **www.cwsa.ca**

International Stoke Mandeville Wheelchair Sports Federation
Stoke Mandeville Sports Stadium
Olympic Village, Guttman Road
Aylesbury, Bucks HP 21 9PP
United Kingdom
+44 (0)-01296-436179
Fax: +44 (0)-01296-436484

Wheelchair Sports, USA
3595 E. Fountain Blvd. Suite L-1
Colorado Springs, CO 80910
719-574-1150
Fax: 719-574-9840
URL: **www.wsusa.org**

Spinal Cord Injuries

National Spinal Cord Injury Association
One Church Street, Suite 600
Rockville, MD 20850
301-588-6959
Fax: 301-588-9414
URL: **www.spinalcord.org**

Spinal Cord Injury Information Network
URL: **www.spinalcord.uab.edu**

Stroke

National Stroke Association
URL: **www.stroke.org**

Traumatic Brain Injury

Brain Injury Association of America
URL: **www.biausa.org**

Brain Injury Society
427 Coney Island Ave.
Brooklyn, NY 11218
718-645-4401
URL: **www.bisociety.org**

Sport Organizations

Aerobics

Disabled Sports USA
Kirk Bauer, Executive Director
451 Hungerford Drive Suite 100
Rockville, MD 20850
301-217-0960
Fax: 301-217-0968
E-mail: dsusa@dsusa.org
URL: **www.dsusa.org**

Air Guns

NRA Disabled Shooting Services
11250 Waples Mill Road
Fairfax, VA 22030
703-267-1495

Archery

Wheelchair Archery, USA
c/o Wheelchair Sports, USA
3595 E. Fountain Blvd. Suite L-1
Colorado Springs, CO 80910
719-574-1150
Fax: 719-574-9840
URL: **www.wsusa.org**

Basketball

National Wheelchair Basketball Association
Charlotte Institute of Rehabilitation
1100 Blythe Blvd.
Charlotte, NC 28203
704-355-1064
URL: **www.nwba.org**

Billiards

National Wheelchair Poolplayer Association
9757 Mount Lompoc Ct.
Las Vegas, NV 89178
URL: **nwpainc.org**

Boating

United States Rowing Association
201 South Capitol Ave. Suite 400
Indianapolis, IN 46225
800-314-4ROW
317-237-5656
Fax: 317-237-5646
E-mail: **members@usrowing.org**
URL: **www.usrowing.org**

Bowling

American Wheelchair Bowling Association
2912 Country Woods Lane
Palm Harbor, FL 34683-6417
Phone/Fax: 727-734-0023
URL: **www.awba.org**

Camping

Office of Special Programs and Populations
National Park Service
U.S. Department of the Interior
800 N. Capitol NW
Washington, DC 20002
202-673-7647

Canoeing

American Canoe Association
Kayaking/Disabled Paddlers Committee
7432 Alban Station Blvd. Suite B-232
Springfield, VA 22150-2311
703-451-0141
Fax: 703-451-2245
URL: **www.acanet.org**

Fencing

United States Fencing Association
1 Olympic Plaza
Colorado Springs, CO 80909
719-578-4511
URL: **www.usfencing.org**

Flying

Challenge Air for Kids and Friends
Love Field, North Concourse
8008 Cedar Springs Road N106-LB24
Dallas, TX 75235
214-351-3353
URL: **www.challengeair.com**

Freedom's Wings International
1832 Lake Avenue
Scotch Plains, NJ 07076
908-232-6354
URL: **www.freedomswings.org**

International Wheelchair Aviators
Big Bear Airport
PO Box 1126
500 W Meadow Lane
Big Bear City, CA 92315
909-585-9663
URL: **www.wheelchairaviators.org**

Football

Parks and Recreation Department
Adapted Recreation Programs
Cabrillo Bathhouse
1118 E Cabrillo Boulevard
Santa Barbara, CA 93103
805-564-5421

Golf

Association of Disabled American Golfers
PO Box 280649
Lakewood, CO 80228-0649
303-922-5228
303-969-0447

National Amputee Golf Association
11 Walnut Hill Road
Amherst, NH 03031-1713
800-633-6242
Fax: 603-672-2987
URL: **www.nagagolf.org**

Hockey

American Sled Hockey Association
Rich DeGlopper
21 Summerwood Court
Buffalo, NY 14223
716-876-7390

Horseback Riding

North American Riding for the Handicapped Association
PO Box 33150
Denver, CO 80233
800-369-7433
Fax: 303-252-4610
URL: **www.narha.org**

Hunting

NRA Disabled Shooting Services
11250 Waples Mill Road
Fairfax, VA 22030
703-267-1495

Motorcycling

Wheelchair Motorcycle Association
101 Torrey Street
Brockton, MA 02301
508-583-8614

Racquetball

U.S. Racquetball Association
1685 West Uintah
Colorado Springs, CO 80904
719-635-5396
URL: **www.usra.org**

Road Racing

U.S. Handcycling Federation
Ian Lawless
115 Du Four St.
Santa Cruz, CA 95060
831-457-7747
E-mail: **info@ushf.org**
URL: **www.ushf.org**

Rowing

United States Rowing Association
201 South Capitol Ave. Suite 400
Indianapolis, IN 46225
800-314-4ROW
317-237-5656
Fax: 317-237-5646
E-mail: **members@usrowing.org**
URL: **www.usrowing.org**

Rugby

United States Quad Rugby Association
Jim Bishop
5861 White Cypress Drive
Lake Worth, FL 33467-6230
561-964-1712
Fax: 561-642-4444
E-mail: **jbishop@quadrugby.com**
URL: **www.quadrugby.com**

Sailing

Access to Sailing
6475 East Pacific Coast Hwy.
Long Beach, CA 90802
562-499-6925
Fax: 562-437-7655
URL: **www.accesstosailing.org**

National Ocean Access Project
451 Hungerford Dr. Suite 100
Rockville, MD 20850
301-217-0960

Scuba Diving

Handicapped Scuba Association
1104 El Prado
San Clemente, CA 92672
949-498-4540
Fax: 949-498-6128
E-mail: **hsa@hsascuba.com**
URL: **www.hsascuba.com**

Shooting

Amateur Trapshooting Association
601 W. National Road
Vandalia, OH 45372
937-898-4638
Fax: 937-898-5472
URL: **www.shootata.com**

NRA Disabled Shooting Services
11250 Waples Mill Road
Fairfax, VA 22030
703-267-1495

National Skeet Shooting Association
5931 Roft Road
San Antonio, TX 78253
210-688-3371
Fax: 210-688-3014
URL: **www.mynssa.com**

Snow Skiing

Disabled Sports USA
Kirk Bauer, Executive Director
451 Hungerford Drive Suite 100
Rockville, MD 20850
301-217-0960
Fax: 301-217-0968
E-mail: **dsusa@dsusa.org**
URL: **www.dsusa.org**

U.S. Disabled Ski Team
PO Box 100
Park City, UT 84060
801-649-9090

Softball/Baseball

Challenger Baseball
Little League Headquarters
PO Box 3485
Williamsport, PA 17701

National Beep Baseball Association
c/o Jeanette Bigger
231 West 1st St.
Topeka, KS 66606-1304
913-234-2156
URL: **www.nbba.org**

National Wheelchair Softball Association
1616 Todd Court
Hastings, MN 55033
612-437-1792
URL: **www.wheelchairsoftball.org**

Swimming

Aquatics Council (Adapted Aquatics)
Dr. Monica Lepore, Chairperson
West Chester University
Department of Kinesiology
West Chester, PA 19382
610-436-2516

Council for National Cooperation in Aquatics
c/o Louise Priest
901 W. New York Street
Indianapolis, IN 46202
317-638-4238

U.S. Wheelchair Swimming, Inc.
Liz DeFrancesco
105 Jenne St.
Santa Cruz, CA 95060
E-mail: **bizde@got.net**

Table Tennis

American Wheelchair Table Tennis Association
Jennifer Johnson
23 Parker St.
Port Chester, NY 10573
914-937-3932
E-mail: **johnsonjennifer@yahoo.com**
URL: **www.awtta.org**

Tennis

National Foundation of Wheelchair Tennis
940 Calle Amanecer Suite B
San Clemente, CA 92672
714-361-3663

United States Tennis Association
URL: **http://www.usta.com/PlayNow/Wheelchair.aspx**

Track and Field

Wheelchair Athletics of the USA/WSUSA
3595 E. Fountain Blvd. Suite L-1
Colorado Springs, CO 80910
719-574-1150
Fax: 719-574-9840
URL: **www.wsusa.org**

Water Skiing

USA Water Ski
1251 Holy Cow Road
Polk City, FL 33868
800-533-2972
Fax: 863-325-8259
URL: **usawaterski.org**

Weightlifting

U.S. Wheelchair Weightlifting Federation (WSUSA)
39 Michael Place
Levittown, PA 19057
215-945-1964
URL: **www.wsusa.org**

Wilderness

Breckenridge Outdoor Education Center
PO Box 697
Breckenridge, CO 80424
970-453-6422
Fax: 970-453-4676
URL: **www.boec.org**

*Cooperative Wilderness Handicapped
Outdoor Group*
PO Box 8128
Idaho State University
Pocatello, ID 83209
208-236-3912
URL: **www.isu.edu/departments/cwhog/index.html**

Outward Bound Wilderness
101 Chapman Street
Ely, MN 55731
218-365-7790
URL: **www.outwardboundwilderness.org**

Pacific Crest Outward Bound School
0110 SW Bancroft
Portland, OR 97201
800-547-3312
URL: **www.outward-bound.org/docs/info/ob-west.htm**

Wilderness Inquiry
808 14th Avenue SE Box 84
Minneapolis, MN 55414-1516
800-728-0719
612-676-9400
URL: **www.wildernessinquiry.org**

Wilderness on Wheels
3131 S Vaughn Way Suite 224
Aurora, CO 80014
303-751-3959
URL: **www.wildernessonwheels.org**

General Resources in Adapted Physical Education and Sport

USOC Committee on Sports for Disabled
Mark Shepherd, COSD Chair
United States Olympic Committee
1750 East Boulder Street
Colorado Springs, CO 80909-5760
719-578-4818

Disabled Sports USA
Kirk Bauer, Executive Director
451 Hungerford Drive Suite 100
Rockville, MD 20850
301-217-0960
Fax: 301-217-0968
E-mail: **dsusa@dsusa.org**
URL: **www.dsusa.org**

National Sports Center for the Disabled
PO Box 1290
Winter Park, CO 80482
970-726-1540
303-316-1540
Fax: 970-726-4112
URL: **www.nscd.org**

National Sports Network
A Sports Program for People With Disabilities
PO Box 47799
St. Petersburg, FL 33743-7799
800-699-4494
Fax: 727-345-7130

*Palaestra: Forum of Sport, Physical Education, and
Recreation for Those With Disabilities (Magazine)*
PO Box 508
Macomb, IL 61455
309-833-1902
E-mail: **challpub@macomb.com**
URL: **www.palaestra.com**

Sports 'N Spokes (Magazine)
PVA Publications
2111 East Highland Street Suite 180
Phoenix, AZ 85016-4780
URL: **www.sportsnspokes.com**

U.S. Organization for Disabled Athletes (USODA)
143 California Avenue
Uniondale, NY 11553
800-25-USODA
516-485-3701

Equipment Companies

This list includes the names of equipment companies, what they make, the number to call to order a catalog or ask questions, and, if available, the Web site address. This information is intended both to help general physical education teachers and to inform parents about equipment availability.

Access to Recreation: Adaptive recreation equipment for people with physical challenges.
800-634-4351 to order catalog
Fax: 805-498-8186 fax
URL: **www.accesstr.com**

American Printing House for the Blind: Product and equipment for children with visual impairments.
URL: **www.aph.org**

Community Playthings: Safe and adapted playground equipment for young children.
800-777-4244 for customer service
Fax: 800-336-5948 (U.S. only)
URL: **www.communityplaythings.com**

Project Adventure Equipment Catalog: A sourcebook for ropes courses and adventure programs.
800-468-8898
URL: **www.pa.org/store**

RehabTool: High-tech assistive, adaptive, and accessibility aids for children and adults with disabilities and special needs.
281-531-6106
Fax: 281-531-6406
E-mail: info@rehabtool.com
URL: **www.rehabtool.com**

S&S Worldwide Games: Sports equipment for every occasion.
800-288-9941 to order catalog
Fax: 800-566-6678
URL: **www.snswwide.com**

Sportime/Abilitations: Sports, recreation, and game equipment with a variety of textures, shapes, and colors, for all individuals, including those with sensory impairments and physical disabilities.
800-850-8602 to order catalog
Fax: 800-845-1535
E-mail: **catalog.request@sportime.com**
URL: **www.sportime.com**
URL: **www.abilitations.com**

Toledo Physical Education Supply: Physical education supply company with inexpensive sports and playground equipment.
800-225-7749 to order catalog
Fax: 800-489-6256
URL: **www.tpesonline.com**

Vital Signs: Instrumentation for rehabilitation, sports medicine, and physical fitness.
608-735-4718 to order catalog
Fax: 608-735-4859
URL: **www2.vital-signs.com**

Wolverine Sports: Sports, gymnastics, and coaching equipment.
800-521-2832 to order catalog
Fax: 800-654-4321
URL: **www.wolverinesports.com**

Additional Resources

Here are a few suggested resources, in addition to the references used in each chapter, to assist the general physical educator with adapted physical education.

Books

American Alliance for Health, Physical Education, Recreation and Dance. (1989). *The best of practical pointers*. Reston, VA: Author.

American Alliance for Health, Physical Education, Recreation and Dance. (1991). *Sports instruction for individuals with disabilities: The best of practical pointers*. Reston, VA: Author.

DePauw, K.P., and Gavron, S.J. (2005). *Disability and sport* (2nd ed.). Champaign, IL: Human Kinetics.

Dunn, J., and Leitschuh, C.A. (2005). *Special physical education: Adapted, individualized, developmental* (8th ed.). Dubuque, IA: Kendall/Hunt.

Friend, M. (2005). *Special education: Contemporary perspectives for school professionals*. Boston: Allyn & Bacon.

Grosse, S.J., and Thompson, D. (1993). *Play and recreation for individuals with disabilities: Practical pointers*. Reston, VA: American Alliance for Health, Physical Education, Recreation and Dance.

Hodge, S., Murata, N., Block, M., & Lieberman, L.J. (2003). Case studies in adapted physical education. Scottsdale, AZ: Holcomb Hathaway.

Horvat, M.A., Block, M.E., & Kelly, L. (2007). *Assessment in adapted physical education*. Champaign, IL: Human Kinetics.

Houston-Wilson, C. (1995). Alternate assessment procedures. In J. Seaman (Ed.), *Physical Best and individuals with disabilities* (pp. 92–97). Reston, VA: AAHPERD.

Kasser, S.L. (1995). *Inclusive games*. Champaign, IL: Human Kinetics.

Kasser, S.L., & Lytle, R.K. (2005). *Inclusive physical activity*. Champaign, IL: Human Kinetics.

Kaufman, K. (2006). *Inclusive creative movement and dance*. Champaign, IL: Human Kinetics.

Lavay, B.W., French, R., & Henderson, H.L. (2006). *Positive behavior management in physical activity settings*. Champaign, IL: Human Kinetics.

Lieberman, L.J. (Ed.) (2007). *Paraeducators in physical education*. Champaign, IL: Human Kinetics.

Lieberman, L.J., and Cowart, J.F. (1996). *Games for people with sensory impairments*. Champaign, IL: Human Kinetics.

Lieberman, L.J., Modell, S., & Jackson, I. (2006). *Going PLACES: A transition guide to physical activity for youth with visual impairments*. Louisville: American Printing House for the Blind.

McCall, R.M., & Craft, D.H. (2000). *Moving with a purpose: Developing programs for preschoolers of all abilities*. Champaign, IL: Human Kinetics.

McCall, R.M., & Craft, D.H. (2004). *Purposeful play*. Champaign, IL: Human Kinetics.

Sherrill, C. (2004). *Adapted physical activity, recreation, and sport: Crossdisciplinary and lifespan* (6th ed.). Boston: WCB/McGraw-Hill.

Special Olympics International. (1989). *Sports Skills Program*. Washington, DC: Author.

Tripp, A., & Zhu, W. (2005). Assessment of students with disabilities in physical education: Legal perspectives and practices. *Journal of Physical Education, Recreation & Dance, 76(2)*, 41–47.

Winnick, J. (2000). *Adapted physical education and sport*. Champaign, IL: Human Kinetics.

Adapted Physical Education Web Sites

Adapted Physical Education National Standards (APENS): Web site for information about the national certification exam for adapted physical education.

www.pecentral.org/adapted/adaptedapens.html

Adapt-Talk: Discussion group addressing adapted physical education; supported by Sportime.

www.sportimeresources.com/forum/forumdisplay.php?f=3

Camp Abilities: Developmental sports camp for children who are blind.

www.campabilities.org

Disability Sports: Web site providing information about adapted physical education, adapted sport, and adapted technology; supported by Michigan State University.

http://edweb6.educ.msu.edu/kin866

Handspeak: Sign language taught in a simple and understandable way; includes sports signs.

www.handspeak.com

National Center on Physical Activity and Disability: Provides tremendous amount of information on physical activity programming for individuals with disabilities.

www.ncpad.org

National Consortium for Physical Education and Recreation for Individuals With Disabilities: Advocacy group promoting adapted physical education and recreation.

www.ncperid.org

Project INSPIRE: Information about inclusion, disabilities, and adapted physical education; supported by Texas Woman's University.

www.twu.edu/INSPIRE

Publications

Active Living: The cross-disability "how-to, where-to, and what-to" magazine for people who want to attain or maintain a healthy, active lifestyle.

www.activelivingmagazine.com

Adapted Physical Activity Quarterly: Official journal of the International Federation of Adapted Physical Activity; the latest scholarly inquiry related to physical activity for special populations.

www.humankinetics.com/APAQ/journalAbout.cfm

Palaestra: Described by its publishers as a "forum of sport, physical education, and recreation for those with disabilities."

www.palaestra.com

Sports 'N Spokes: Covers the latest in competitive wheelchair sports and recreational opportunities.

www.sportsnspokes.com/sns

Directors of Special Education for U.S. States and Territories

The first part of this list is arranged alphabetically by state, the second part by territory.

Alabama

Special Education Services
State Department of Education
PO Box 302101
Montgomery, AL 36130-2101
334-242-8114
TTY: 334-242-8406
Fax: 334-242-9192
URL: **www.alsde.cdu/html/sections/section_detail.asp?section=65&footer=sections**
E-mail: **speced@alsde.edu**

Alaska

Teaching and Learning Support
Alaska Department of Education and Early Development
801 West 10th Street Suite 200
Juneau, AK 99801-1894
907-465-2800 (general information)
TTY/TTD: 907-465-2815
Fax: 907-465-4156
URL: **www.eed.state.ak.us/tls/support/support_chart.html**

Arizona

Exceptional Student Services
Department of Education
1535 West Jefferson Street Bin 24
Phoenix, AZ 85007
602-542-3184
800-352-4558
TTY: 602-542-1410
Fax: 602-542-5404
URL: **www.ade.state.az.us/ess**
E-mail: **jgasawa@ade.az.gov**

Arkansas

Special Education
Department of Education Building
Room 105-C
4 State Capitol Mall
Little Rock, AR 72201-1071
501-682-4221
Fax: 501-682-5159
URL: **http://arkansased.org/**
E-mail: **dsydoriak@arkedu.k12.ar.us**

California

Special Education Division
State Department of Education
515 L Street Suite 270
Sacramento, CA 95814
916-445-4602
Fax: 916-327-3706
URL: **www.cde.ca.gov/sp/se**
E-mail: **aparker@cde.ca.gov**

Colorado

Special Education Services
Department of Education
201 East Colfax Avenue
Denver, CO 80203
303-866-6694
TTY: 303-860-7060
Fax: 303-866-6811
URL: **www.cde.state.co.us/index_special.htm**
E-mail: **sped@cde.state.co.us**

Connecticut

Bureau of Special Education and Pupil Services
State Department of Education
25 Industrial Park Road
Middletown, CT 06457
860-807-2025
Fax: 860-807-2047
URL: **www.state.ct.us/sde**
E-mail: **george.dowaliby@po.state.ct.us**

Delaware

Exceptional Children & Early Childhood Education
Delaware Department of Education
401 Federal Street, Suite 2
Dover, DE 19901
302-735-4210
Fax: 302-739-2388
URL: **www.doe.state.de.us**
E-mail: **mtoomey@doe.k12.de.us**

District of Columbia

Office of Special Education
825 North Capitol Street NE 6th Floor
Washington, DC 20002
202-442-4800
Fax: 202-442-5517
URL: **www.k12.dc.us**
E-mail: **specialeducation@k12.dc.us**

Florida

Clearinghouse Information Center
Department of Education
Bureau of Instructional Support and Community Services
325 West Gaines Street
Tallahassee, FL 32399-0400
850-488-1879
Fax: 850-487-2679
URL: **www.fldoe.org/ese**
E-mail: **CICBISCS@mail.doe.state.fl.us**

Georgia

Division for Exceptional Students
Department of Education
1870 Twin Towers East
205 Jesse Hill Jr. Drive SE
Atlanta, GA 30334
404-656-3963
Fax: 404-651-6457
URL: **www.doe.k12.ga.us/ci_exceptional.aspx**
E-mail: **pbragg@doe.k12.ga.us**

Hawaii

State Department of Education
Special Education Services Branch
637 18th Avenue, Bldg. C, Rm. 201
Honolulu, HI 96816
808-733-4400
Fax: 808-733-4841
URL: **http://doe.k12.hi.us/specialeducation/**

Idaho

Special Education Department
Department of Education
PO Box 83720
Boise, ID 83720-0027
208-332-6910
800-432-4601
TTY: 800-377-3524
Fax: 208-334-4664
URL: **www.sde.idaho.gov/SpecialEducation/default.asp**
E-mail: **rbrychen@sde.state.id.us**

Illinois

Office of Special Education
Illinois State Board of Education
Mail Code E-228
100 North First Street
Springfield, IL 62777-0001
217-782-4826
866-262-6663
TTY: 217-782-1900
Fax: 217-782-0372
URL: **www.isbe.state.il.us/spec-ed**
E-mail: **griffel@isbe.net** or **jshook@smtp.isbe.state.il.us**

Indiana

Division of Special Education
Department of Education
State House, Room 229
Indianapolis, IN 46204-2798
317-232-0570
877-851-4106
TTY: 317-232-0570
Fax: 317-232-0589
URL: **www1.indstate.edu/coe/iseas**
E-mail: **marrab@speced.doe.state.in.us**

Iowa

State Department of Education: Special Education
Student and Family Support Services
Department of Education
Grimes State Office Building
Des Moines, IA 50319-0146
515-281-5735
URL: **www.state.ia.us/educate**
E-mail: **Lana.Michelson@iowa.gov**

Kansas

Student Support Services
Kansas State Department of Education
120 SE 10th Avenue
Topeka, KS 66612-1182
785-296-3869
Fax: 785-296-1413
TTY: 785-296-6338
URL: **www.kansped.org**
E-mail: **criley@ksde.org**

Kentucky

Division of Exceptional Children Services
State Department of Education
500 Mero Street Eighth Floor
Frankfort, KY 40601
502-564-4970
TTY: 502-564-4770
Fax: 502-564-6721
URL: **www.kde.state.ky.us**
E-mail: **marmstro@kde.state.ky.us**

Louisiana

Division of Special Populations
PO Box 94064
Baton Rouge, LA 70804-9064
225-342-3633
TTY: 225-219-4588
Fax: 225-342-5880
URL: **www.doe.state.la.us**
E-mail: **vberidon@mail.doe.state.la.us**

Maine

Office of Special Services
State Department of Education
23 State House Station
Augusta, ME 04333-0023
207-624-6650
TTY: 207-624-6800
Fax: 207-624-6651
URL: **www.maine.gov/education/speced**
E-mail: **dstockford@doe.k12.me.us**

Maryland

Division of Special Education/Early Intervention
Services
Department of Education
200 West Baltimore Street Fourth Floor
Baltimore, MD 21201
410-767-0238
TTY: 800-735-2258
Fax: 410-333-8165
URL: **www.msde.state.md.us**
E-mail: **cbaglin@msde.state.md.us** or **nFeather@
msde.state.md.us**

Massachusetts

Massachusetts Director of Special Education
State Department of Education
350 Main Street
Malden, MA 02148-5023
781-388-3388
Fax: 781-388-3396
URL: **www.doe.mass.edu/sped**
E-mail: **MMittnacht@doe.mass.edu**

Michigan

Office of Special Education and Early Intervention
Services
Department of Education
608 West Allegan
Lansing, MI 48933
517-373-0923
TTY: 517-373-9434
Fax: 517-373-7504
URL: **www.michigan.gov/mde/0,1607,7-140-6530_
6598---,00.html**
E-mail: **RowellF@state.mi.us**

Minnesota

Division of Special Education
Department of Children, Families, and Learning
1500 Highway 36 West
Roseville, MN 55113-4266
651-582-8289
Fax: 651-582-8729
URL: **http://children.state.mn.us**
E-mail: **norena.hale@state.mn.us**

Mississippi

Office of Special Education
Mississippi Department of Education
PO Box 771
359 North West Street Suite 338
Jackson, MS 39205-0771
601-359-3498
Fax: 601-359-2198
URL: **www.mde.k12.ms.us**
E-mail: **thoover@mde.k12.state.ms.us** or **dennis@
mde.k12.ms.us**

Missouri

Division of Special Education
Department of Elementary and Secondary Education
PO Box 480
Jefferson City, MO 65102
573-751-5739
Fax: 573-526-4404
URL: **http://dese.mo.gov/divspeced/**
E-mail: **mfriedeb@mail.dese.state.mo.us**

Montana

Division of Special Education
Office of Public Instruction
PO Box 202501
Helena, MT 59620-2501
406-444-4429
Fax: 406-444-3924
URL: **www.opi.state.mt.us/SpecEd**
E-mail: **tharris@mt.gov**

Nebraska

Special Populations Office
Department of Education
301 Centennial Mall South
PO Box 94987
Lincoln, NE 68509-4987
402-471-2471
888-806-6287 (NE Residents only)
TTY: 402-471-2471
Fax: 402-471-5022
URL: **www.nde.state.ne.us/SPED/sped.html**

Nevada

Educational Equity Team
State Department of Education
700 East Fifth Street Suite 113
Carson City, NV 89701
775-687-9171
TTY: 800-326-6888
Fax: 775-687-9123
URL: **www.doe.nv.gov**

New Hampshire

Special Education Services
Department of Education
101 Pleasant Street
Concord, NH 03301-3860
603-271-3741
TTY: 800-735-2964
Fax: 603-271-1953
URL: **www.ed.state.nh.us/EDUCATION/doe/
organization/Instruction/bose.htm**

New Jersey

Office of Special Education Programs
Department of Education
PO Box 500
Trenton, NJ 08625-0500
609-633-6833
TTY: 609-984-8432
Fax: 609-984-8422
URL: **www.state.nj.us/education**
E-mail: **bgantwer@doe.state.nj.us**

New Mexico

New Mexico State Department of Special Education
300 Don Gaspar Avenue
Santa Fe, NM 87501
505-827-1457
Fax: 505-827-6791
URL: **www.ped.state.nm.us/seo/index.htm**
E-mail: **acurtis@ped.state.nm.us**

New York

Office of Vocational and Educational Services for Individuals with Disabilities
One Commerce Plaza, Room 1624
Albany, NY 12234
518-486-7584
800-222-5627
TTY: 518-474-5652
Fax: 518-473-5387
URL: **www.vesid.nysed.gov**
E-mail: **vesidspe@mail.nysed.gov**

North Carolina

Exceptional Children Division
North Carolina Department of Public Instruction
301 North Wilmington Street
Raleigh, NC 27601-2825
919-807-3969
Fax: 919-807-3243
URL: **www.ncpublicschools.org/ec**
E-mail: **lharris@dpi.state.nc.us**

North Dakota

Office of Special Education
Department of Public Instruction
600 East Boulevard Avenue 10th Floor
Bismarck, ND 58505-0440
701-328-2277
TTY: 701-328-4920
Fax: 701-328-4149
URL: **www.dpi.state.nd.us/speced**
E-mail: **landerso@mail.dpi.state.nd.us**

Ohio

Office for Exceptional Children
State Department of Education
25 South Front Street Second Floor
Columbus, OH 43215
614-466-2650
Fax: 614-728-1097
URL: **www.ode.state.oh.us/GD/Templates/Pages/
ODE/ODEPrimary.aspx?page=2&TopicRelationID
=967**
E-mail: **john.herner@ode.state.oh.us/exceptional_
children**

Oklahoma

Special Education Services
State Department of Education
2500 North Lincoln Boulevard Room 411
Oklahoma City, OK 73105-4599
405-521-3351
TTY: 405-521-4875
Fax: 405-522-3503
URL: **http://sde.state.ok.us**
E-mail: **darla_griffin@mail.sde.state.ok.us** or
john_corpolongo@mail.sde.state.ok.us

Oregon

Office of Special Education
Department of Education
255 Capitol Street NE
Salem, OR 97310-0203
503-378-3600
TTY: 503-378-2892
Fax: 503-378-7968
URL: **www.ode.state.or.us/search/results/?id=40**
E-mail: **Robbi.Perry@state.or.us**

Pennsylvania

Bureau of Special Education
Pennsylvania Department of Education
333 Market Street Seventh Floor
Harrisburg, PA 17126-0333
717-783-6913
TTY: 717-787-7367
Fax: 717-783-6139
URL: **www.pde.psu.edu**
E-mail: **fwarkomski@state.pa.us**

Rhode Island

Office of Special Populations
State Department of Education
Shepard Building Fourth Floor
255 Westminster Street
Providence, RI 02903
401-222-3505
Fax: 401-222-6030
URL: **www.ride.ri.gov/Special_populations/default.
aspx**
E-mail: **phyllis.pezzullo@ride.ri.gov**

South Carolina

Office of Exceptional Children
Department of Education
Rutledge Building 1429 Senate Room 808
Columbia, SC 29201
803-734-8806
Fax: 803-734-4824
URL: **http://ed.sc.gov/agency/Standards-and-
Learning/Exceptional-Children/**
E-mail: **Sdurant@ed.sc.gov**

South Dakota

Office of Educational Services & Support
700 Governors Drive
Pierre, SD 57501-2291
605-773-3678
TTY: 605-773-6302
Fax: 605-773-3782
URL: **http://doe.sd.gov/oess/specialed/index.asp**
E-mail: **michelle.powers@state.sd.us**

Tennessee

Division of Special Education
Department of Education
Fifth Floor Andrew Johnson Tower
710 James Robertson Parkway
Nashville, TN 37243-0380
615-741-2851
TTY: 615-741-2237
Fax: 615-532-9412
URL: **www.tennessee.gov/education/speced/**
E-mail: **jfisher@mail.state.tn.us**

Texas

Division of Special Education
Texas Education Agency
1701 North Congress Avenue
Austin, TX 78701
512-463-9414
800-252-9668
TTY: 512-475-3540
Fax: 512-463-9560
URL: **www.tea.state.tx.us/special.ed**
E-mail: **sped@tea.tetn.net**

Utah

Services for At-Risk Students
Utah State Office of Education
250 East 500 South
Salt Lake City, UT 84111-3204
801-538-7587
Fax: 801-538-7991
URL: **www.usoe.k12.ut.us/sars**
E-mail: **mtaylor@usoe.k12.ut.us**

Vermont

Family and Educational Support Team
State Office Building
120 State Street
Montpelier, VT 05620-2501
802-828-5118
Fax: 802-828-3140
URL: http://education.vermont.gov/new/html/pgm_sped.html
E-mail: mmartin@doe.state.vt.us or dkane@doe.state.vt.us

Virginia

Office of Special Education
Department of Education
PO Box 2120
Richmond, VA 23218-2120
804-225-2402
800-292-3920
TTY: 800-422-1098
Fax: 804-371-8796
URL: www.doe.virginia.gov/VDOE/sess
E-mail: dougcox@mail.va.k12.edu

Washington

Special Education Section
Old Capitol Building
PO Box 47200
Olympia, WA 98504
360-725-6075
TTY: 360-586-0126
Fax: 360-586-0247
URL: www.k12.wa.us/specialed
E-mail: speced@ospi.webnet.edu

West Virginia

Office of Special Education
Department of Education
Building 6 Room 304
1900 Kanawha Boulevard East
Charleston, WV 25305
304-558-2696
800-642-8541 (WV residents only)
TTY: 800-642-8541
Fax: 304-558-3741
URL: http://wvde.state.wv.us
E-mail: dbodkins@access.k12.wv.us/ose

Wisconsin

Division for Learning Support: Equity and Advocacy
Department of Public Instruction
125 South Webster Street
PO Box 7841
Madison, WI 53707-7841
608-266-1649
800-441-4563
TTY: 608-267-2427
Fax: 608-267-3746
URL: www.dpi.state.wi.us/dpi/dlsea/index.html
E-mail: michael.thompson@dpi.state.wi.us

Wyoming

Special Education Unit
State Department of Education
Second Floor Hathaway Building
2300 Capitol Avenue
Cheyenne, WY 82002-0050
307-777-7417
Fax: 307-777-6234
URL: www.k12.wy.us/se.asp
E-mail: rwalk@educ.state.wy.us

Federated States of Micronesia

Office of Special Education
Special Education
Federated States of Micronesia National Government
Kolonia, Pohnpei, FM 96941
691-320-2609
Fax: 691-320-5500
URL: www.literacynet.org/micronesia/doe.html
E-mail: mkeller@mail.fm

Guam

Division of Special Education
Department of Education
PO Box DE
Agana, GU 96910
671-475-0549
TTY: 671-475-0550
Fax: 671-475-0562
URL: www.icdri.org/Education/education_on_guam.htm
E-mail: guamsped@ite.net

Republic of Palau

Special Education Coordinator
PO Box 189
Palau, PW 96940
680-488-2568
Fax: 680-488-5808
URL: wdcrobcolp01.ed.gov/Programs/EROD/org_list_by_territory.cfm?territory_cd=pw
E-mail: spedcor@palaunet.com

Adapted from EROD database Aug. 16, 2001. Please report any discrepancies to mheeg@aspensys.com.

Parent Web Sites

Attention-Deficit/Hyperactivity Disorder

www.help4adhd.org

This is the Web site for the National Resource Center on AD/HD. In the search box, type in "parents" to call up a page titled "Parenting a Child with AD/HD." Here you can find local support groups for parents and help for your child.

Cerebral Palsy

www.ucp.org/index.cfm

The Web site for United Cerebral Palsy provides links for parents and families about employment opportunities, health and wellness, and much more.

Deafness

www.agbell.org/DesktopDefault.aspx

The Web site of the Alexander Graham Bell Association for the Deaf and Hard of Hearing includes a parent section offering support and information to families and friends of a child who is deaf. It includes message boards, resources, and news for parents.

Developmental Cognitive Disabilities

http://education.state.mn.us/mde/Learning_ Support/Special_Education/Categorical_ Disability_Information/%20 Developmental_Cognitive_Disabilities/ index.html

This site, provided by the Minnesota Department of Education, provides resources for parents, including fact sheets and a manual for DCD.

Diabetes

www.diabetes.org/for-parents-and-kids/ resources.jsp

This resource page on the Web site of the American Diabetes Association lists books, magazines, and articles that specifically address raising children who have diabetes.

www.childrenwithdiabetes.com/index_cwd. htm

This site (Children with Diabetes) tells you about camps, conferences, and chat rooms for parents of children with diabetes.

Down Syndrome

www.ndss.org

The Web site of the National Down Syndrome Society provides information about research, communities, support groups, and much more.

www.ds-health.com/ds_sites.htm

This site provides many links related specifically to Down syndrome. It also lists sites made by people who have Down syndrome.

HIV/AIDS

http://kidshealth.org/parent/infections/std/hiv.html

This site (KidsHealth for Parents) tells parents about the general health of children with HIV, their growth and development, the signs and symptoms, how it can be transmitted, and other information that can assist parents who have a child with HIV or want to talk with their children about it.

Intellectual Disability

www.thearc.org

This site provides support for parents, families, and other people involved with an intellectual disability. Chapters can be found throughout the United States, and support networks are available online.

Multiple Sclerosis

www.nationalmssociety.org/site/
PageServer?pagename=HOM_ABOUT_
peds_network

The Web site of the National Multiple Sclerosis Society provides information for parents and families of children with MS.

Muscular Dystrophy

www.parentprojectmd.org

The Web site of the Parent Project of Muscular Dystrophy offers news releases, educational services, treatment, emotional issues, and more for parents of children with muscular dystrophy.

Spina Bifida

www.sbhao.on.ca/SBsupport.asp

This site (Spirit, Breakthrough & Hope) is provided by the Spina Bifida & Hydrocephalus Association of Ontario. It provides information about spina bifida itself, various medical treatments, current research, and associations around the world for persons with spina bifida.

Spinal Cord Injuries

www.spinalcord.org

The Web site of the National Spinal Cord Injury Association includes an A–Z index of topics, and you can search for sites and resources just for parents, families, and caregivers of people with a spinal cord injury.

Traumatic Brain Injury

http://education.state.mn.us/mde/Learning
_Support/Special_Education/Categorical
_Disability_Information/Traumatic_Brain_
Injury/index.html

This site from the Minnesota Department of Education provides resources for parents, including a brief and a manual for TBI.

Tourette Syndrome

www.tsa-usa.org/

This is the official site of the Tourette Syndrome Association. Parents can use it to learn about medical research, news, and events and to subscribe to the group's newsletter.

http://tourettenowwhat.tripod.com/

This site (Tourette Syndrome—Now What?) offers various links for information about Tourette syndrome, including one about a camp for children with Tourette syndrome.

Visual Impairments

www.spedex.com/napvi/

This is the official Web site for the National Association for Parents of Children with Visual Impairments. Here you can find information about research, publications, and conferences, as well as a parent directory and much more.

Inspirational Books About Role Models

Driscoll, J. (2000). *Determined to win.* Colorado Springs, CO: Waterbook Press.

Jean Driscoll has won the Boston Marathon eight times. She was born with spina bifida and uses a wheelchair. This book is her story.

Irwin, B. (1993). *Blind courage.* Waco, TX: WRS Group.

Bill Irwin, who is blind, hiked from Georgia to Maine on the Appalachian National Scenic Trail. This is his story.

Maynard, K. (2005). *No excuses.* Washington, DC: Regnery.

Kyle Maynard was born with short stumps for arms and very short legs. He wrestled his way to the state championships in Georgia. This is his inspiring story.

Ralston, A. (2004). *Between a rock and a hard place.* New York: Atria Books.

Aron Ralston found himself in a canyon pinned between a rock and a cliff. He made a dramatic yet life-saving move and cut off part of his arm. This story tells how he uses his prosthesis to climb rocks, hike, and ride a mountain bike.

Reeve, C. (1999). *Still me.* New York: Ballantine Books.

Christopher Reeve had a remarkable life both before and after his life-changing spinal cord injury. Here he tells his own story.

Runyan, M., & Jenkins, S. (2002*). No finish line: My life as I see it.* New York: Berkley Trade.

Marla Runyan, who is legally blind, is a world-class runner who competed in the Paralympics and the Olympics. This is her life story so far.

Steber, R. (2005). *No end in sight.* Prineville, OR: Two Star.

This book tells the story of Rachel Scdoris, a young woman with a visual impairment who competed in several Iditarod races.

Weihenmayer, E. (2002). *Touch the top of the world.* New York: Penguin.

Climber Erik Weihenmayer tells his story of climbing the highest peak on each continent. He happens to be blind.

Wellman, M., & Flinn, J. (1992). *Climbing back.* Waco, TX: WRS.

This is the story of Mark Wellman, a very experienced climber who continued climbing after he fell and became paralyzed; since his injury, he has climbed many very difficult rock faces.

Wilkins, S., & Dunn, J. (1988). *The real race.* Carlisle, UK: Paternoster Press.

Skip Wilkins experienced a spinal cord injury after high school. He later competed in the Paralympics in both table tennis and track and field. This is his inspiring story.

Adapted Physical Education National Standards (APENS)

The APENS are national standards for adapted physical education. These standards are the basis for a national exam that certifies teachers for adapted physical education (Kelly, 2006). Go to www.cortland.edu/APENS for more information.

Standard 1—Human Development

The foundation of proposed goals and activities for individuals with disabilities is grounded in a basic understanding of human development and its applications to those with various needs. For the adapted physical education teacher, this implies familiarity with theories and practices related to human development. The emphasis within this standard focuses on knowledge and skills helpful in providing quality APE programs.

Standard 2—Motor Behavior

Teaching individuals with disabilities requires some knowledge of how individuals develop. In the case of APE teachers, it means having knowledge of typical physical and motor development as well as understanding the influence of developmental delays on these processes. It also means understanding how individuals learn motor skills and apply principles of motor learning during the planning and teaching of physical education to students with disabilities.

Standard 3—Exercise Science

As an adapted physical educator, you must understand that modifications to the scientific principles of exercise and the application of these principles may be needed when teaching individuals with disabilities to ensure that all children with disabilities enjoy similar benefits of exercise. While there is a wealth of information in the foundational sciences, the focus of this standard will be on the principles that address the physiological and biomechanical applications encountered when working with diverse populations.

Standard 4—Measurements and Evaluation

This standard is one of the foundation standards underscoring the background an adapted physical educator should have in order to comply with the mandates of legislation and meet the needs of students. Understanding the measurement of motor performance, to a large extent, is based on a good grasp of motor development and acquisition of motor skills covered in other standards.

Standard 5—History and Philosophy

This standard traces facts regarding legal and philosophical factors involved in current day practices in adapted physical education. This information is important to understand the changing contribution that physical education can make in their lives. Major components of each law that related to education and physical activity are emphasized. The review of history and philosophy related to special and general education is also covered in this area.

Standard 6—Unique Attributes of Learners

Standard 6 refers to information based on the disability areas identified in the Individuals with Disabilities Education Act (IDEA) found within school age population. Material is categorically organized in order to present the information in a systematic matter. This organization is not intended to advocate a categorical approach to teaching children with disabilities. All children should be treated as individuals and assessed to determine what needs they have.

Standard 7—Curriculum Theory and Development

As you are planning to teach physical education to students with disabilities, you should recognize that certain Curriculum Theory and Development concepts, such as selecting goals based on relevant and appropriate assessments, must be understood by APE teachers. As you have no doubt discovered, Curriculum Theory and Development is more than writing unit and lesson plans. Nowhere does this come into play more than when you are planning a program for a student with a disability.

Standard 8—Assessment

This standard addresses the process of assessment, one that is commonly taught as part of the basic measurement and evaluation course in a physical education degree curriculum. Assessment goes beyond data gathering to include measurements for the purpose of making decisions about special services and program components for individuals with disabilities.

Standard 9—Instructional Design and Planning

Instructional design and planning must be developed before an APE teacher can provide services to meet legal mandates, educational goals, and most importantly the unique needs of individuals with disabilities. Many of the principles addressed earlier in human development, motor behavior, exercise science, and curriculum theory and development are applied to this standard in order to successfully design and plan programs of physical education.

Standard 10–Teaching

A major part of any APE position is teaching. In this standard many of the principles addressed earlier in such standard areas as human development, motor behavior, and exercise science are applied to this standard in order to effectively provide quality physical education to individuals with disabilities.

Standard 11–Consultation and Staff Development

As more students with disabilities are included in the general education program, teachers will provide more consultation and staff development activities for colleagues. This will require sensitivity and excellent communication skills. The dynamics of interdisciplinary cooperation in the consultation process requires knowledge of several consultative models. This standard identifies key competencies an adapted physical educator should know related to consultation and staff development.

Standard 12–Student and Program Evaluation

Program evaluation is a process of which student assessment is only a part. It involves evaluation of the entire range of educational services. Few physical educators are formally trained for program evaluation, as national standards for programs have only recently become available. Therefore, any program evaluation that has been conducted is typically specific to the school or district or limited to a small range of parameters such as number of students scoring at a certain level of a physical fitness test. Adapted physical education programs or outcomes for students with disabilities are almost never considered in this process.

Standard 13–Continuing Education

The goal of this standard is to focus on APE teachers remaining current in their field. A variety of opportunities for professional development are available. Course work at a local college or university is just one avenue. APE teachers can take advantage of workshops, seminars and presentations at conferences, conventions or in-service training. Distance learning opportunities are also becoming abundant.

Standard 14–Ethics

A fundamental premise of the Adapted Physical Education National Standards Project is that those who seek and meet the standards to be certified as adapted physical educators will strive at all times to adhere to the highest of ethical standards in providing programs and services for children and youth with disabilities. This standard has been developed to ensure that its members not only understand the importance of sound ethical practices, but also adhere to and advance such practices.

Standard 15–Communication

In recent years, the role of the professional in APE has evolved from being a direct service provider to include communication with families and other professionals in order to enhance program instruction for individuals with disabilities. This standard includes information regarding the APE teacher effectively communicating with families and other professionals using a team approach in order to enhance service delivery to individuals with disabilities.

References

AAPAR. (2007). APEAS II: Adapted physical education assessment scale, revised. Reston, VA: Author.

Andrews, S.E. (1998). Using inclusion literature to promote positive attitudes toward disabilities. *Journal of Adolescent & Adult Literacy* 41(6), 420–426.

Auxter, D., Pyfer, J., & Heuttig, C. (2005). *Principles and methods of adapted physical education* (10th ed.). St. Louis: Mosby.

Barfield, J.P., Hannigan-Downs, S.B., & Lieberman, L.J. (1998). Implementing a peer tutor program: Strategies for practitioners. *The Physical Educator* 55(4), 211–221.

Batista, P.J., & Pittman, A. (2005). Peer-grading passes the Supreme Court test. *Journal of Physical Education, Recreation & Dance*, 76(2), 10-12.

Blinde, E.M., & McCallister, S.G. (1998). Listening to the voices of students with physical disabilities. *Journal of Physical Education, Recreation & Dance*, 69, 64–68.

Block, M.E. (1998). Don't forget the social aspects of inclusion. *Strategies* 12(2), 30–34.

Block, M.E. (1999). Did we jump on the wrong bandwagon? Problems with inclusion in physical education. *Palaestra*, 15(3), 30–36.

Block, M.E. (2003a). Inclusion: Common problems—practical solutions. *Teaching Elementary Physical Education*, 14, 6.

Block, M.E. (2003b). Placement of students with disabilities in physical education: More than inclusion or segregation. *Revista da Soboma*, 8, 1–5.

Block, M.E. (2007). *A teacher's guide to including students with disabilities in general physical education* (3rd ed.). Baltimore: Brookes.

Block, M.E., French, R., & Silliman-French, L. (2007). Accommodating students with behavior challenges. In M.E. Block (Ed.), *A teacher's guide to including students with disabilities in general physical education* (3rd ed., pp. 205–237). Baltimore: Brookes.

Block, M.E., Lieberman, L.J., & Conner-Kuntz, F. (1998). Authentic assessment in adapted physical education. *Journal of Physical Education, Recreation & Dance*, 69(3), 48–56.

Briggs, D. (1975). Across the ages. *Times Educational Supplement*, 15, 9.

Broer, S., Doyle, M., & Giangreco, M. (2005). Perspectives for students with intellectual disabilities about their experiences with paraeducator support. *Exceptional Children*, 71, 415–430.

Bruininks, R.H., & Bruininks, R.D. (2005). *Bruininks-Oseretsky Test of Motor Development Proficiency* (2nd ed.). Circle Pines, MN: American Guidance Service.

Burton, A.W., & Miller, D.E. (1998). *Movement skill assessment*. Champaign, IL: Human Kinetics.

Butler, S.A., & Hodge, S.R. (2001). Enhancing student trust through peer assessment in physical education. *Physical Educator, 58*, 30-42.

Byra, M., & Marks, M. (1993). The effect of two pairing techniques on specific feedback and comfort levels of learners in the reciprocal style of teaching. *Journal of Teaching in Physical Education*, 12, 286–300.

Campbell, J.M. (2007). Middle school students' response to self-introduction of a student with autism: Effects of perceived similarity, prior awareness, and educational message. *Remedial and Special Education*, 28, 163–173.

Carson, L.M., Bulger, S.M., & Townsend, J.S. (2007). Enhancing responsible decision making in physical activity. In W.E. Davis & G.E. Broadhead (Eds.), *Ecological task analysis and movement* (pp. 141–147). Champaign, IL: Human Kinetics.

Causton-Theoharis, J., & Mamgren, K. (2005, July/August). Building bridges: Strategies to help paraprofessionals promote peer interaction. *Teaching Exceptional Children, 37*, 18–24.

Chadsey, J., & Gun Han, K. (2005). Friendship facilitating strategies: What do students in middle school tell us? *Teaching Exceptional Children, 38*, 52–57.

Colette, G. (2005). Inclusion, impact and need: Young children with visual impairment. *Child Care in Practice*, 11, 179–190.

Collier, D. (2005). Instructional strategies for adapted physical education. In J.P. Winnick (Ed.), *Adapted physical education & sport* (pp. 109–130). Champaign, IL: Human Kinetics.

Conatser, P., Block, M., & Lepore, M. (2000). Aquatic instructors' attitudes toward teaching students with disabilities. *Adapted Physical Activity Quarterly* 17(2), 197–207.

Copeland, S.R., McCall, J., Williams, C.R., Guth, C., Carter, E.W., Fowler, S.E., et al. (2002, September/October). High school peer buddies: A win-win situation. *The Council for Exceptional Children*, 16–21.

Cullinan, D., Sabornie, E.J., & Crossland, C.L. (1992). Social mainstreaming of mildly handicapped students. *The Elementary School Journal*, 92, 339–352.

d'Arripe-Longueville, F., Gernigon, C., Huet, M., Cadopi, M., & Winnykamen, F. (2002). Peer tutoring in a physical education setting: Influence of tutor skill level on novice learners' motivation and performance. *Journal of Teaching in Physical Education*, 22(1), 105–123.

Davis, R.W., Kotecki, J.E., Harvey, M.W., & Oliver, A. (2007). Responsibilities and training needs of paraeducators in physical education. *Adapted Physical Activity Quarterly*, 24, 70–83.

Davis, W., & Broadhead, G.D. (2007). *Ecological task analysis and movement*. Champaign, IL: Human Kinetics.

Davis, W., & Burton, A. (1991). Ecological task analysis: Translating movement behavior theory into practice. *Adapted Physical Activity Quarterly 8*(2), 154–177.

Delquadri, J., Greenwood, C.R., Whorton, D., Carta, J.J., & Hall, R.V. (1986). Classwide peer tutoring. *Exceptional Children, 52*, 535–542.

DePaepe, J.L. (1985). The influence of three least restrictive environments on the content, motor-ALT, and performance of moderately mentally retarded students. *Journal of Teaching in Physical Education, 5*, 34–41.

DePauw, K., & Gavron, S. (2005). *Disability sport* (2nd ed.). Champaign, IL: Human Kinetics.

Downing, J.E., Ryndak, D., & Clark, D. (2000). Paraeducators in inclusive classrooms: Their own perspectives. *Remedial and Special Education, 23*(2), 157–164.

Dunn, J.M., & Leitschuh, C.A. (2006). *Special physical education* (8th ed.). Dubuque, IA: Kendall/Hunt.

Dunn, J.M., Morehouse, J.W., & Fredericks, H.D. (1986). *Physical education for the severely handicapped: A systematic approach to data based gymnasium*. Austin, TX: PRO-ED.

Ernst, M., & Byra, M. (1998). Pairing learners in the reciprocal style of teaching: Influence of student skill, knowledge and socialization. *The Physical Educator, 55*(1), 24–37.

Falvey, M.A., Givner, C.C., & Kimm, C. (1995). What is an inclusive school? In R.A. Villa and J.S. Thousand (Eds.), *Creating an inclusive school* (pp. 34–58). Alexandria, VA: Association for Supervision and Curriculum Development.

Federal Register. (August 23, 1977). *Education for All Handicapped Children Act of 1975*, Public Law 94-142.

Fittipaldi-Wert, J., & Brock, S. (2007). I can play too: Disability awareness activities for your physical education class. *Strategies, 20*, 30–33.

Foley, J., Tindall, D.W., Lieberman, L.J., & Kim, S. (2007). How to develop disability awareness using the sport education model. *Journal of Physical Education, Recreation & Dance, 78*, 32–36.

Folio, M.R., & Fewell, R.R. (2000). *Peabody Developmental Motor Scales* (2nd ed.). Austin, TX: PRO-ED.

Folsom-Meek, S.L., & Aiello, R. (2007). Instruction strategies. In L.J. Lieberman (Ed.), *Paraeducators in physical education: A training guide to roles and responsibilities*. Champaign, IL: Human Kinetics.

Franck, M., Graham, G., Lawson, H., Lougherty, T., Ritson, R., Sanborn, M., et al. (1992). *Outcomes of quality physical education programs*. Reston, VA: National Association of Sport and Physical Education.

Frankenburg, W.K., & Dodds, J.B. (1990). *The Denver II Developmental Screening Test*. Denver: University of Colorado Medical Center.

French, N.K. (2003). *Managing paraeducators in your school*. Thousand Oaks, CA: Corwin Press.

French, R., Henderson, H., Kinnison, L., & Sherrill, C. (1998). Revisiting Section 504, physical education and sport. *Journal of Physical Education, Recreation & Dance, 69*(7), 57–63.

Friend, M. (2005). *Special education: Contemporary perspectives for school professionals*. Boston: Pearson.

Fronske, H. (Ed.). (2005). *Teaching cues for sport skills*. Needham Heights, MA: Allyn & Bacon.

Getchell, N., & Gagen, L. (2006). Adapting activities for all children: Considering constraints can make planning simple and effective. *Palaestra, 22*(1), 20–27, 43, 48.

Giangreco, M.F., Edelman, S., Luiselli, T.E., & MacFarland, S. (1997). Helping or hovering? Effects of instructional assistant proximity on students with disabilities. *Exceptional Children, 64*, 7–18.

Goodwin, D. (2001). The meaning of help in PE: Perceptions of students with physical disabilities. *Adapted Physical Activity Quarterly, 18*, 289–303.

Goodwin, D., & Watkinson, J. (2000). Inclusive physical education from the perspective of students with physical disabilities. *Adapted Physical Activity Quarterly, 17*, 144–160.

Greenwood, C.R., Carta, J.J., & Hall, R.V. (1988). The use of peer tutoring strategies in classroom management and education instruction. *School Psychology Review 17*(4), 258–275.

Gregory, G.H., & Chapman, C. (2007). *Differential instructional strategies*. Thousand Oaks, CA: Corwin Press.

Grenier, M., Dyson, B., & Yeaton, P. (2005). Cooperative learning that includes students with disabilities. *Journal of Physical Education, Recreation & Dance, 6*, 29–35.

Grenier, M., Rogers, R., & Iarrusso, K. (2008). Including students with Down syndrome in adventure programming. *Journal of Physical Education, Recreation & Dance, 79*, 30–35.

Halle, J.W., Gabler-Halle, D., & Bembren, D.A. (1989). Effects of a peer-mediated aerobic conditioning program on fitness measures with children who have moderate and severe disabilities. *Journal of the Association for Persons with Severe Handicaps, 14*, 33–47.

Hardin, B. (2005). Physical education teachers' reflections on preparation for inclusion. *The Physical Educator, 62*, 44–57.

Hart, S. (2001). Homework in physical education: Strategies for promoting healthy lifestyles through supplementary home tasks. *Strategies, 15*, 30–32.

Hauge, J.M., & Babkie, A.M. (2006). 20 ways to develop collaborative special educator–paraprofessional teams: One para's view. *Intervention in School and Clinic, 42*, 51–53.

Henderson, H.L., French, R., & Kinnison, L. (2001). Reporting grades for students with disabilities in general physical education. *Journal of Physical Education, Recreation & Dance, 72*(6), 50–55.

Horton, M. (2001, November). Utilizing paraprofessionals in the general physical education setting. *Teaching Elementary Physical Education*, 22–25.

Houston-Wilson, C. (1995). Alternate assessment procedures. In J. Seaman (Ed.). *Physical Best and Individuals with Disabilities: A handbook for inclusion in fitness programs*. Reston, VA: American Alliance for Health, Physical Education, Recreation and Dance.

Houston-Wilson, C., Dunn, J.M., van der Mars, H., & McCubbin, J.A. (1997). The effect of peer tutors on motor performance in integrated physical education classes. *Adapted Physical Activity Quarterly, 14*(4), 298–313.

Houston-Wilson, C., & Lieberman, L.J. (1999). Becoming involved in the individualized education program: A guide for regular physical educators. *Journal of Physical Education, Recreation & Dance, 70*(3), 60–64.

Houston-Wilson, C., Lieberman, L.J., Horton, M., & Kasser, S. (1997). Peer tutoring: A plan for instructing students of all abilities. *Journal of Physical Education, Recreation & Dance, 6*, 39–44.

Hughes, C., Fowler, S.E., Copeland, S.R., Agran, M., Wehmeyer, M.L., & Church-Pupke, P.P. (2004). Supporting high school students to engage in recreational activities with peers. *Behavior modification, 28,* 3–27.

Individuals With Disabilities Education Improvement Act of 2004, U.S. Public Law 108-446, *Federal Register* (2004).

Jackson, C.W., & Larkin, M.J. (2002). Teaching students to use grading rubrics. *Teaching Exceptional Children, 35,* 40–44.

Joukowsky, A.A.W., III, & Rothstein, L. (2002). *Raising the bar: New horizons in disability sport.* Brooklyn, NY: Umbrage Editions.

Johnson, M. (Ed.). (2006). *Disability awareness—Do it right! Your all-in-one how-to guide: Tips, techniques and handouts for a successful Awareness Day from the Ragged Edge Online community.* Louisville, KY: Advocado Press.

Johnson, M., & Ward, P. (2001). Effects of classwide peer tutoring on correct performance of striking skills in 3rd grade physical education. *Journal of Teaching in Physical Education, 20,* 247–263.

Kalyvas, V., & Reid, G. (2003). Sport adaptation, participation, and enjoyment of students with and without disabilities. *Adapted Physical Activity Quarterly, 20,* 182–199.

Kasser, S., & Lytle, R. (2005). *Inclusive physical activity.* Champaign, IL: Human Kinetics.

Kelly, L.E. (2006). *Adapted Physical Education National Standards* (2nd ed.). Champaign, IL: Human Kinetics.

Killoran, J., Templeman, T., Peters, J., & Udell, T. (2001). Identifying paraprofessional competencies for early intervention and early childhood special education. *Teaching Exceptional Children, 34*(1), 68–73.

Kiphard, E. (1983). Adapted physical education in Germany. In R. Eason, T. Smith, and F. Caron (Eds.), *Adapted physical activity from theory to application* (pp. 25-32). Champaign, IL: Human Kinetics.

Kowalski, E., Daggett, S., Speedling, R., & Houston-Wilson, C. (2002). *Statewide assessment for inclusive physical education.* Paper presented at the New York State Alliance for Health, Physical Education, Recreation & Dance Conference, Villa Roma, NY.

Kowalski, E., Lieberman, L.J., & Daggett, S. (2006). Getting involved in the IEP process. *Journal of Physical Education, Recreation & Dance.*

Kowalski, E., Lieberman, L.J., Pucci, G., & Mulawka, C. (2005). Implementing IEP or 504 goals and objectives into general physical education. *Journal of Physical Education, Recreation & Dance, 76*(7), 33–37.

Kowalski, E., McCall, R., Aiello, R. & Lieberman, L.J. (2009). Utilizing IEP goal banks effectively. *Journal of Physical Education, Recreation & Dance, 80,* 44-48, 52.

LaMaster, K., Gall, K., Kinchin, G., & Siedentop, D. (1998). Inclusion practices of effective elementary specialists. *Adapted Physical Activity Quarterly, 15*(1), 64–81.

Lavay, B.W., French, R., & Henderson, H.L. (2006). *Positive behavior management in physical activity settings.* Champaign, IL: Human Kinetics.

Lavay, B.W., French, R., & Henderson, H.L. (2007). A practical plan for managing the behavior of students with disabilities in general physical education. *Journal of Physical Education, Recreation & Dance, 78,* 42–48.

Lepore, M., Gayle, G.W., & Stevens, S. (2007). *Adapted aquatics programming* (2nd ed.). Champaign, IL: Human Kinetics.

Lieberman, L.J. (1999). Physical fitness and adapted physical education for children who are deafblind. In *Deafblind training manual* (pp. 313-345). Logan, UT: SKI-HI Institute Press.

Lieberman, L.J. (Ed.). (2007). *Paraeducators in physical education.* Champaign, IL: Human Kinetics.

Lieberman, L.J., Arndt, K.L., & Daggett, S. (2007). Promoting leadership in physical education and recreation. *Journal of Physical Education, Recreation & Dance, 78,* 46–50.

Lieberman, L.J., & Cowart, J.F. (1996). *Games for people with sensory impairments.* Champaign, IL: Human Kinetics.

Lieberman, L.J., & Cruz, L. (2001, July). Blanket medical excuses from physical education: Possible solutions. *Teaching Elementary Physical Education,* 27–31.

Lieberman, L.J., Dunn, J.M., van der Mars, H., & McCubbin, J.A. (2000). Peer tutors' effects on activity levels of deaf students in inclusive elementary physical education. *Adapted Physical Activity Quarterly, 17*(1), 20–39.

Lieberman, L.J., Houston-Wilson, C., & Aiello, R. (2001). *Developing and implementing a peer tutor program.* Paper presented at the American Alliance for Health, Physical Education, Recreation and Dance National Conference, Cincinnati, Ohio.

Lieberman, L.J., Houston-Wilson, C., Brock, S., Aldrich, K., & Kolb, L. (2000). *Setting up a peer tutor training program for your inclusive program.* Paper presented at the New York State Association for Health, Physical Education, Recreation and Dance Conference, Hudson Valley, NY.

Lieberman, L.J., Houston-Wilson, C., & Kozub, F. (2002). Perceived barriers to including students with visual impairments and blindness into physical education. *Adapted Physical Activity Quarterly, 19*(3), 364–377.

Lieberman, L.J., Lytle, R., & Clarcq, J. (2008). Getting it right from the start: Employing the Universal Design for Learning approach to your curriculum. *Journal of Physical Education, Recreation & Dance, 79,* 32–39.

Lieberman, L.J., & McHugh, B.E. (2001). Health-related fitness of children with visual impairments and blindness. *Journal of Visual Impairment and Blindness, 95*(5), 272–287.

Lieberman, L.J., Newcomer, J., McCubbin, J.A., & Dalrymple, N. (1997). The effects of cross-aged peer tutors on the academic learning time in physical education of students with disabilities in inclusive elementary physical education classes. *Brazilian International Journal of Adapted Physical Education, 4,* 15–32.

Lieberman, L.J., Robinson, B., & Rollheiser, H. (2006). Youth with visual impairments: Experiences within general physical education. *RE:View, 38,* 35–48.

Lieberman, L.J., Stuart, M.E., Hand, K., & Robinson, B. (2006). An investigation of the motivational effects of talking pedometers among youth with visual impairments and deafblindness. *Journal of Visual Impairment and Blindness, 100*(12), 726–736.

Long, E., Irmer, L., Burkett, L., Glasenapp, G., & Odenkirk, B. (1980). PEOPEL. *Journal of Physical Education and Recreation, 51,* 28–29.

Loovis, M.E., & Loovis, C.L. (1997). A disability awareness unit in physical education and attitudes of elementary school students. *Perceptual Motor Skills, 84,* 768–770.

Lytle, R., Lieberman, L.J., & Aiello, R. (2007). Motivating paraeducators to be actively involved in physical education programs. *Journal of Physical Education, Recreation & Dance, 78,* 26–30, 50.

Macdonald, C., & Block, M.E. (2005). Self-advocacy in physical education for students with physical disabilities. *Journal of Physical Education, Recreation & Dance, 76*, 45–48.

Mach, M. (2000). Using assistants for physical education. *Strategies, 14*(2), 8.

Martin, J., & Smith, K. (2002). Friendship quality in youth disability sport: Perceptions of a best friend. *Adapted Physical Activity Quarterly, 19*, 472–482.

Mauerer, K. (2004). *The use of paraprofessionals in general physical education*. Unpublished masters degree thesis, SUNY Brockport.

Melograno, V.J. (1994). Portfolio assessment: Documenting authentic student learning. *Journal of Physical Education, Recreation & Dance, 65*(8), 50–61.

Melograno, V.J. (2006). *Professional and student portfolios for physical education* (2nd ed.). Champaign, IL: Human Kinetics.

Menear, K.S., & Davis, T. (2007). Modifying physical activities to include individuals with disabilities: A systematic approach. *Journal of Physical Education, Recreation & Dance, 78*, 37–41.

Meyer, A., & O'Neill, L.M. (2000). Supporting the motivation to learn: How Universal Design for Learning can help. *The Exceptional Parent, 30*(6), 35.

Meyer, A., & Rose, D.H. (2000). Universal design for individual differences. *Educational Leadership, 58*(3), 39–43.

Mills v. Board of Education of the District of Columbia, 348 F. Supp. 966 (1972).

Mitchell, S., & Oslin, J. (2007). Ecological task analysis in games teaching: Tactical games model. In W.E. Davis & G.E. Broadhead (Eds.), *Ecological task analysis and movement* (pp. 161–177). Champaign, IL: Human Kinetics.

Morley, D., Bailey, R., Tan, J., & Cooke, B. (2005). Inclusive physical education: Teachers' views of including pupils with special education needs and/or disabilities in physical education. *European Physical Education Review, 11*, 84–107.

Mpofu, E. (2003). Enhancing social acceptance of early adolescents with physical disabilities: Effects of role salience, peer interaction, and academic support interventions. *International Journal of Disability, Development and Education, 50*, 435–454.

National Association for Sport & Physical Education. (2004). *Moving into the future: National standards for physical education* (2nd ed.). St. Louis: Mosby.

Nirje, B. (1969). The normalization principle. In R.J. Flynn and K.E. Nitsch (Eds.), *Normalization, social integration, and community services* (pp. 31–49). Baltimore, MD: University Park Press.

Obrusnikova, I., Valkova, H., & Block, M. (2003). Impact of inclusion in general physical education on students without disabilities. *Adapted Physical Activity Quarterly, 20*, 230–245.

O'Connell, M., Lieberman, L., & Petersen, S. (2006). The use of tactile modeling and physical guidance as instructional strategies in physical activity for children who are blind. *Journal of Visual Impairment & Blindness, 100*(8).

Odem, S.L., Brantlinger, E., Gersten, R.H., Thompson, B., & Harris, K.R. (2005). Research in special education: Scientific methods and evidence-based practices. *Exceptional Children, 71*, 137–148.

Pangrazi, R.P. (2007). *Dynamic physical education for elementary school children* (15th ed.). San Francisco: Pearson Benjamin Cummings.

Pennsylvania Association for Retarded Children v. Commonwealth of Pennsylvania, 343 F. Supp. 279 (U.S. District Court 1972).

Petersen, J.C., & Piletic, C.K. (2006). Facility accessibility: Opening the doors to all. *Journal of Physical Education, Recreation & Dance, 77*, 38–44.

Picket, A.L. (2002, Fall). Paraeducators: The evolution in their roles, responsibilities, training, and supervision. *Impact, 15*(2), [online]. Minneapolis: University of Minnesota, Institute on Community Integration. Retrieved from http://ici.umn.edu/products/impact/152.

Piletic, C., Davis, R., & Aschemeier, A. (2005). Paraeducators in physical education. *Journal of Physical Education, Recreation & Dance, 76*(5), 47–55.

Place, K., & Hodge, S. (2001). Social inclusion of students with physical disabilities in general physical education: A behavioral analysis. *Adapted Physical Activity Quarterly, 18*, 389–404.

Powers, L.E., Wilson, R., Matuszewski, J., Phillips, A., Rein, C., Schumacher, D., et al. (1996). Facilitating adolescent self-determination: What does it take? In D.J. Sands & M. Wehmeyer (Eds.), *Self-determination across the lifespan: Independence and choice for people with disabilities* (pp. 257–284). Baltimore: Brookes.

Rehabilitation Act of 1973, Public Law 93-112.

Riggs, C., & Mueller, P. (2001). Employment and utilization of paraeducators in inclusive settings. *Journal of Exceptional Children, 35*(1), 54–62.

Rink, J.E. (1998). *Teaching physical education for learning*. Boston: McGraw-Hill.

Rose, D.H., & Meyer, A. (2002). *Teaching every student in the digital age: Universal Design for Learning*. Alexandria, VA: Association for Supervision and Curriculum Development.

Salend, S.J., & Garrick-Duhaney, L.M. (2002). What do families have to say about inclusion? *Teaching Exceptional Children, 35*, 62–66.

Schuldberg, J. (2005). It's easy to make judgments if it's not familiar: The use of simulation kits to develop self-awareness and reduce ageism. *Journal of Social Work Education, 41*, 441–455.

Seaman, J.A., DePauw, K.P., Morton, K.B., & Omoto, K. (2003). *Making connections: From theory to practice in adapted physical education*. Scottsdale, AZ: Holcomb Hathaway.

Shephard, R.J. (1990). *Fitness in special populations*. Champaign, IL: Human Kinetics.

Sherrill, C. (1988). *Leadership training in adapted physical education*. Champaign, IL: Human Kinetics.

Sherrill, C. (1998). *Adapted physical activity, recreation, & sport* (5th ed.). Boston: McGraw-Hill.

Sherrill, C. (2004). *Adapted physical activity, recreation, & sport* (6th ed.). Boston: McGraw-Hill.

Sherrill, C. (2005). Will the Individuals with Disabilities Education Act—2004 affect us? *Palaestra, 21*, 54–56.

Short, F.X. (2005). Individualized education programs. In J.P. Winnick (Ed.), *Adapted physical education and sport* (4th ed., pp. 47–60). Champaign, IL: Human Kinetics.

Siedentop, D., Hastie, P.A., & van der Mars, H. (2004). *Complete guide to sport education*. Champaign, IL: Human Kinetics.

Silliman-French, L., Candler, C., French, R., & Hamilton, M.L. (2007). I have students with physical and motor problems: How can an APE, OT or PT help? *Strategies, 21*, 15–19.

Sinibaldi, R. (2001). Peers: Partners and equals, exceptional and regular students. *Strategies, 14*(4), 9–13.

Smith, T.K. (1997). Authentic assessment: Using a portfolio card in physical education. *Journal of Physical Education, Recreation & Dance, 68*(4), 48–52.

Special Olympics International. (1989). *Sport skills program*. Washington, DC: Author.

Spooner, F., Baker, J., Harris, A., Ahlgrim-Delzell, L., & Browder, D. (2007). Effects of training in Universal Design for Learning on lesson plan development. *Remedial and Special Education, 28*, 108–116.

Suomi, J., Collier, D., & Brown, L. (2003). Factors affecting social experiences of students in elementary physical education classes. *Adapted Physical Activity Quarterly, 22*, 186–202.

Tapasak, R., & Walther-Thomas, C. (1999). Evaluation of a first-year inclusion program. *Remedial and Special Education, 20*(4), 216–225.

Thousand, J.S., Villa, R.A., & Nevin, A.I. (2007). Differentiating instruction: Collaborative planning and teaching for universally designed learning. Thousand Oaks, CA: Corwin Press.

Trautman, M.L. (2004). Preparing and managing paraprofessionals. *Intervention in School and Clinic, 39*, 131–139.

Tripp, A., French, R., & Sherrill, C. (1995). Contact theory and attitudes of children in physical education programs toward peers with disabilities. *Adapted Physical Activity Quarterly, 12*(4), 323–332.

Tripp, A., & Zhu, W. (2005). Assessment of students with disabilities in physical education: Legal perspectives and practices. *Journal of Physical Education, Recreation & Dance, 76*(2), 41–47.

Ulrich, D.A. (2000). *The Test of Gross Motor Development*. Austin, TX: PRO-ED.

The University of the State of New York/The State Education Department (Office of Educational Services for Individuals with Disabilities). (2005, December). *Regulations of the Commissioner of Education, Part 200*. Albany, NY.

Verderber, J.M.S., Rizzo, T.L., & Sherrill, C. (2003). Assessing student intention to participate in inclusive physical education. *Adapted Physical Activity Quarterly, 20*, 26–45.

Wallace, T., Shin, J., Bartholomay, T., & Stahl, B.J. (2001). Knowledge and skills for teachers supervising the work of paraprofessionals. *The Council for Exceptional Children, 67*, 520–533.

Ward, P., & Ayvazo, S. (2006). Classwide peer tutoring in physical education: Assessing its effects with kindergartners with autism. *Adapted Physical Activity Quarterly, 3*, 233–244.

Ward, P., & Lee, M. (2005). Peer-assisted learning in physical education: A review of theory and research. *Journal of Teaching in Physical Education, 24*, 205–225.

Waugh, L., Bowers, T., & French, R. (2007). Use of picture cards in integrated physical education. *Strategies, 20*, 18–20.

Webster, G.E. (1987). Influence of peer tutors upon academic learning time-physical education of mentally handicapped students. *Journal of Teaching in Physical Education, 7*, 393–403.

Wehmeyer, M.L., Agran, M., & Hughes, C. (1998). *Teaching self-determination to students with disabilities: Basic skills for basic transition*. Baltimore: Brookes.

Wessel, J.A., & Zittel, L.L. (1995). *Smart start: Preschool movement curriculum designed for children of all abilities*. Austin, TX: PRO-ED.

Wessel, J.A., & Zittel, L.L. (1998). *I CAN Primary Skills K–3*. Austin, TX: PRO-ED.

Wheeler, J.J., & Richey, D.D. (2005). Behavior management: Principles and practices of positive behavior supports. Upper Saddle River, NJ: Pearson.

White, G., Casebolt, K., & Hull, S. (2004). Low-organized games: An approach to inclusion. *Strategies, 18*, 27–29.

Wiggins, G. (1997). Practicing what we preach in designing authentic assessment. *Educational Leadership, 54*(4), 18–25.

Wilson, S., & Lieberman, L. (2000). Disability awareness in physical education. *Strategies, 13*(6), 12, 29–33.

Winnick, J.P. (Ed.). (2005). *Adapted physical education and sport* (4th ed.). Champaign, IL: Human Kinetics.

Winnick, J.P., & Short, F.X. (1985). *Physical fitness testing for the disabled: Project UNIQUE*. Champ

Winnick, J.P., & Short, F.X. (1999). *The Brockport Physical Fitness Test Manual: A Health-Related Test for Youths with Physical and Mental Disabilities*. Champaign, IL: Human Kinetics.

Wiskochil, B., Lieberman, L.J., Houston-Wilson, C., & Petersen, S. (2007). The effects of trained peer tutors on academic learning time-physical education on four children who are visually impaired or blind. *Journal of Visual Impairment and Blindness, 101*, 339–350.

Wolfensberger, W. (1972). *Normalization*. Toronto: National Institute on Mental Retardation.

Yell, M.L. (1998). The legal basis of inclusion. *Educational Leadership, 56*(2), 70–73.

Zittel, L.L. (1994). Gross motor assessment of preschool children with special needs: Instrument selection consideration. *Adapted Physical Activity Quarterly, 11*(3), 245–260.

Index

About The Authors

Lauren J. Lieberman, PhD, is a professor in the department of physical education and sport at the State University of New York (SUNY) at Brockport. She has three degrees in adapted physical education (APE) and has taught higher education since 1995. She taught at the Perkins School for the Blind in the deaf blind program. She also has written five books on adapted physical education and has consulted throughout the United States and internationally on issues relating to including children with disabilities in physical education. She is past chair of the Adapted Physical Activity Council.

Lieberman started Camp Abilities, a developmental sports camp for children with visual impairments. This camp is replicated in eight states and Guatemala. In her free time, she enjoys playing ultimate Frisbee, running, mountain biking, kayaking, and hiking.

Cathy Houston-Wilson, PhD, is a professor in the department of physical education and sport at SUNY Brockport. She is a frequent presenter on APE at conferences and workshops and has taught APE in a residential facility as well as in public schools. She continues to be involved in teaching students with disabilities in campus settings and has coached many students in Special Olympic events and at the Empire State Games for the Physically Challenged.

Houston-Wilson is past president of the Adapted Physical Education section of New York State AHPERD, and she also served as secretary of the National Consortium on Physical Education and Recreation for Individuals with Disabilities. In her leisure time, she likes to ski, jog, and Jazzercise.

CD-ROM User Instructions

System Requirements

You can use this CD-ROM on either a Windows-based PC or a Macintosh computer.

Windows

- IBM PC compatible with Pentium processor
- Windows 98/2000/XP/Vista
- Adobe Reader 8.0
- 4x CD-ROM drive

Macintosh

- Power Mac recommended
- System 10.4 or higher
- Adobe Reader
- 4x CD-ROM drive

User Instructions

Windows

1. Insert the *Strategies for Inclusion* CD-ROM. (Note: The CD-ROM must be present in the drive at all times.)
2. Select the "My Computer" icon from the desktop.
3. Select the CD-ROM drive.
4. Open the file you wish to view. See the "00Start.pdf" file for a list of the contents.

Macintosh

1. Insert the *Strategies for Inclusion* CD-ROM. (Note: The CD-ROM must be present in the drive at all times.)
2. Double-click the CD icon located on the desktop.
3. Open the file you wish to view. See the "00Start" file for a list of the contents.

For customer support, contact Technical Support:

Phone: 217-351-5076 Monday through Friday (excluding holidays) between 7:00 a.m. and 7:00 p.m. (CST).
Fax: 217-351-2674
E-mail: support@hkusa.com